Whitey Ford: A Biography

Whitey Ford

A Biography

MILES COVERDALE, JR.

McFarland & Company, Inc., Publishers
Jefferson, North Carolina, and London

LIBRARY OF CONGRESS CATALOGUING-IN-PUBLICATION DATA

Coverdale, Miles.
    Whitey Ford : a biography / Miles Coverdale, Jr.
        p.   cm.
    Includes bibliographical references and index.

        ISBN-13: 978-0-7864-2514-3
        ISBN-10: 0-7864-2514-8 (softcover : 50# alkaline paper) ∞

    1. Ford, Whitey, 1928–   2. Baseball players—United
States—Biography.   I. Title.
GV865.F613C68   2006
796.357092 — dc22   2006009578

British Library cataloguing data are available

Cover photograph: Ford before Game 6 of the 1960 World Series
against the Pirates (National Baseball Hall of Fame Library,
Cooperstown, N.Y.)

Manufactured in the United States of America

McFarland & Company, Inc., Publishers
  Box 611, Jefferson, North Carolina 28640
    www.mcfarlandpub.com

To my mother — Anne Backman —
an avid New York Giants fan
who instilled in me a love of baseball and
provided constant encouragement
during the writing of this book

Contents

Preface   1

One: Growing up on the Sandlots   3

Two: Making the Majors   8

Three: Back from the Army   19

Four: "Next Year" Unfortunately Arrives   36

Five: Chasing Twenty Wins   53

Six: Ford vs. Spahn   72

Seven: A Great Season Interrupted by Injuries   87

Eight: A Disappointing Season   102

Nine: Pirates Steal Series, with Help from Stengel   108

Ten: Ford Finally Wins Twenty   123

Eleven: Another Near No-Hitter and Another Title   144

Twelve: Ford vs. Koufax   161

Thirteen: Chasing Ruth Again   175

Fourteen: End of an Era   194

Fifteen: Where Ford Ranks   211

APPENDIX A: CAREER STATISTICS   219

APPENDIX B: FORD'S YANKEES RECORD 236 CAREER WINS   220

APPENDIX C: CAREER WINNING PERCENTAGE LEADERS   223

APPENDIX D: CAREER ERA LEADERS   224

APPENDIX E: ERA DIFFERENTIAL VERSUS LEAGUE   225

APPENDIX F: COMPARISON OF BEST LEFT-HANDERS IN MODERN   226
            BASEBALL HISTORY

APPENDIX G: YANKEES CAREER WINS LIST   228

        Chapter Notes   229
        Bibliography   233
        Index   235

Preface

I grew up on Long Island during the 1950s and '60s, one of the golden eras of baseball and a great time to be a New York Yankees fan. Starting with the year I was born, 1949, the Yankees won 14 pennants in 16 years and nine world championships. The Yanks had a host of great players during those years, including MVPs Yogi Berra (1952, 1954, 1955), Roger Maris (1960, 1961) and Phil Rizzuto (1950). They had an outstanding trio of starting pitchers in the early '50s (Allie Reynolds, Vic Raschi and Eddie Lopat) and they had a succession of fine supporting players such as Hank Bauer, Billy Martin, Moose Skowron, Elston Howard, Bobby Richardson and Tony Kubek. But the two pillars on which this Yankee dynasty was built were Mickey Mantle and Whitey Ford. Mantle was the more spectacular of the two with his 536 home runs, many of them of the tape-measure variety. But Ford was the guy the Yanks gave the ball to when they really needed a win.

Brought up by the Yanks midway through the 1950 season, Ford proceeded to win nine straight games in the heat of the pennant race and then won the final game of the Yankees' World Series sweep of the Phillies. After two years of military service, Ford returned for the last 12 years of this remarkable Yankee run and was the most dependable pitcher in baseball. His winning percentage during this period was .714, as compared to the team's winning percentage of .607 when Ford was not involved in the decision. Furthermore, he was always at his best in the big games. If the phrase "money pitcher" wasn't coined to describe Ford, it certainly could have been. Three times he won both of his starts in the World Series, and he still holds the World Series records for wins (10) and consecutive scoreless innings (33). He was known as the "Chairman of the Board" because he always seemed to be in control when the money was on the line.

There were four other truly great pitchers during his era: Warren Spahn, Sandy Koufax, Bob Gibson and Juan Marichal. Spahn had higher career totals than Ford in most categories because he was incredibly durable, winning 20 games 13 times and piling up 363 career wins, the all-time record for left-handers. However, over a comparable number of years, Ford had the edge. Ford had only 14 seasons of at least 100 innings while Spahn had 20, but Whitey won at least two-thirds of his decisions eleven times versus five for Spahn. Whitey's ERA was at least three-quarters of a run better than his league's ERA every year of his career until his last full season, while Spahn met this standard in only 70 percent of his seasons.

On the other end of the spectrum, Koufax had the best five consecutive seasons (1962–1966) of any pitcher in baseball history, but the early part of his career was mediocre and he had to quit at the age of 31 due to traumatic arthritis in his left elbow. Gibson and Marichal had fabulous careers, but numbers don't lie — Ford's numbers were better. His career winning percentage of .690 was the best in the 20th century among pitchers with at least 200 decisions and his career ERA of 2.75 was not only the best of his era among starting pitchers but also is the lowest of any starting pitcher who has retired since 1930.

However, statistics don't come close to painting a complete picture of Whitey Ford. Ford was an artist on the mound, winning with his head as much as with his arm. He did not have an overpowering fastball, but he kept a book on all of the hitters and won with pinpoint control and guile, not to mention the guts of a burglar. He had a reputation for being cocky, and Mantle once said of him: "He *was* real cocky, very confident of himself, which is probably why he was such a great pitcher.... He had so much confidence on the mound that it seemed that it [spread] through the rest of the team when he was pitching.... I felt like we were never going to get beat when he pitched." But as cocky as he was on the field, he was just as humble and unassuming off of it. He cared little about individual statistics and he always tried to deflect the credit for his success to others. Never once did he try to blame a teammate for a loss. If a teammate botched a play in the field behind him to put him in a hole, you couldn't tell that from watching Ford — his demeanor wouldn't change at all. He would simply call for the ball and get back to business.

Ford was never involved in incidents with opposing players and he seldom argued with umpires. In fact, according to Mantle in one of his autobiographies, Ford never argued with anyone. He was one of the most popular ballplayers of his era — with teammates, opposing players, fans and the media. Even after a tough loss, Ford would sit and calmly answer all of the writers' questions. I can't remember ever hearing or reading anything negative about him. Nobody ever disproved Leo Durocher's famous saying that "Nice guys finish last" more than Whitey Ford.

ONE

Growing Up on the Sandlots

The greatest pitcher in Yankee history grew up not far from Yankee Stadium. Edward Charles "Whitey" Ford was born on October 21, 1928, the only child of Jim and Edna Ford, who lived on 66th Street in Manhattan. When Whitey was five, the family moved to 34th Avenue in Astoria, Queens, a close-knit neighborhood of second-generation Irish, Italian and Polish families. Although this was during the Depression, Whitey has great memories of his childhood and says he never felt deprived. His father worked for Consolidated Edison and his mother worked as a bookkeeper for the local A&P store.

Ford was a pretty good athlete as a boy, playing baseball and stickball in the summer, football in the fall, and roller hockey in the winter. He probably inherited his athletic genes from his father, a pretty fair baseball player who played on the Con Ed semipro team. Whitey's mother came from an athletic family as well: two of her brothers were semipro baseball players in Astoria.

All summer long, Whitey and his friends played sandlot baseball until dark on fields next to the Madison Square Garden Bowl on Northern Boulevard and 43rd Street, about a mile from the neighborhood. They got much more playing time than kids of today who play organized Little League baseball and get only a few at-bats or innings pitched per day. When they weren't on the sandlots, Whitey and his friends played stickball against a wall in the neighborhood, using a rubber ball and a broomstick. The strike zone was marked in chalk on the wall, giving Whitey some early practice throwing strikes.

Ford was always a Yankees fan. His two uncles who played semipro baseball would take him by subway to Yankee Stadium, where they would pay 25 cents apiece to sit in the bleachers and root for the Yanks. Whitey's favorite player was Joe DiMaggio, and like most New York City boys of that era, he dreamed of one day playing for the Yankees.

Ford played for his first team when he was 10. The Astoria Indians were a pickup team from the neighborhood that played teams from other neighborhoods, and the other boys on the team were reluctant to let young Eddie

Ford (front row, second from left) with his Thirty-fourth Avenue Boys sandlot team. Whitey pitched this team to the 1946 city sandlot championship at the Polo Grounds with a 1–0 win and was signed by the Yankees the following week. (Whitey Ford Collection)

(as he was called until he played in the minor leagues) join the team because of his small size. However, Eddie's best friend, Johnny Martin, was the team's best player and Johnny insisted on adding Eddie to the team. After Ford got the game-winning hit in the bottom of the ninth inning of his first game, the other players on the Astoria Indians were glad to have him on the team. This was the first of many times in his life that he would have to answer questions about his size by performing well before he could climb up the baseball ladder to the major leagues.

Whitey played his first organized baseball at 13 for the Thirty-fourth Avenue Boys. He and his buddy Johnny Martin were the best players on the team, with Ford playing first base and Martin catching. The team was pretty good but had stiff competition from another Astoria team that had a pitcher named Billy Loes. Although Ford and Loes couldn't have guessed it at the time, 11 years later they would face each other as the starting pitchers in the fourth game of the 1953 World Series. A couple of other kids from the neighborhood went on to fame and fortune as well, including a kid named Anthony Benedetto who later changed his name to Tony Bennett.

When Ford and Martin graduated from the eighth grade in 1942, they faced a dilemma. They both wanted to be baseball players, but the local high school didn't have a baseball team. Therefore, they decided to enroll at Manhattan School of Aviation Trades, riding a bus one hour each way. With the country at war, learning an aviation trade seemed like a good idea to young Eddie, and he would be able to play for the school's baseball team, which competed in the city vocational school league.

Ford proved to be a mediocre student and an even less promising airplane mechanic. As his last two years of high school approached, he realized that he didn't want to be an airplane mechanic but he had not had the academic curriculum necessary to prepare him for college. At that point, he resolved to concentrate all of his efforts on becoming a professional baseball player so that he could make a living. That spring he pitched and played first base for the Aviation Trades varsity baseball team, winning six straight games before losing the city vocational school championship game to a team from the Bronx.

Two life-changing events occurred when Ford was 17. First, an Irishman named Joe Foran moved his family into the apartment building across the street from the Fords. Joe had been brought over to the United States by a soccer team in the Bronx and was working as a carpenter in addition to playing soccer. Foran's daughter Joan was three years younger than Eddie, who first took notice of the girl that he would marry five years later.

The second event occurred in April of 1946 when Ford and Martin attended a tryout held by the Yankees at the Stadium. Though only 5'9" and 150 pounds, Eddie was a pretty good hitter who figured his ticket to professional baseball was as a first baseman. Long-time Yankees scout Paul Krichell was running the tryout. Ford did not impress Krichell as a hitter but the scout watched him take infield practice and noticed that he had a strong arm and a natural left-handed break on the ball. He asked Ford if he had ever pitched, and when Eddie answered in the affirmative, Krichell told him to stick to pitching, that he was too small to make the majors as a first baseman. After watching Ford pitch to several batters, Krichell took the youngster aside and showed him how to throw his curveball at varying speeds and with a varying amount of break to it. He thought that Ford had the potential and the moxie to perhaps play professional baseball someday, but he wasn't impressed enough to offer the kid a contract. Nevertheless, the advice and encouragement that Eddie got from the famed Yankees scout that day focused him on pitching, and he went to work on perfecting the variations of the curveball that Krichell had taught him.

Eddie was determined to be the best pitcher in the vocational school league his senior year, but as things turned out, he wasn't even the best pitcher on his own team. A junior pitcher named Vito Valentinetti joined the team and beat him out for the number one pitching spot. Valentinetti was bigger and stronger than Ford and he had enough ability that he would eventually have a brief career in the major leagues, pitching for the Cubs, Senators and three other teams from 1956 through 1959 and compiling a career record of 13–14. Ford was relegated to playing first base and hit about .350, but he won only three games as the team's number two pitcher and attracted no notice from the major league scouts who scoured the city looking for prospects.

Ford's baseball fortunes rose sharply in the summer after that senior season as he went 18–0 as the number one pitcher for the Thirty-fourth Avenue Boys in the Queens-Nassau sandlot baseball league. The team was 36–0 overall, with Eddie playing first base when he wasn't pitching. Although he still hadn't attracted any notice from scouts, he was about to get his first big break and he took full advantage of it.

On September 28, 1946, the Thirty-fourth Avenue Boys played a team from the Bronx for the *Journal American* city sandlot championship at the Polo Grounds, home park of the New York Giants. Ford had a two-hit shutout after nine innings but the opposing pitcher had a no-hitter and the game was still scoreless. Eddie took matters into his own hands by doubling to break up the no-hitter leading off the top of the 10th, and he came around to score on another double. Ford then went out and struck out the side in the bottom of the 10th (giving him a total of 18 strikeouts in the game) to nail down a 1–0 win and the championship. For his heroics he was awarded the Lou Gehrig Trophy as the game's most valuable player.

(Twenty-four years later, Whitey's son Eddie won the same trophy. Eddie went on to play baseball for Whitey's Yankees teammate Bobby Richardson at the University of South Carolina and was signed by the Boston Red Sox as a shortstop. He got as far as triple A but never got a major league at-bat, although ironically he got a hit off rookie southpaw Ron Guidry of the Yanks that helped win a 1977 spring training game for Boston and nearly got Guidry sent down to the minors. Fortunately, Yankees general manager Gabe Paul convinced manager Billy Martin and owner George Steinbrenner to keep Guidry, who went on to become one of the three best pitchers in Yankees history, with career statistics roughly equivalent to those of Lefty Gomez.)[1]

After his sterling performance in the game at the Polo Grounds, Ford sat back and waited for the contract offers to come in. He was hoping for some of the big bonus money that major league teams were starting to throw around, but once again his size worked against him and the offers were quite modest. The Red Sox offered him $1,000 and then raised their offer to $3,000 after the Giants offered Whitey $2,000. The Dodgers also offered $3,000. Finally Whitey heard from the team he really wanted to play for when Krichell called and offered him $5,500. Since Ford would have signed with the Yankees even if their offer hadn't been the highest, his decision was an easy one and he verbally accepted the Yankees' offer. But before he signed the contract, the Giants upped their offer to $6,500. Ford would have honored his verbal commitment but Kritchell upped the Yankees' offer to $7,000 to close the deal and Whitey signed his first Yankee contract. Half of the $7,000 was paid up front as a bonus and the other half was paid when he reported to spring training and was called first-year salary so that he wouldn't run afoul of the "bonus baby" rule that would have prevented the Yanks from farming him out for seasoning.

Ford cashed his $3,500 bonus check and suddenly had 70 $50 bills in his pocket — more money than he had ever seen. He decided to buy a radio-record player for his parents that cost $181, and when he pulled out the wad of bills, the store owner called the police, figuring there was no way an 18-year-old kid in that neighborhood could have that kind of money unless he stole it. Whitey's mother had to explain to the police that the kid's story about getting a bonus from the New York Yankees was true, and Whitey's surprise was ruined.

Ford's friend Johnny Martin never got an offer to play pro ball. Four years later, Whitey would become good friends with another kid named Martin, a brash second baseman for the Yankees' Kansas City farm team who would follow Whitey to New York.

At the age of 18, Eddie Ford was the envy of the neighborhood and was on track to achieve his childhood dream of playing professional baseball — hopefully for the Yankees. He had put all his eggs in one basket and had succeeded due to hard work, determination and a bit of luck. His father had left Consolidated Edison during the war to join the Merchant Marine and was now home working in a local poultry market. If not for his spectacular outing at the Polo Grounds, Eddie had no prospects and might have ended up working for his father in the poultry market instead of helping the Yankees win 11 pennants and six world championships.

Note

Much of the material for this chapter was obtained from the following sources:

Whitey Ford and Phil Pepe, *Slick: My Life in and Around Baseball* (New York: William Morrow, 1987), 23–38.

Whitey Ford, Mickey Mantle, and Joseph Durso, *Whitey and Mickey: A Joint Autobiography of the Yankee Years* (New York: Viking Press, 1977), 3–7.

Milton J. Shapiro, *The Whitey Ford Story* (New York: Julian Messner, 1962), 9–31.

Two

Making the Majors

In early 1947, Whitey reported to spring training in Edenton, North Carolina, with the Yankees' Binghamton farm club. All of the rookies in the Yankees organization were sent there for evaluation and assignment, and manager Lefty Gomez couldn't remember all of their names. He gave everybody nicknames that he would be able to remember and he gave Ford the name "Whitey" because of his blond hair.

Whitey was eventually assigned to Butler (Pennsylvania) in the Class C Middle Atlantic League at a salary of $250 a month. In 24 games for Butler he was 13–4 with a 3.84 ERA, but he was still only 5'9" and 150 pounds and he didn't think he had much of a chance to reach the major leagues. Nevertheless, the minor leagues were still preferable to getting a real job. As Whitey said in *Slick:* "I was doing what I enjoyed and they were paying me for it."[1]

The following season he was promoted to Norfolk in the Class B Piedmont League. He was expecting a raise but instead got cut to $200 a month. His only pitches at the time were a curveball and a mediocre (in his own words) fastball, yet he had an excellent season: 16–8, 16 complete games and a 2.58 ERA. He had grown an inch to his final height of 5'10" and was starting to fill out, reaching 170 pounds by the end of the season. As a result, he started to develop a little more pop on his fastball and he led the league in strikeouts with 171 in 216 innings.

After the season, he went to Mexico to play winter ball, against the wishes of the Yankees' front office. The Mexican team offered him $400 a month and Whitey needed the money. Besides, after the Yankees had cut his pay to $200 a month, who were they to tell him he couldn't earn money in the off-season? The good news was that Whitey learned to throw a changeup while he was in Mexico. The bad news was that he got so sick with amoebic dysentery that he almost died. His weight dropped all the way down to 130 pounds.

Whitey was nowhere near fully recovered when he reported to Binghamton in the Class A Eastern League in the spring of 1949. His manager there was George Selkirk, who had taken over in right field for the Yankees in 1935 after they traded Babe Ruth to the Boston Braves. After Whitey passed out on the mound during a spring training game, the Yankees flew him to Lenox Hill Hospital in New York to get rid of the amoebic dysentery. It took 19 days in the hospital for Whitey to get rid of the bug, but within a few weeks of being discharged his weight was back up to 155 pounds and he was regaining his strength. He returned to Binghamton in May, six weeks into the season. In his best "I told you so" tone, Yankees general manager George Weiss said: "Ford's develop-

Ford during spring training in 1950, his rookie year. (National Baseball Hall of Fame Library, Cooperstown, N.Y.)

ment as a pitcher was set back a year by his refusal to take our advice."[2]

Once he finally got healthy, Whitey burned up the Eastern League. He was 16–5 and led the league in ERA (1.61) and strikeouts (151), allowing only 118 hits in 168 innings. His fastball was getting faster as he got stronger and was made even more effective by the changeup he had learned in Mexico. Most importantly, his control was improving: he walked only 2.9 batters per nine innings while striking out 8.1 batters per nine innings. Binghamton went from last at midseason to fourth, beat Scranton in the Eastern League playoffs to get to the finals and then beat Wilkes-Barre to win the league championship.

It was at this point that Whitey really started to believe that he would make the majors. "Most kids dream about growing up and becoming a major league baseball player," Ford said in *Slick*. "I dreamed, too, but I never really thought I would make it because as a kid I always was too small. In fact, it wasn't until my third year in the minor leagues that I even began to think I had a chance to make the majors."[3] A popular story told frequently by Stengel was that Whitey called him anonymously after the Eastern League playoffs and told him that if he wanted to win the pennant, he should "bring Ford up from Binghamton." Whitey has always denied the story, saying that what really happened was that he called Paul Krichell and asked if the Yanks could bring him up for the last two weeks of the season to pitch batting practice or pinch-run, just to get a taste of life in the majors. Krichell told him no but also told him that if he behaved himself (in other words, no winter ball in Mexico) the Yankees would bring him to spring training the following spring.

Although Whitey arrived in St. Petersburg for spring training hopeful of making the team, he knew that it would be an uphill battle. The Yankees had one of the best starting rotations in baseball, comprised of the "big three" of Allie Reynolds, Vic Raschi and Eddie Lopat, plus left-hander Tommy Byrne, who had won 15 games the previous year. The bullpen was also strong, led by Joe Page.

There were other rookies in camp in the same boat, including a brash second baseman named Billy Martin and "Golden Boy" Jackie Jensen, the Rose Bowl hero from the University of California. Right-hander Lew Burdette was another pitching hopeful. Although the rookies were in awe of the veterans and pretty much kept to themselves, Whitey got to meet his hero, Joe DiMaggio. He also got good pitching instruction for the first time in his career. None of his minor league managers had been pitchers and there had been no pitching coaches. Now he had Yankees pitching coach Jim Turner helping him. Even more importantly, veteran left-hander Eddie Lopat took Whitey under his wing. "Steady Eddie" (who also was from New York City) taught Whitey the importance of studying the hitters and keeping a book on them, recording what pitches and pitch locations were successful against each hitter and which weren't. Lopat also taught Ford the importance of changing speeds and moving the ball around from one spot to another. Ford would always have the reputation of being one step ahead of the hitters, and it was in the spring of 1950 that he started the transition from thrower to pitcher.

When he finally got to pitch in some exhibition games, Whitey pitched well against the Phillies but then got hit hard by the Tigers on a day that his elbow was bothering him. Shortly thereafter he was sent down to Kansas City, the top Yankees farm team. Kansas City had a terrible team that year but Ford pitched well, going 6–3 with a 3.22 ERA and eight complete games in 12 starts. Then on June 30, he got the call he'd been waiting for. The Yanks were four games behind the Detroit Tigers (with Cleveland and Boston right on their heels) and needed pitching. Age the age of 21, Whitey had made the majors.

He joined the Yankees in Boston on July 1 after taking the overnight train from New York and arriving at seven o'clock in the morning. Stengel used him in relief that afternoon in a blowout loss to the Red Sox, and Whitey was hit hard. He found out later that he'd been tipping his pitches: the Boston first-base coach (Earle Combs of the 1927 Yankees) could tell if he was about to throw a fastball or a curve and was tipping off the hitters. Turner and Lopat helped him correct the problem the following day.

Whitey made his first major league start on July 6 at Yankee Stadium and pitched well for six innings, limiting the Philadelphia Athletics to three hits and one run. However, he weakened in the seventh and was touched for three runs.

Ford during spring training in 1950. (National Baseball Hall of Fame Library, Cooperstown, N.Y.)

He left for a pinch hitter trailing 4–3, but the Yanks won the game on Yogi Berra's ninth-inning double, with Tom Ferrick getting the win in relief. For his next scheduled start at the Stadium on July 17, Whitey set an unofficial club record by scrounging 73 of his teammates' free tickets so his family and friends could attend the game. With his Astoria cheering section on hand he picked up his first major league win, pitching 7⅔ innings to beat the White Sox, 4–3. Once again it was Berra and Ferrick who came to his aid: Yogi with a two-run double in the seventh inning to give New York the lead, and Ferrick by getting out of a bases-loaded jam in the eighth inning and pitching a scoreless ninth to preserve the win. Ferrick also saved Whitey's second win, a 6–3 victory over the St. Louis Browns that pulled the Yanks within half a game of the Tigers in the AL standings.

During a brief demotion to the bullpen following an early exit in a 4–3 Yankees win over Chicago, Whitey pitched 8⅓ scoreless innings in three relief appearances. Meanwhile the Yanks lost eight of 13 games with Ford out of the starting rotation and now trailed both Detroit and Cleveland. Whitey was reinserted into the rotation on August 15 and recorded his first

major league shutout, blanking the Washington Senators 9–0 on three hits.

New York was still in third place (four games behind Detroit and one behind Cleveland) when they sent their two southpaw "Eddies" to the mound for a Sunday double-header against the Athletics on August 20 in Philadelphia. (Ford was referred to by the newspapers as "Eddie Ford" throughout the 1950 season. There was no mention of the nickname "Whitey." It wasn't until 1953, when he was reunited with some of his minor league teammates, that the nickname given him by Lefty Gomez was resurrected.) In the first game of the twin bill, Eddie Lopat posted his 14th win of the year with the help of Joe DiMaggio's 23rd home

Ford in August 1950 after being called up by the Yankees midway through the season. (National Baseball Hall of Fame Library, Cooperstown, N.Y.)

run of the season, and then Ford pitched his second straight complete game, limiting the Athletics to six hits in a 5–2 win. The Yanks slipped past the Indians into second place but still trailed the Tigers by three games.

Whitey raised his record to 5–0 his next time out with a 10–0 four-hit shutout of the St. Louis Browns. Hank Bauer went 5 for 5 to personally out hit the Browns and Yogi Berra homered and drove in four runs. The only time Ford's shutout was threatened was in the fifth inning when two singles sandwiched around a strikeout put runners on the corners with one out, but Whitey struck out the next two batters. He had now allowed just two runs in his last 35⅓ innings, and one of those had been unearned.

So far, Stengel had started Whitey only against second-division teams, preferring to go with his veteran "big three" and Byrne against the Tigers, Indians and Red Sox. Casey finally gave Ford a start against the Indians on August 30 because the Yanks had a midweek double-header at the Stadium. Again the Yanks counted on their two Eddies and again they got two victories. In the opener, Ford pitched seven strong innings head to head with the great Bob Feller before leaving the game after bruising his right hip in a collision with big Luke Easter while covering first base. The Yankees won the game 4–3 on an eighth-inning pinch single by Tommy Henrich but Tom Ferrick got the win in relief. Lopat hurled a six-hit shutout to win the nightcap 3–0 and put the Yanks into first place for the first time since June 9.

Lopat and Ford won another double-header 12 days later against the Senators, with Whitey throwing a neat three-hitter to win the opener 5–1 and Lopat winning the nightcap 6–2 in relief of Tommy Byrne. Fellow rookie Jackie Jensen supported Ford in the first game with three hits, including his first major league homer. The two wins gave the Yanks a half-game lead over Detroit and a game-and-a-half lead over the surging Red Sox.

A loss to Cleveland the following day dropped New York back into second, and they trailed the Tigers by half a game when the two teams met in mid-September for a crucial three-game series at Briggs Stadium. After the teams split the first two games, Stengel shocked everybody by picking his cocky rookie to pitch the rubber game instead of Allie Reynolds. Pitching in front of 56,548 hostile fans in what was by far the most important game of his life up to that point, Whitey was as cool and calm as could be. He was opposed by veteran right-hander Dizzy Trout (13–4 on the season), and the two dueled through five scoreless innings. Then Joe DiMaggio hit his 30th home run of the year in the sixth inning to give Whitey a 1–0 lead. However, back-to-back doubles by Gerry Priddy and Vic Wertz tied the score at one in the eighth inning. There was still only one out, but Casey showed great confidence in the 21-year-old Ford by leaving him in. Whitey coolly retired the next two batters on ground outs and the game moved into the ninth inning.

The Yanks got a runner to second with one out in the top of the ninth and Ford due up. Whitey was sure that Stengel would pinch-hit for him, but Casey left him in the game to bat for himself. He drew a walk, and Gene Woodling followed with an RBI single to give New York a 2–1 lead. Phil Rizzuto then doubled, scoring Ford and putting runners on second and third. Detroit manager Red Rolfe opted to walk Berra to fill the bases for ex-teammate Joe DiMaggio, and the proud DiMaggio singled sharply to left to score two more runs. That hit knocked out Trout; Rolfe replaced him with veteran left-hander Hal Newhouser, who finally retired the Yankees after another three runs had crossed the plate. Ford made quick work of the Tigers in the bottom of the ninth to secure the 8–1 win, which put the Yankees in first place to stay. Whitey allowed only six hits and required just two putouts from his outfielders; he struck out five and induced one ground ball after another. When asked by the writers after the game if that was the biggest game he had ever won, Whitey replied with a straight face: "Well, no. I remember pitching the Maspeth Ramblers to a 17–11 victory over the Astoria Indians. That was a good one, too."[4]

At the end of his game article in the *New York Times* the following day, John Drebinger noted that former Purdue football player Bill Skowron would join the Yanks in Chicago in a few days to work out with the team for the last two weeks of the season. He also noted that "highly touted Mickey Mantle, brilliant 18-year-old shortstop prospect, also will join the Yanks on this jaunt. Mantle, a switch-hitter, batted at a .390 clip for Joplin during the past season."[5]

Four days after his big win in Detroit, Ford notched his eighth win without a loss with a three-hitter against the White Sox at Comiskey Park. Although he lost his

Ford going through his fan mail in late September 1950 after winning his first eight decisions. He finished the season 9–1. (National Baseball Hall of Fame Library, Cooperstown, N.Y.)

shutout in the fourth inning when a hit batter, a single and a sacrifice fly scored a Chicago run, the Yanks already had six runs by then and they coasted to an 8–1 win that enabled them to retain their half-game lead over Detroit. Just about the only anxious moment Whitey had was when he overslept and almost missed the start of the game. Roommate Yogi Berra was supposed to wake him up but forgot, and Whitey was still sound asleep when trainer Gus Mauch noticed an hour before the game that the day's starting pitcher hadn't shown up yet. After a frantic phone call woke him up, Whitey took a cab to the ballpark and arrived just in time to warm up. A few of the veterans (including Allie Reynolds and Hank Bauer) stopped by to tell him: "Hey, rookie, don't go fooling around with our money," but they were pretty happy with him after he threw his third three-hitter in five weeks.

Whitey made his last start of the regular season on September 25, going the route to beat the Senators 7–4 in the second game of a double-header after Allie Reynolds had won the first game. The two wins put the Yanks on the verge of clinching their 17th American League pennant, as they were now three and a half games ahead with only six to play. (They clinched it four days later.) Whitey's record was now an amazing 9–0, tying the American League record for consecutive wins by a rookie.[6] The Yanks were a perfect 12–0 in games started by Ford. Since New York won the pennant by only three games over Detroit and four over Boston, they needed every one of his wins.

Stengel used Whitey in relief two days later against the Athletics and he gave up a ninth-inning home run to Sam Chapman that won the game for Philadelphia and spoiled his perfect record. He finished 9–1 with seven complete games, and his ERA of 2.81 would have won the AL title (ahead of Early Wynn's 3.20) had he pitched enough innings. Boston's Walt Dropo was an easy winner of the AL Rookie of the Year Award (he hit .322 with 34 homers and a league-leading 144 RBI), but Whitey finished second in the balloting.

Joe DiMaggio had missed 16 games with injuries during the season and had suffered through one of the worst slumps of his career, but he had finished with a rush to raise his final batting average up to .301, with 32 homers and 122 RBIs. Joltin' Joe was overshadowed by two of his teammates: Yogi Berra (.322, 28 HR and 124 RBI) and Phil Rizzuto (.324, 200 hits, 125 runs), who was voted American League MVP not just for his offensive production but also for his outstanding defensive play at shortstop. Johnny Mize had stepped in for the injured Tommy Henrich at first base and hit 25 homers in only 90 games. On the mound, the Yanks had gotten good production out of their big three of Raschi (21–8), Lopat (18–8) and Reynolds (16–12) and Byrne had chipped in with another 15 wins, but they had needed their rookie left-hander to put them over the top.

Their opponents in the 1950 World Series were the Philadelphia Phillies, nicknamed the "Whiz Kids" because of their young ages. The Phillies had a comfortable lead with just a few weeks left in the season but then became the "Phading Phils" (the precursors of the 1964 Phillies) and found themselves needing to win the last game of the season at Ebbets Field to avoid a playoff with the Dodgers for the pennant. They dodged a bullet in that game when center fielder Richie Ashburn made a perfect throw to the plate in the bottom of the ninth to cut down what would have been the winning run, and then Dick Sisler homered in the 10th off Don Newcombe to give Robin Roberts his 20th win and the city of Philadelphia its first National League pennant in 35 years.

Though not expected to beat the Yanks, the Phillies had an interesting team. For Robin Roberts, this was the first of six consecutive 20-win seasons that would land him in the Hall of Fame. But it was relief pitcher Jim Konstanty who was voted National League MVP after appearing in 74

Ford and Casey Stengel after Whitey beat the Philadelphia Phillies to complete a Yankees sweep of the 1950 World Series. Ford won the game 5–2, losing a shutout on an error with two out in the ninth inning. (AP/Wide World Photos)

games with a 16–7 record and 22 saves. Left-hander Curt Simmons (17–8) also had an excellent year, but his National Guard unit was activated in late September and he missed the World Series.

The Phillies also had some good hitters. Right fielder Del Ennis finished first in the league in RBIs (126), fourth in batting (.311) and fifth in home runs (31). Left fielder Dick Sisler, though not as good as his Hall-of-Fame father George Sisler (who hit .340 lifetime with seasons of .420 and .407), hit .296 with 83 RBIs. Center fielder Richie Ashburn hit .303 and third baseman Willie "Puddin' Head" Jones contributed 25 homers and 88 RBIs. The most interesting story, however, was the comeback of first baseman Eddie Waitkus from his critical injury two years before. Waitkus had been an All-Star in 1948 when he hit .295 for the Cubs, but he had been shot in the chest by a deranged female admirer in Chicago after he was traded to the Phillies. (It was his story on which the movie *The Natural* was based.) He had not been expected to ever play again, but he played nearly every game for the Phillies in 1950 and hit .284.

The last few days of the NL pennant race had left the Phillies' pitching rotation in a shambles for the Series. With neither Roberts nor Simmons available for the opener at Shibe Park in Philadelphia, manager Eddie Sawyer gambled on Konstanty, who hadn't started a game all season and had averaged only two innings per appearance. The gamble almost paid off as Konstanty limited the Yanks to just four hits and one run in eight innings, but Vic Raschi was even better, pitching a two-hit shutout to win 1–0. After this game, Whitey innocently told announcer Dizzy Dean that he now understood how Dizzy had won 30 games in a season in the National League, rendering Dean speechless for perhaps the first time in his life.

Game 2 was another great pitching duel. Robin Roberts (pitching on short rest) and Allie Reynolds battled through nine innings to a 1–1 standoff. In the top of the 10th, DiMaggio drove a ball deep into the left-field pavilion of Shibe Park, and Reynolds blanked the Phillies in the bottom half of the inning for a 2–1 victory. As good as Roberts was, the gopher ball was frequently his downfall: he allowed a staggering 505 dingers in his career.

Game 3 at Yankee Stadium was a matchup of veteran left-handers: Eddie Lopat for the Yanks and Ken Heintzelman for the Phils. Heintzelman was 3–9 that year and nearing the end of an undistinguished career (77–98), but just the year before he had been 17–10 with five shutouts and the fifth-best ERA in the NL (3.02). He pitched a good game against the Yanks and deserved to win. He had a 2–1 lead with two out and nobody on in the bottom of the eighth, but then his control deserted him and he walked Jerry Coleman, Berra and DiMaggio to load the bases. Sawyer replaced him with Konstanty, who got pinch hitter Bobby Brown to hit an easy grounder to Granny Hamner at shortstop. Unfortunately for the Phils, Granny booted the ball as the tying run scored. Konstanty got Mize to pop up to end the inning, but instead of being one inning away from a win with the best relief pitcher in baseball on the mound, it was a new ballgame.

Hamner led off the top of the ninth and attempted to atone for his error by ripping a ball into the gap in left-center. It looked like a sure triple, but DiMaggio made a great play to cut it off and hold it to a double. After Hamner was bunted over to third, he was thrown out at the plate when Dick Whitman (batting for Konstanty) grounded to Joe Collins at first. Had the Phillies still been ahead at the time, Konstanty surely would have hit for himself and stayed in the game.

When the Phillies took the field for the bottom of the ninth, Russ Meyer came in to pitch and Jimmy Bloodworth replaced Mike Goliat at second for defensive purposes. Meyer retired the first two Yankees, but then Woodling and Rizzuto hit consecutive balls to Bloodworth that he couldn't handle. Both were scored as hits, but either ball could have gotten the Phils into extra innings. Instead, Coleman followed with his third hit of the game and the Yanks had a three-games-to-none lead in the Series.

Ford was given the honor of closing out the Phillies in Game 4. His opposing pitcher was rookie right-hander Bob Miller, who was 11–6 that year for the Phillies with a 3.57 ERA. Miller didn't get out of the first inning. Gene Woodling reached on an error by Goliat; one out later, he scored on a single by Berra. Yogi went from first to third on a very wild pitch and then scored on a double by DiMaggio. Miller's workday was over, and poor over-worked Jim Konstanty came in for the 77th time that season. (Maybe that's why his record fell to 4–11 the following season.) Konstanty got out of the inning with no further damage and blanked the Yanks over the next four innings.

Meanwhile, Ford was shutting out the Phillies, pitching out of jams in the first and fourth innings. Even as a rookie, Ford had ice water in his veins. Arthur Daley in the next day's *New York Times* said he had "the brass of a burglar" and he was in complete control.[7] When Konstanty finally ran out of gas in the bottom of the sixth inning, the Yanks removed any further suspense from the Series by scoring three runs on a lead-off homer by Berra, a hit batter, a triple by Brown and a sacrifice fly by Bauer.

The only remaining question was whether Ford would pitch a shutout in his first World Series game. He sailed into the ninth inning with a five-hitter and a 5–0 lead but gave up a single to Willie Jones leading off. Then he hit Del Ennis; a force at second put men on first and third with one out. Ford bore down and struck out Hamner, his seventh strikeout of the game. When he got Andy Seminick to loft an easy fly ball to Woodling in left, the game should have been over, but Gene lost it in the sun and dropped it, allowing two runs to score. When Goliat followed with a single under Rizzuto's glove to bring the tying run to the plate, Casey came out and got Ford, much to the displeasure of the 68,098 in attendance at the Stadium who wanted to see the rookie finish the game. Reynolds came in and fanned pinch hitter Stan Lopata to put the Phillies out of their misery. It was the Yankees' 13th World Series victory and sixth sweep.

For two weeks, Whitey was on top of the world. He had achieved his dream of making the major leagues, and for his hometown team, the best team in baseball. To be on a world championship team in his rookie year was the icing on the cake, and to pitch the clinching game in front of his family and friends was a Hollywood storyline.

Two weeks after the World Series, Ford stopped by his local draft board to check on his status and found out that he was being drafted into the army, with a reporting date of November 19. The toast of New York City would be doing his pitching for Uncle Sam for the next two years.

THREE

Back from the Army

The start of what would become a lifelong friendship between Whitey Ford and Mickey Mantle was a brief meeting between the two at Whitey's wedding reception on April 14, 1951. Ford had been stationed at Fort Monmouth (New Jersey) since the previous fall but had been granted a two-week furlough so that he could get married to Joan Foran, his long-time sweetheart. The wedding took place in Long Island City and the reception was held at Donahue's Bar in Astoria. The Yanks had played an exhibition game against the Dodgers that day at Yankee Stadium in preparation for their home opener, and after the game the entire team took a bus to the reception to join in the celebration. Mantle was too shy to go inside, so he stayed on the bus with several other players.

Ford had actually met Mantle the previous September when the Yanks had let Mickey travel with the team on the final road trip of the regular season so that he could get a taste of life in the majors. Ford remembers saying hello to the rookie a few times and getting only a grunt in return. While his first impression was that Mantle was a real hayseed, Whitey was definitely impressed with the power that Mickey exhibited in batting practice. It was obvious that the hayseed could hit a ton.

When Whitey and Joan found out that several players had stayed outside, they went out to the bus to say hello. That was the first time he actually had a conversation with his future buddy. The newlyweds delayed their Florida honeymoon a few days because the Yankees asked Whitey to throw out the first ball on Opening Day, in his army uniform. When he got back to Fort Monmouth he pitched for their baseball team for a while, but the commanding officer wanted him to pitch three times a week so he quit the team and played for a local softball team to stay in shape. It was certainly quite a change from the previous year when he had won the deciding game of the World Series. In October, when Bobby Thomson hit his famous home run to beat the Dodgers in the National League playoff, Whitey was on KP duty peeling potatoes.

Ford was discharged in November of 1952 and held out briefly before signing for the 1953 season. He had been paid at an annual rate of $5,000 for his half season in 1950, and after helping the Yanks win the pennant and the World Series, he felt he deserved a raise to $10,000 for the 1953 season. General manager George Weiss felt otherwise, telling Whitey that he had to prove he could still pitch after being in the army for two years. Weiss initially offered only $7,000 but eventually came up to $8,000, telling Ford that the offer would drop back down to $7,000 if he wasn't on the next plane to St. Petersburg, where the Yankees were training. Whitey relented and reported to camp, where he was given uniform number 16. (He had worn number 19 in 1950.)

Whitey was not in the starting rotation at the start of the season, as Stengel decided to go with his veteran "Big 3" of

Ford reporting to Fort Monmouth (New Jersey) for two years of army duty, seven weeks after winning the final game of the 1950 World Series against the Philadelphia Phillies. (National Baseball Hall of Fame Library, Cooperstown, N.Y.)

Raschi, Reynolds and Lopat plus Johnny Sain, who had been acquired from the Braves in 1951 to help fill the gap created by Ford's absence. Casey wanted to give Whitey a chance to work his way back into form and used him just once (in relief) in the Yankees' first 10 games as New York sprinted out to an 8–2 record.

The highlight of the first week of the season was Mantle's most

Whitey and the former Joan Foran cut their wedding cake after getting married on April 14, 1951, in Astoria (Queens), New York. (AP/Wide World Photos)

famous home run, a 565-footer at Griffith Stadium in Washington. Batting right-handed against Chuck Stobbs with a man on in the fifth inning, Mickey hit a ball that soared over the left-center-field bleachers and struck a 60-foot-high beer sign on a football scoreboard perched atop the rear wall of the bleachers, 460 feet from home plate. The ball caromed off the beer sign and kept on going, clearing the street in back of the ballpark and landing in the back yard of a house at 434 Oakdale Street, where it was tracked down by Yankees publicity director Arthur "Red" Patterson. Since the spot where the ball landed was measured by Patterson to be 105 feet from

Ford in spring training after returning to the Yankees in the spring of 1953. (National Baseball Hall of Fame Library, Cooperstown, N.Y.)

the back wall of the stadium, the home run was reported to have traveled 565 feet, making it the longest in major league history in an official game. If not for the scoreboard, the ball would easily have traveled more than 600 feet. This epic blast (which was witnessed by only 4,206 spectators) was the genesis of the term "tape-measure homer." No one had ever before cleared those bleachers in a game, although Eddie Lopat (the winning pitcher that day) recalls that Mantle had hit a ball off the football scoreboard on the fly in batting practice that very day.[1]

During the two years that Ford had been in the army, Mantle had been schooled by Billy Martin and had acquired some street smarts and a modicum of sophistication. Since Ford and Martin had become friendly during their rookie year with the Yanks in 1950, when Whitey returned he fell in with Martin and Mantle and the triumvirate that would drive George Weiss crazy was formed. All three were tremendously competitive players on the field but partied hard off the field. Casey began telling them they were "whiskey slick," and Mantle and Ford called each other "Slick" for the rest of their careers. Mantle, in particular, was intent on living the high life because his father, his grandfather and two uncles had all died of Hodgkin's disease soon after reaching the age of 40, and Mickey figured the same fate would befall him as well so he resolved not to get cheated by life.

Ford finally got a start in New York's 11th game of the season and pitched eight strong innings in a 4–2 Yankee win, although he didn't get credit for the win because the Yanks didn't win the game until the bottom of the ninth, when Gene Woodling hit a three-run homer. Whitey picked up his first win of the season in his next start, beating the White Sox 6–1 with the help of Mantle's fourth homer of the young season. At one point in the game an error and a misplayed bunt put Ford in a bases-loaded jam with nobody out, but he bore down and retired the side on a foul pop and two strikeouts.

After beating the Indians 11–1 in Cleveland on May 5, Ford faced the Tribe again seven days later at Yankee Stadium and turned in a real masterpiece. For five innings, the Indians couldn't manage a hit off Whitey. Then, much to the disappointment of the crowd of 57,440, the no-hitter went down the drain in the unlikeliest of fashions. Leading off the sixth, opposing pitcher Early Wynn topped a ball weakly down the third-base line and began lumbering toward first. Third baseman Gil McDougald missed a running barehanded stab at the ball and couldn't make a play. The official scorer had no choice but to rule the play a hit, and the no-hitter was gone. Ford cruised through the rest of the game without allowing another hit (striking out the side in the eighth) and picked up his third major league shutout, a 7–0 one-hitter. A two-run first-inning triple by Mantle was all the support Whitey needed.

Ford remained unbeaten on the season with a 7–2 win over Washington in which he knocked in two runs himself, and then he was the beneficiary of an 18–2 explosion by the Yankees against the White Sox in Chicago on June 3, collecting three more RBIs as he ran his season's record to 5–0. A 7–2 win over St. Louis (with relief help from Allie Reynolds) ran Whitey's streak to six.

Ford and Wynn squared off again on June 3 when the Yanks took on the second-place Indians in the opener of a four-game series in Cleveland. Whitey trailed 1–0 after six innings due to a fifth-inning homer by Dale Mitchell (best known as the final out in Don Larsen's perfect game), but the Yanks rallied with three in the seventh and Reynolds preserved Ford's seventh straight win. Whitey was now 16–0 in his major league career as a starter, his only loss having come in relief at the tail end of the 1950 season. This remains the best start ever for a major league pitcher.

The win over Cleveland was also New York's 15th straight win and increased their lead over the Indians to seven and a half games. Ed Lopat beat the Indians the following day for *his* seventh straight win (making the

Yankees' two left-handed Eddies 14–0 on the season) and the Yanks went on to sweep the series to run their winning streak to 18 and take most of the suspense out of the American League pennant race.

The Yankees were now just one shy of the AL record of 19 consecutive victories shared by the 1947 Yanks and the 1906 White Sox, and their next game looked like the mismatch of that (or any other) season as they took on the last-place St. Louis Browns at Yankee Stadium. The Browns had lost their last 14 games and were on their way to a 100-loss season. The opposing pitchers made the game even more of a mismatch: Ford against right-hander Duane Pillette, whose 22–38 career record entering the game was hardly a match for Whitey's 16–1 record.

Perhaps the law of averages caught up with Ford and the Yanks in this game as they struggled against their lowly opponents. But it was a season-long problem that really hurt Ford in this game: lack of control. Though he is remembered as a pitcher with pinpoint control, Whitey's control was actually a problem for him in his early years, as evidenced by the fact that he walked the exact same number of batters in 1953 as he struck out — 110 in 207 innings, or 4.8 per nine innings. (His career average was 3.1 walks per nine innings, with an average well below that during the second half of his career.) Against the Browns, two walks led to a run in the second inning and another walk preceded a home run by Vic Wertz in the fifth, so the Yanks trailed 3–0 when they batted in the bottom of the fifth, having squandered several scoring opportunities against Pillette. Forty-year-old Johnny Mize got the Yanks on the board with a pinch-hit RBI single (the 2,000th hit of his career), but Pillette kept the Yankees at bay until one out in the eighth, when he got in a jam and was replaced by Satchel Paige. Ol' Satch was just three weeks shy of his 47th birthday but he snuffed out the New York rally and retired the Yanks easily in the ninth to secure an improbable win for the Browns. Mantle helped him out by bunting foul with two strikes in the ninth, a fact that Ford needled him about for years thereafter. "I knew I couldn't hit Paige," Mickey said years later, "but I knew that if I could poke it past him, I could beat him to first base."[2] The defeat was Ford's first as a starting pitcher, in his 23rd major league start.

The Yankees' 18-game winning streak, though not a record, was the longest in the majors from that time until the Oakland A's broke the AL record in 2002 with a 20-game winning streak. They resumed winning, and when Ford beat Hal Newhouser and the Tigers 6–3 on June 21 on homers by Mantle, Martin and Berra, the Yanks led the Tribe by 11½ games. Then, inexplicably, New York lost nine straight games (their longest losing streak since 1945) and allowed Cleveland to creep within five games, with Chicago just another half game back. Vic Raschi finally ended the skid with a win over the Red Sox on July 2 and Ford followed that up with a two-hit shutout

against Philadelphia, allowing just a couple of seeing-eye ground balls
through the infield in a 4–0 win. Whitey reached the halfway point of the
season with a 9–2 record.

The White Sox passed Cleveland and were within four games of New
York when Ford faced the Browns in the second game of a July 16 double-
header in St. Louis. When Phil Rizzuto and Billy Martin both booted double-play grounders to put Ford in a 3–0 first-inning hole, the sparse St.
Louis crowd of 7,901 smelled another upset, but Whitey shut out the Browns
over the final eight innings and the Yankees restored order with a 7–3 win.
Berra supplied the exclamation point with a two-run ninth-inning homer
off one of Satchel Paige's eephus pitches.

Ford started New York on another winning streak in early August by
collecting four hits and striking out eight in an 11–3 win over St. Louis at
the Stadium. The Yanks then swept three games from Detroit, but the White
Sox trailed New York by just five games when they came into Yankee Stadium on August 7 for a crucial four-game series. With the Yanks trailing
1–0 in the first game, Mantle came up with two men on, slammed a ball
into the gap in left-center and never stopped running. Yogi Berra and Billy
Martin added homers as Ed Lopat beat the Sox, 6–1. Then the Yanks delivered the knockout blow in an August 8 double-header.

The first game was a tight pitching duel between Ford and Cuban right-
hander Sandy Consuegra and the game was still scoreless when the Yanks
batted in the bottom of the ninth. After a walk to Woodling and a sacrifice
by Martin, Stengel sent Mize up to hit for Ford. Big Jawn came through
with a line single to left to win it for the Yanks 1–0 and give Ford his 13th
win of the season. Although he allowed just five hits in recording his third
shutout of the campaign, he was trumped by New York right-hander Bob
Kuzava, who pitched an even-better game in the nightcap. Kuzava pitched
a one-hit shutout (losing the no-hitter with one out in the ninth on a clean
double by Bob Boyd), and the White Sox were suddenly eight games back.
The only bad news for New York was that Mantle had injured his right knee
making a fine play in the first game and would be out indefinitely.

Even with Mantle sidelined, the Yanks unloaded on Washington pitching for 28 hits in Ford's next start and led 22–0 after seven innings. Whitey
had collected four hits for the second time in 10 days and had allowed just
three, but Casey decided to give him the rest of the day off. It appeared the
Yanks would break the major league record for the most lopsided shutout
win (shared by the 1901 Tigers and 1939 Yankees), but rookie left-hander
Steve Kraly (making just his second major league appearance) gave up a
run and the Yanks had to settle for a 22–1 win. Ford's record improved to
14–4 and when he beat Philadelphia 10–3 on August 17 for his 15th win, he
seemed like a good bet to win 20 games. However, a loss and a no-decision

in his next two starts left him with only six scheduled starts remaining in which to reach that coveted milestone.

Ford picked up the first of his needed wins on September 1, beating Chicago 3–2 on a homer by Mantle, who had returned to the lineup wearing a brace on his injured knee. Whitey went 2-for-2 at the plate to raise his season's batting average to .292, right behind Mantle (.304) and Berra (.293). But then Whitey lost a start when a two-game series against Washington was washed out, and those meaningless games were never made up. After waiting eight days between starts due to the rainouts, Ford beat Chicago again with a five-hitter, 9–3. He was now 5–0 on the season against the White Sox and 17–5 overall, but he had only three starts remaining.

All hope of winning 20 games evaporated in Ford's next start when his wildness resulted in an early exit against the Indians. New York rebounded to win the game 8–5 on a homer by Yogi Berra, but Johnny Sain got the win. The Yanks clinched their fifth consecutive AL flag in this game, becoming the first team in major league history to win five consecutive pennants, a record that has been matched only by the 1960–64 Yankees.

With 13 days still remaining in the season, Stengel could have given Ford three more starts to give him a chance to win 20, but saving him for the World Series was more important. Homers by Mantle and Martin helped Whitey pick up his 18th win in a 10–8 slugfest at Fenway Park, but an error by Berra and two walks (one with the bases loaded) led to two ninth-inning runs and a 2–1 loss to Boston in his final start of the regular season.

The Yankees' final margin of victory was 8½ games over the Indians and 11½ over the White Sox. Berra finished second to Cleveland's Al Rosen in the MVP balloting after batting .296 with 27 homers and 108 RBIs, while Mantle batted .295, hit 21 homers and scored 105 runs despite playing in only 127 games due to his knee injury. The two left-handed Eddies finished 1–2 in the league in winning percentage, with Lopat finishing 16–4 (.800) and Ford 18–6 (.750). Lopat's 2.42 ERA also led the league, with Ford (3.00) tied for fourth. Thirty-eight-year-old Allie Reynolds and 36-year-old Johnny Sain combined for 27 wins and 22 saves as they both split time between starting and relieving, while Vic Raschi was 13–6. Due to the five-man starting rotation employed by Stengel and the fact that he was held out of the rotation for the first 10 games of the season, Ford got only 30 starts, which prevented him from winning 20. He did accumulate a team-leading (for pitchers) 20 hits, batting .267 with 20 runs produced to aid his own cause.

For the second year in a row, the Yanks' World Series opponents were the Brooklyn Dodgers. On paper, the Dodgers were the better team that year. They won the NL pennant by 13 games with a record of 105–49, still one of the best records (based on winning percentage) in major league history.

They led the major leagues by wide margins in hits, runs, homers (208), and batting average (.285). Roy Campanella outdid Berra by hitting .312 with 41 homers and a league-leading 142 RBIs and winning his second MVP Award. Duke Snider outdid Mantle, making a run at the Triple Crown by finishing fourth in batting (.336), second in home runs (42) and third in RBIs (126). Right fielder Carl Furillo won the batting title with a .344 average and rookie second baseman Junior Gilliam led the NL with 17 triples and was voted Rookie of the Year. First baseman Gil Hodges had a better year than anybody on the Yankees, batting .302 with 31 homers and 122 RBIs. Jackie Robinson switched to third base and left field and had his last great year, batting .329 with 109 runs scored and 17 stolen bases in only 21 attempts. Six of the eight Dodger regulars (Campanella, Snider, Furillo, Hodges, Robinson and shortstop Pee Wee Reese) made the NL All-Star team. While one has to keep in mind that their batting statistics were somewhat inflated by playing half their games at cozy Ebbets Field, clearly the "Boys of Summer" were at their peak in 1953.

Their pitching wasn't too shabby either, even though Don Newcombe was in the army. Carl Erskine (20–6) and Russ Meyer (15–5) finished 1–3 in the NL in winning percentage, and Preacher Roe (11–3), Billy Loes (14–8), Clem Labine (11–6) and rookie Johnny Podres (9–4) rounded out a deep pitching staff. Of course, they usually had quite a few runs to work with.

So if not for the Dodgers' history of World Series failure (0–6), they would have been heavily favored to beat the Yanks in the Series. Brooklyn fans had good reason to think that their time had finally come.

Dodger manager Charlie Dressen led with his ace (Erskine) in Game 1 at Yankee Stadium, while Stengel went with the Chief — Allie Reynolds. Since Lopat and Ford were clearly the Yankees' best pitchers that year, and since normally you'd want a southpaw to pitch in Yankee Stadium because of its Death Valley in left and left-center, most Yankee fans had expected the two southpaws to pitch the two games at the Stadium. But Stengel was famous for playing hunches and he went with his veteran right-hander who was just 13–7 on the season but was 6–2 lifetime in World Series play.

Erskine lasted just one inning, yielding a run-scoring triple by Hank Bauer and a bases-loaded triple by Billy Martin. Gilliam and Berra traded homers in the fifth inning to make the score 5–1, but Reynolds tired in the top of the sixth, yielding a lead-off homer to Hodges and a two-run, pinch-hit homer by George Shuba. Johnny Sain relieved Reynolds and yielded the tying run in the top of the seventh, but Joe Collins broke the tie with a home run in the bottom of the seventh and Sain shut out the Dodgers over the final two innings to nail down a 9–5 Yankee win.

Game 2 was a great match-up between two junk-balling southpaws, Lopat and Roe. The Yanks scored a run in the first on a sacrifice fly by Berra, but

Brooklyn third baseman Billy Cox doubled in two runs in the fourth inning to give Roe and the Dodgers a 2–1 lead that lasted until the bottom of the seventh, when Martin hit a solo homer to tie the score. After Lopat retired the Dodgers in the top of the eighth, Bauer singled in the bottom half of the inning and was on first with two out and Mantle up. Roe threw a changeup that Mickey deposited deep into the left-field stands for two runs, to the delight of most of the 66,786 fans in attendance. Lopat finished off the Dodgers in the ninth to give the Yankees a 4–2 win and a two-games-to-none lead in the Series.

Ford (left) and Billy Martin practice putting while waiting for Mickey Mantle to arrive during spring training in 1953. (National Baseball Hall of Fame Library, Cooperstown, N.Y.)

Dressen brought Erskine back to face Raschi in Game 3 at Ebbets Field and this time Carl had his best stuff. He fanned Mantle and Joe Collins four times each with a big overhand curveball. Gil McDougald and Gene Woodling each drove in a run for the Yanks, but Robinson had a double and two singles off Raschi, driving in one run and scoring another. With the score tied 2–2 in the bottom of the eighth, Roy Campanella showed why he was the league's MVP. Campy had been hit on the hand by a Reynolds fastball in Game 1 and the hand was painfully swollen, but he connected off Raschi for a solo homer over the left-field wall that gave Erskine a 3–2 lead.

Erskine had 12 strikeouts entering the ninth; the Series record was 13. He fanned pinch-hitter Don Bollweg on three pitches to tie the record. Then Casey sent Johnny Mize up to bat for Raschi. The Big Cat had just finished the final season of his Hall-of-Fame career with a .312 lifetime average and he was still a dangerous pinch hitter. Throughout the game, he had been sitting in the dugout needling his teammates: "How can you guys keep swinging at that pitch in the dirt?" So they all watched with interest when the veteran got his chance. Three pitches later, Mize was strikeout victim number 14 after chasing a curve in the dirt. Erskine walked the next batter but got Collins to tap weakly back to the mound to end the game. (Joe was just glad not to strike out for the fifth time, which would have set a record.)

Ford finally got to pitch in Game 4 at Ebbets Field, opposed by right-hander Billy Loes in a matchup of second-year pitchers from the sidewalks of Astoria. In his one previous World Series game, Ford had lost a shutout in the ninth inning because of a dropped fly ball, and he would be victimized by poor Yankee fielding with abnormal frequency in Series play throughout his career. This time it happened in the very first inning when Hank Bauer overran a fly ball by Junior Gilliam for a double, leading to three Dodger runs, the last two on a double by Snider after Robinson took out Rizzuto to break up a double play and keep the inning alive. Stengel yanked Ford after that inning and Brooklyn scored a run off Tom Gorman in the fourth to go up 4–0.

After a two-run homer by McDougald in the fifth cut the lead in half, Snider rocked Johnny Sain for a homer in the bottom of the sixth and then knocked in his fourth run of the game with a double in the seventh. Loes cruised into the ninth with a 7–2 lead but then loaded the bases with nobody out and was replaced by Clem Labine. After Labine fanned Rizzuto and retired Mize on a short fly ball, Mantle ripped a single to left to score one run but Martin was thrown out at the plate to end the game. Mantle was still limping noticeably from his August knee injury and a pulled thigh muscle, and he needed to have both legs wrapped with elastic bandages from his ankles to his hips in order to be able to play, a practice that would continue for the rest of his career.

With the Series now tied at two games apiece, 36,775 fans jammed Ebbets Field for Game 5. Right-hander Jim McDonald (who was 9–7 during the regular season as a spot starter and reliever) was a surprise starter for the Yankees against rookie left-hander Johnny Podres. Although Podres would have some memorable days against the Yanks in Series play, this wasn't one of them. Gene Woodling led off the game with a home run and the Yanks took a 2–1 lead in the third when Hodges booted a grounder with a man on third and two out. When Podres proceeded to hit Bauer and walk Berra to load the bases with Mantle coming up, Dressen brought in right-hander Russ Meyer in order to turn Mickey around to bat lefty. His bad right knee was buckling when he batted lefty; in addition, he had been hit on the hand by a line drive during batting practice and had needed to have it frozen with Xylocaine in order to be able to play.

Meyer's first pitch to Mantle was a knee-high curveball on the outside corner, and Mickey rode it high and far the opposite way into the upper deck in left-center field for the fourth grand-slam homer in Series history. After the game, Meyer said: "When you throw your best pitch and a guy hits it like Mantle did, there's just nothing you can do about it."[3] Until the day he died, Mantle always said that this homer was one of his biggest thrills in baseball. It was also the turning point of the '53 Series.

After Mantle's homer, Game 5 turned into a slugfest, except that it was the infielders on both teams doing the slugging instead of the sluggers. Cox and Gilliam homered for Brooklyn while Martin and McDougald homered for the Yanks. McDonald pitched into the eighth with a 10–2 lead before the Dodgers knocked him out with four runs; Kuzava and Reynolds closed out an 11–7 Yankees win. In what would be the only World Series appearance of his career, McDonald was the winning pitcher despite allowing 12 hits.

Ford got a chance to pitch in the right ballpark when the Series moved back to the Bronx for Game 6, in front of a crowd of 62,370. He was opposed by Erskine, trying to pitch on only two days of rest.

The Yanks took a 2–0 first-inning lead on RBIs by Berra and Martin and came back for more in the second. Rizzuto singled and went to third on a single by Ford. A sacrifice fly by Woodling plated the third Yankees run, and an infield hit by Collins and an error by Erskine moved Whitey around to third. When Berra followed with a fly ball to deep right-center, a fourth Yankees run seemed assured, but Ford had left third base too early and had to go back to tag up again. By the time he headed back to the plate, Snider had thrown the ball in to Gilliam, who relayed it to Campanella to nail the embarrassed Ford at the plate. That lost run would loom large later on.

Ford shut the Dodgers out until the sixth, when Jackie Robinson created a run for Brooklyn by doubling, stealing third and then racing home on a grounder to short. Whitey retired the Dodgers easily in the seventh, striking out Snider for the third time in the game. He had allowed just six hits, had struck out seven and appeared to be in complete control, but Stengel lifted him after seven innings and brought in Reynolds to pitch the eighth. The Chief retired the Dodgers in the eighth but walked Snider with one out in the ninth. When Furillo followed with a homer into the right-field stands, the score was tied and Ford's fine effort had been wasted. Reynolds struck out the next two batters to retire the side, which meant that the run Ford had squandered on the base paths back in the second inning had cost him what would have been his second Series-clinching win in two World Series.

Bauer led off the bottom of the ninth with a walk. With one out, Mantle beat out an infield hit, with Bauer advancing to second. That brought up Martin, who singled to center to score Bauer with the Series-winning run. It was Billy's 12th hit of the Series, a new record for a six-game Series. (Sam Rice and Pepper Martin had previously gotten 12 hits in a seven-game Series.) The RBI was Martin's eighth, giving him one more than Mantle. For his heroics, Martin received the Babe Ruth Award as the Series MVP. The Dodgers hit .300 as a team in the Series but lost to the Yankees for the fifth time in five tries; they were now 0–7 in their history in Series play. For the Yankees, the championship was their 16th in 20 trips to the World Series, including 15 of their last 16.

By winning his fifth World Series in a row, Casey eclipsed Joe McCarthy, who had piloted the 1936–1939 Yankees to four consecutive championships. Ten of the players on the '53 team had been with Casey for all five championships: Bauer, Berra, Coleman, Lopat, Mize, Raschi, Reynolds, Rizzuto, Silvera and Woodling. Mantle and Martin had each played in the last three.

Over the years, many people have said that Stengel's contribution to the Yankees has been overrated — that with the talent he had at his disposal, all he ever had to do was fill out the lineup card and then sit back and watch. They point to his mediocre managing record with other teams as evidence. While there were certainly some years when the Yanks were so much better than everybody else that it didn't take a genius to manage them, 1953 was not one of those years. The '53 Yanks did not have the best talent in baseball; with the exception of Mantle, Berra and Ford, they were a mix of aging veterans and overachievers like Martin, Bauer and Woodling who squeezed every last drop of performance out of average natural ability. In terms of talent, they were no match for the '27 Murderers' Row Yankees of Ruth, Gehrig, Lazzeri and Combs; the '36 Yankees of Gehrig, Lazzeri, DiMaggio, Dickey, Gomez and Ruffing; or the '61 Yankees of Mantle, Maris, Berra and Ford. What they lacked in talent, the '53 Yankees made up for with heart. No one will ever claim that this Yankees team was the greatest team of all time, but it remains the only team in baseball history to have won five straight World Series. Only the Montreal Canadiens in hockey and the Boston Celtics in basketball have ever won five consecutive world championships.

Though deprived of a well-deserved win, Ford was happy to get his second World Series ring and even happier to get his World Series check for $8,281, which was slightly more than he had been paid for the entire regular season. The Fords used the money for a down payment on their first house, in Glen Cove on Long Island.

A number of Yankees stars held out prior to the 1954 season, including Mantle, Rizzuto and all four of the team's star pitchers. Lopat signed first (for $27,500) and then Reynolds signed for $40,000, matching Raschi's 1953 salary as the highest salary ever paid to a Yankees pitcher at the time.

General manager George Weiss then shocked Yankees fans by selling long-time ace Vic Raschi to the Cardinals because he refused to accept a substantial cut from his 1953 salary. Raschi had been 120–50 as a Yankee and had helped them win six titles. But after winning 21 games three straight years (1949–1951), Raschi's win total had slipped to 16 in 1952 and to 13 in 1953, and Weiss felt he deserved a cut. When Raschi ignored the offer, Weiss shipped him off to St. Louis, thereby sending a message to the other hold-outs, whom he called "independently wealthy men through the winning of five pennants and world championships [who] have become too complacent."[4] Rizzuto fell into line three days later (signing for $40,000), and the following day Mantle and Ford signed contracts for $22,500 and $20,000, respectively.[5]

The Yanks received a blow during spring training when World Series hero Billy Martin was drafted into the army. He would miss nearly two full seasons and was replaced by Gil McDougald and Jerry Coleman.

Two rookies made a big impression during training camp. Elston Howard — the first black player signed by the organization — came to camp listed as an outfielder but was converted to catcher with coaching from Yankee great Bill Dickey. He was sent down to the minors at the end of spring training to gain experience as a catcher, but it was clear that he would be back. The other rookie to draw raves from Stengel was 24-year-old right-hander Bob Grim, who would take Raschi's spot in the rotation and win 20 games to capture the AL Rookie of the Year Award.

The five-year period 1949–1953 had been a time of transition for the Yankees. The 1949 team that beat the Dodgers in the World Series had been built around DiMaggio, Henrich, Rizzuto, Berra and pitchers Raschi, Reynolds and Lopat. By 1953, DiMaggio and Henrich were gone and the others (with the exception of Berra) were nearing the end of the line. The torch had been passed to the next generation of Yankees stars, headed by Mantle and Ford. They fully expected to win their sixth straight World Series in 1954, and in fact they won more games that year than in any of the previous five. Unfortunately for them, the 1954 Cleveland Indians had what was then the best regular-season record in American League history: 111 wins and only 43 losses. They broke the record held by the 1927 Yankees, whose record was 110–44.

Despite the expansion of the schedule from 154 games to 162 in 1961, the Indians' 1954 record of 111 wins was unsurpassed until the 1998 Yankees won 114 games. With all due respect to the Atlanta Braves of the 1990s (with their three Cy Young Award winners)[6] and the 1971 Baltimore Orioles (with their four 20-game winners),[7] the '54 Indians had the greatest pitching staff in history. Their five starting pitchers posted a combined record of 93–36, led by Bob Lemon (23-7), Early Wynn (23-11) and Mike

Garcia (19–8), who were 2–3–1 in the AL in earned run average. Fourth starter Art Houtteman (15–7) had the fifth-highest winning percentage in the league, and their *fifth* starter was 35-year-old Bob Feller, who still had enough gas in the tank to post a 13–3 record. In the bullpen they had Hal Newhouser, the only pitcher in major league history to win back-to-back MVP Awards—in 1944 when he was 29–9 and 1945 when he was 25–9. These six pitchers amassed an amazing 1,209 victories and 24 20-win seasons in their careers, and four of them (Feller, Newhouser, Lemon and Wynn) are in the Hall of Fame. The best measure of the Cleveland pitching staff's dominance that season is that their *team* ERA of 2.78 was bettered by only one non-Indian pitcher in the entire league. At the plate, Bobby Avila won the AL batting crown, Larry Doby led the league in homers and RBIs, and 1953 MVP Al Rosen had another good year.

The Yankees stayed close to the Indians for most of the season, trailing by just three games in the loss column as late as September 4. Ford got off to a terrible start and fell to 2–4 on Memorial Day after losing 1–0 to the Senators on an unearned run. He started to turn his season around with an 8–3 win over the first-place Indians on June 4 and then threw back-to-back gems in mid-June. First he beat Chicago 2–0 with a two-hitter, striking out eight and retiring the last 14 batters he faced. He followed that up four days later with a three-hit 2–0 shutout against the Baltimore Orioles (who had been the St. Louis Browns the previous season), beating Duane Pillette, who exactly one year before had ended the Yankees' 18-game winning streak and had handed Whitey his only career loss to the Browns in the process. He again finished strong, retiring the last 13 Orioles in a row. The most encouraging sign was that he walked a total of just one batter in the two shutouts and struck out 14. However, his control failed him again in his next several starts and he was just 6–6 at the halfway point of the season, with the Yankees trailing the Indians by four and a half games.

Despite his mediocre start, Ford was picked by Stengel to start the All-Star Game for the American League and he responded with three shutout innings, with the only hit off him a single by Stan Musial. (The game eventually turned into a slugfest that was won by the AL, 11–9.) For the remainder of the season, Whitey continued to pitch like an all-star. He started his hot streak with a 4–1 win over Boston, yielding just an unearned run in eight innings of work. Then he beat the Orioles 3–2 with a complete-game seven-hitter as the Yanks won their 11th straight game on a ninth-inning homer by Irv Noren. The Bombers now trailed the Tribe by just half a game, with the third-place White Sox another three and a half games back.

New York's winning streak was stopped at 13 but Ford kept on winning, beating the White Sox 4–1 with a complete game and scoring the first two Yankees runs himself on hits by Mantle. That win finally pulled New York even with Cleveland in the AL standings. The Indians invaded the Stadium on July 23 for a big three-game series and the Yanks had Lopat, Reynolds and Ford lined up to pitch. But after losing the first two games to Early Wynn and Bob Lemon, the Yanks needed Ford to stop the bleeding.

New York scored first off right-hander Mike Garcia on a sacrifice fly by Noren, and Ford took a shutout into the sixth inning before wildness and bad luck put the Yanks in a 3–1 hole. Whitey walked Jim Hegan to start the inning and the latter came around to score on a two-out single by Bobby Avila. After Ford walked Larry Doby and Al Rosen to load the bases, Vic Wertz tried to check his swing but the ball hit his bat and blooped over the shortstop for a two-run single. But Whitey shut the door after that and his teammates brought him even again the following inning on a two-run pinch double by Eddie Robinson, who was batting for Ford. The two teams then battled into the 11th inning until Andy Carey's single scored Mantle with the run that pulled the Yanks back within a game and a half of the Indians.

The Yanks then moved on to Chicago, where Ford stopped the White Sox 10–0 with a four-hitter and added a two-run double for good measure. Five days later he faced the Indians again in front of 60,643 fans at Cleveland's Municipal Stadium and this time he went the distance, throwing a four-hitter to beat the Tribe 2–1 on a two-run single by Berra. His control nearly hurt him again when he walked two batters to load the bases with two out in the fourth, but he fanned Jim Hegan to get out of the jam and shut the Indians down the rest of the way. The win pulled the Yanks within a game and a half of the leaders.

After splitting the next two games with Cleveland and losing two out of three to Detroit, the Yanks put together a 10-game winning streak that kept them in the race. Unfortunately the Indians were winning 13 out of 14 during this stretch and added a game to their lead. Ford contributed two of the 10 New York wins, striking out eight in a complete-game 8–2 win over Boston and beating Philadelphia 6–1 with a five-hitter. In the latter game he walked eight batters but was tough when he needed to be, striking out nine. The win was his seventh straight and raised his record to 13–6.

If one had to pick the series in which the Yankees' 1954 pennant plans went awry, it would be the three-game series against the Red Sox in Boston on August 20–22. The Yanks sent rookie sensation Bob Grim (16–4 entering the game) to the hill in the opener, and New York appeared to have consecutive win No. 11 well in hand when they carried a 3–1 lead into the bottom of the seventh. Then a double by ill-fated Harry Agganis[8] scored Ted Williams and Jackie Jensen with the tying runs and Boston pitcher Willard Nixon won his own game in the eighth inning with a 400-foot RBI double. The 4–3 win was Nixon's fourth straight win over New York that season and it dropped the Yanks three and a half games behind Cleveland.

That loss was nothing compared to the one the Yanks suffered the following evening at Fenway Park. A three-run pinch homer by Bauer gave New York a 6–5 lead entering the last of the ninth, but a walk to Williams and a triple by Agganis tied the score. The Yanks tallied two in the top of the 10th but gave them right back in the bottom half of the inning when Sammy White reached Johnny Sain for a two-run homer. This game was so important to Stengel that he brought in Ford (who had pitched nine innings just three days before) to relieve Sain. Whitey pitched two hitless innings (striking out four) and then put the Yankees ahead 9–8 in the top of the 12th with a sacrifice fly.

After fanning Ted Lepcio to open the bottom of the 12th, Ford needed just two outs to close out the Sox. Then a single and two walks filled the bases for Billy Goodman, who hit a line drive right back at Ford. Whitey caught the ball and appeared to have an easy game-ending double play at first, but he whirled and threw to second — too late to get the runner. When Don Lenhardt followed with a two-run single to center to end the four-hour marathon, the Yankees' pennant chances were jolted. When Williams homered, doubled, singled and drove in four runs in an 8–2 Red Sox win the following day, the Indians were five and a half games up on the Yanks and receding into the distance.

Ford snapped New York's three-game losing streak two days later with a 9–2 win over the Orioles and then capped off a six-game winning streak with a complete-game 4–1 win over Chicago, losing a shutout on a bad-hop grounder. Whitey was now 11–1 in his career against the White Sox and the Yanks were hanging on, four and a half games behind Cleveland, as the Indians arrived at the Stadium on August 31 for a showdown three-game series.

The Yanks needed to take at least two out of three but lost the first game when Early Wynn bested Grim, 6–1. Ed Lopat evened the series with a 4–1 win over Mike Garcia, and Ford faced Bob Lemon (winner of 11 consecutive decisions) in the rubber match. The Indians scored first on a solo homer by Sam Dente and the Yanks trailed 1–0 until Mantle's 27th homer leading off the bottom of the sixth brought them even. An RBI single by Andy Carey and an error by Cleveland first baseman Vic Wertz gave Whitey a 3–1 lead, and he stymied the Indians on two hits until Larry Doby homered with one out in the ninth to cut New York's lead to 3–2. Allie Reynolds came on to get the last two outs and the Yanks crept to within three and a half games of the Indians with 22 games remaining. The win was Ford's 10th in his last 11 decisions, with the only loss coming in the relief appearance against Boston. Overall he was 16–7 on the season.

The Yanks then proceeded to stumble, winning just four of their next nine to drop three games further off the pace with just 13 games left, only two of which would be against the Indians. Anticipating the kill, a major league record crowd of 86,563 jammed Municipal Stadium for a September 12 double-header, breaking the record of 86,288 set in the same stadium for Game 5 of the 1948 World Series.[9] Ford and Lemon squared off again in the opener and the score was knotted at one after six innings. Whitey's shoulder was hurting, however, so Stengel pinch-hit for him in the seventh, to no avail. Al Rosen's two-run double off Allie Reynolds in the bottom half of the inning was enough to give Lemon his 22nd victory of the year and Wynn picked up his 21st win in the nightcap to administer the coup de grace, 3–2.

The Yanks finished eight games behind the Indians with 103 wins, breaking the American League record for wins by a runner-up (previously 100) and missing the major league record by one.[10] Ford made one more start in the final weeks, finishing the season on a frustrating note by losing to the Senators 3–2 on an unearned run that he walked home in the ninth inning. His eight walks that day gave him 101 for the season in only 210.7 innings, an average of 4.3 walks per nine innings that was only a slight improvement over his 4.8 average of the previous season. His control lapses continued to be his biggest weakness, but his average of 7.26 hits allowed per nine innings was the second best in the league.

After his mediocre first half of the season, Ford's second-half mark of 10–2 gave him a final record of 16–8 in only 28 starts. His ERA of 2.82 (eighth best in the AL) trailed leader Mike Garcia by only 0.18 and was nearly a run better than the league average ERA of 3.72. Stengel's practice of pitching Ford only every fifth, sixth or even seventh day had deprived Whitey of at least five starts, compared to the other top pitchers in the league. (Wynn and Lemon had 36 and 33 starts, respectively.) The low number of starts, along with his poor start and his wildness, had kept him from winning 20 games. As long as Casey was managing the Yanks, it would be very difficult for Whitey to win 20.

The 1954 World Series seemed strange without the Yankees, and it had taken a record number of wins to break their streak. Yet, despite their record-breaking season, when *Sports Illustrated* published a special issue in 1991 ranking "baseball's 20 greatest teams of all time," the 1954 Cleveland Indians were missing from the list. The reason? They were swept in the World Series by the New York Giants. The Giants stole the first game of the Series at the Polo Grounds on a 259-foot pinch-hit home run by Dusty Rhodes after Willie Mays made his famous over-the-shoulder catch to keep them in the game, and the Indians never recovered.

FOUR

"Next Year" Unfortunately Arrives

The Yankees' pitching staff underwent radical change in 1955. Allie Reynolds had retired at the end of the 1954 season, Vic Raschi was in Kansas City, and Eddie Lopat and Johnny Sain would be traded during the season (Lopat to Baltimore and Sain to Kansas City). Tommy Byrne and 1954 AL Rookie of the Year Bob Grim joined Ford in the starting rotation along with Bob Turley and Don Larsen, both of whom had been acquired from Baltimore in a huge off-season trade involving 18 players. Turley had been the key man in the trade; "Bullet Bob" was one of the hardest throwers in the American League. He had been 14–15 in 1954 for a pitiful Orioles team that had won only 54 games and he had led the AL in strikeouts with 185. Larsen had been 3–21 with an ERA of 4.37 in 1954, but two of his three wins had been against the Yankees, who were impressed enough to acquire him. Rookie right-hander Johnny Kucks also joined the Yankee pitching staff in 1955, pitching both as a starter and as a reliever.

The Yankees' season started with a bang as they demolished the Washington Senators 19–1 at Yankee Stadium in the season opener. Whitey pitched a two-hitter but lost his shutout in the sixth inning in bizarre fashion. The game was played in a biting cold drizzle, and with two out and men on first and third, Whitey slipped off the pitching rubber without going through with his pitching motion. A balk was called, giving the Senators their only run. Whitey personally out hit the entire Washington team, garnering three singles and driving in four runs. Mickey Mantle, Yogi Berra and Bill "Moose" Skowron all homered to lead the onslaught.

Ford and Mantle teamed up again five days later in Baltimore. Mickey hit a two-run homer while Whitey blanked the Orioles on three hits, 6–0. No Baltimore runner reached second base, and Whitey again contributed on offense, singling and coming around to score on a double by Irv Noren.

After giving up just five hits in his first 18 innings of the season, Whitey yielded seven hits to the Red Sox in his next start. However, he spaced them out nicely and shut Boston out 3–0. In three consecutive complete games, the run he had balked home against Washington was the only run he had allowed. Home runs by Berra and Hank Bauer staked Whitey to a 2–0 lead, and then he knocked in the third run himself with a seventh-inning single.

Ford's 21-inning scoreless streak came to an end on April 28 when he was chased in the first inning by the White Sox, who reached him for four runs en route to a 13–4 win over the Yanks. A week later, Whitey made another early exit when he couldn't find the plate in the third inning against Cleveland, but New York rallied for an 11–5 win. Curiously, manager Casey Stengel used Ford in relief against Cleveland before his next start, and again Whitey was hit hard.

When Whitey started against Detroit at the Stadium on May 13, it had been three weeks since his last win. He regained his touch against the Tigers, shutting them out until two were out in the seventh when Ray Boone reached him for a two-run homer. That was all Detroit got, and it wasn't nearly enough to offset the best hitting performance of Mantle's career. Batting left-handed in the first inning, Mickey lined a home run into the right-center-field bleachers with Andy Carey on base to give the Yanks a 2–0 lead. His RBI single in the third stretched the lead to 3–0, and then he hit a towering home run into the bleachers above the 407-foot sign in right center in the fifth inning, again batting left-handed. After the Tigers closed the gap to 4–2 on Boone's homer, Mantle put the icing on the cake in the eighth inning. Batting from the right-hand side off southpaw Bob Miller, Mickey launched his third home run of the game into the right-center-field bleachers to cap a 5–2 Yankees win. In addition to being the first time anybody had ever hit three homers into the distant bleachers at Yankee Stadium in the same game, this was also the first time in American League history that a player had homered from both sides of the plate in the same game. (Jim Russell and Red Schoendienst had accomplished the feat in the National League.)[1] Mantle was the eighth Yankee to hit three homers in a game, as he joined a select group that included Ruth, Gehrig, DiMaggio, Lazzeri, Dickey, Keller and Mize.

This game highlighted a trend that continued throughout the careers of Ford and Mantle: Mickey always seemed to hit well when his buddy was pitching. In 1955 he hit 37 homers, and 16 of them came in Whitey's 33 starts. "Everybody enjoyed playing behind Whitey," said Mickey. "He had so much confidence in himself that he lifted the whole team. I know he lifted me. I felt we would never get beat when he pitched."[2]

Back in form, Ford shut out the White Sox 1–0 in his next start four days later, with Mantle scoring the only run of the game on a ground out after stealing third against Chicago southpaw Billy Pierce. Whitey needed only 105 pitches to polish off the White Sox as he induced one ground ball after another. Andy Carey recorded eight assists, two short of the AL record for third basemen.

After pitching well (one earned run) but getting a no-decision in a 7–5 New York win over Baltimore at the Stadium, Whitey faced the Orioles again five days later in Baltimore. Backed by a three-run homer by substitute first baseman Eddie Robinson and an RBI triple by Mantle, Ford tossed a five-hitter to beat the Orioles 6–2 and raise his season's record to 6–1. With their 11th win in 12 games, the Yanks moved out to a three-game lead over Cleveland in the AL pennant race, with Chicago one game further back.

The Yanks stayed hot (winning six of their next seven games), but the Indians kept pace. Ford improved to 7–1 by beating Kansas City on June 1, scattering seven hits and throwing four double-play balls in a complete-game 6–1 win. It was Whitey's 50th career win against only 16 losses, a winning percentage of .758.

On June 5, Ford and Mantle teamed up again in a 3–2 win over the White Sox at Comiskey Park, although Whitey didn't get the win. Batting right-handed against Billy Pierce, Mantle became the second man (Jimmie Foxx being the first) to hit a ball over the left-field roof on the fly. The roof extends back 160 feet from the 360-foot mark, and this blast reportedly shattered the windshield of a car about 550 feet from home plate.[3] Andy Carey also homered, but then made two errors in the seventh inning that allowed the White Sox to tie the game at 2–2. Ford was gone by the time Billy Hunter won the game for New York with an inside-the-park home run in the 10th inning. The lead over Cleveland was now four games; it grew to four and a half games the following night when Mantle's 450-foot home run into the center-field seats at Detroit's Briggs Stadium was one of five Yankee homers that helped rookie Johnny Kucks beat the Tigers 7–5 for his fifth win of the season.

Ford got another no-decision in his next start, a 7–3 Yankees win over Detroit. The Yanks moved on to Cleveland where they dropped three out of four to the Indians, reducing New York's lead in the AL standing to two and a half games over Chicago and three and a half over Cleveland. After the two teams split the first two games of the series, future Hall of Famers Early Wynn and Bob Lemon beat the Yanks in a double-header in front of 69,532 fans at Municipal Stadium, with Ford taking the loss in relief in the nightcap, pitching 5⅔ innings three days after his previous start.

Ford's luck didn't improve in his next start on June 17 at Yankee Stadium. Chicago grabbed a 1–0 lead on a third-inning homer by Walt Dropo and right-hander Dick Donovan blanked New York until the eighth inning when Mantle hit a ball 10 rows back into the upper deck in right field (his 15th homer of the season and seventh in support of Ford) to tie the game. But Whitey couldn't keep it that way in the top of the ninth, yielding a run in somewhat bizarre fashion. With Nellie Fox on second and one out, Stengel ordered former AL batting champion George Kell to be intentionally walked on a 3 and 1 count. However, Kell reached out and tried to hit the fourth ball, fouling it off. With the count now 3 and 2, Stengel changed his mind and signaled for Ford to pitch to Kell, whereupon the latter lined a single to left to score what proved to be the winning run.[4] The loss cut the Yankees' lead over Chicago to one game and dropped Ford's record to 7–3. After winning his first three starts of the season in spectacular fashion, Ford had gone 4–3 during the following eight weeks.

On June 21, just two nights after hitting his 100th career homer at the age of 23, Mantle became the first player in the 32-year history of Yankee Stadium to hit a ball into the bleachers in dead center field, directly above the 461-foot sign. The ball cleared the 30-foot wall and landed in the ninth row, 486 feet from home plate, where a fan caught the ball and showed a Yankees official the exact seat he had been in.[5] Mickey hit this one right-handed off Kansas City southpaw Alex Kellner. He hit another homer (his league-leading 18th of the season) the following day with Ford pitching, as Whitey went the route to post his eighth win in a 6–1 victory over Kansas City at the Stadium. The Yanks were now two games ahead of Chicago and four games up on Cleveland.

The Indians were the next visitors to Yankee Stadium, and Ford squared off against Bob Lemon in the second game of a June 26 double-header after Early Wynn had beaten the Yanks in the opener 5–0. After an RBI single by Berra in the first inning gave New York a 1–0 lead, Lemon left the game with an injury and was replaced by Herb Score, Cleveland's sensational rookie southpaw. Score shut out the Yanks on one hit (a single by Ford) over the next five innings, striking out nine. (He would lead the AL in strikeouts that season with 245 and win the Rookie of the Year Award.) After Score was lifted for a pinch hitter, Mantle's RBI double in the seventh inning gave Ford another run to work with. That was all Whitey needed as he pitched a four-hit shutout to stretch New York's lead in the AL standings to three games. In both the first and seventh innings, Ford sandwiched two walks around a hit to load the bases with only one out, but both times he coolly pitched out of trouble.

Ford won his 10th game of the season in his next start with a complete-game 7–2 win over the Senators at Yankee Stadium, but picked up his fourth loss when he was chased in the fourth inning by the Orioles in a 4–0 Yankee loss.

That loss started a frustrating couple of weeks for Ford. After no-hitting the Senators for four innings in the first game of a July 10 double-header, he faltered in the fifth inning and blew a 4–0 lead that Mantle had helped build with two long home runs. Reliever Tom Morgan replaced Whitey and lost the game, 6–4. The Yanks salvaged the second game of the double-header (aided by Mantle's third homer of the day) to reach the All-Star break with a five-game lead over the Indians.

Ford surrendered another big lead two days later in the All-Star Game in Milwaukee. After Billy Pierce and Early Wynn shut out the National League over the first six innings, Ford took over in the seventh with a 5–0 lead that Mantle had sparked with a three-run homer off Robin Roberts in the first inning. That lead evaporated over the next two innings as the NL hitters nibbled him to death with five singles (two by Willie Mays), aided by two AL errors. Stan Musial eventually won the game for the National League 6–5 with a 12th-inning homer off Boston's Frank Sullivan.

Ford pitched well in his first start after the All-Star Game but lost a 2–1 pitching duel to southpaw Billy Hoeft of the Detroit Tigers. Whitey pitched a complete game but had one bad inning, yielding a walk and successive two-out singles to Harvey Kuenn, Bill Tuttle and Al Kaline in the fifth. The loss narrowed the Yanks' AL lead to three games.

The Yanks briefly dropped out of first place but Ford helped rectify that with a 7–3 win over Kansas City in the first game of a July 24 double-header. A home run by Skowron and a two-run triple by Mantle paced the offense, and Jim Konstanty came on in relief to get the final four outs. When Berra clouted a two-run ninth-inning homer to give Johnny Kucks a 2–0 win in the nightcap, the Yanks moved a game ahead of both Chicago and Cleveland.

After losing two out of three to Chicago at the Stadium, the Yanks again slipped a couple of percentage points in back of the White Sox, with the Indians and Red Sox only one and three games back, respectively. They needed a win when Ford opened a three-game set against the Athletics at home on July 29, and Whitey came through with a complete-game five-hitter, striking out seven. After an unearned run allowed Kansas City to tie the game at 1–1, Ford took matters into his own hands in the bottom of the seventh by hitting his first major league home run off old teammate Vic Raschi. Unfortunately, another old teammate, 39-year-old Enos Slaughter (traded to Kansas City early in the season), followed suit with a solo homer in the top of the eighth to tie the game again. The Yanks finally prevailed when Joe Collins singled Mantle home with the eventual winning run in the bottom of the eighth. Ford raised his record to 12–5 as New York kept pace with Chicago, Cleveland and Boston, all of whom won their games.

The Yanks then went into a tailspin, losing seven of their next 11 games to drop into third place, just half a game ahead of the fourth-place Red Sox. Ford was the losing pitcher in the last of these games, going the distance against Boston on August 9 in front of a Yankee Stadium crowd of 61,678 but losing, 4–1. Though he yielded just five hits, two of them were homers.

The Yankees turned their season around after that loss to Boston, winning 10 of their next 11. Included in that streak were back-to-back doubleheader sweeps of the Orioles. In the opener of the first of these twin bills, a pair of two-run homers by Bauer and Mantle helped Ford to a 7–2 win over his old mentor, Eddie Lopat, who had been sold to the Orioles two weeks before. The Yankees crushed Baltimore 20–6 in the nightcap and continued pounding Oriole pitchers the following day. After Bauer's ninth-inning homer won the first game 5–4, Mantle homered from both sides of the plate in the nightcap to knock in four runs and lead New York to a 12–6 win. In addition to making him the first player in major league history to switch-hit homers in the same game twice, the two homers gave him 29 for the season, a career high. The sweep allowed the Yanks to slide into first place, half a game ahead of the idle Indians.

After a split of two games with Boston, the Yanks maintained a one-game lead over both Chicago and Cleveland on August 19 by beating Baltimore 8–0 on a two-hit shutout by Ford. First-inning homers by Gil McDougald and Mantle got the Yanks off and running and the only hits off Ford were a pop-fly double in the second inning and a clean single in the sixth. The shutout was Whitey's fifth of the season and improved his record to 14–6. The Yanks won Ford's next start as well, 3–2 over the Tigers on back-to-back ninth-inning homers by Berra and Mantle, but Whitey had been lifted for a pinch hitter (after giving up only three hits) and did not get credit for the win.

After losing two out of three in Cleveland and dropping into a dead heat with the Indians (half a game ahead of the White Sox), the Yanks moved on to Chicago for a key double-header on August 28. They quickly staked Ford to a 4–0 lead in the opener, thanks to an RBI single by Rizzuto and a three-run homer by Mantle, his 34th of the season. Walt Dropo ruined Ford's shutout with a solo homer, but a two-run homer by Berra put the game out of reach and Whitey cruised to his 15th win, 6–1. He struck out a season-high nine batters in recording his 15th complete game of the season. Despite losing the nightcap to Billy Pierce, 3–2, the Yanks slipped back into first when the Indians dropped a pair to Washington. However, they lost two of their last three games in August to close the month tied for second with Cleveland, half a game behind Chicago.

The Yanks returned home to the Stadium for a weekend series with Washington. Friday night marked the return to the Yankees of Billy Martin, who had been in the army for two years. Whitey got the start and totally dominated the Senators during the first six innings, not allowing anything even resembling a hit. But Washington right-hander Bob Porterfield managed to keep the Yanks off the scoreboard for the first five innings, so the game was still scoreless when the Yanks batted in the bottom of the sixth. Then Martin and Berra singled and Mantle launched his 36th homer deep into the right-field stands for a 3–0 Yankee lead.

Ford's best previous bid for a no-hitter, back in 1953 against Cleveland, had been broken up with one out in the seventh inning. History repeated itself as Washington right fielder Carlos Paula broke up Ford's no-hitter with a line-drive single to left with one out in the seventh. Mickey

Vernon, who had drawn a walk to open the inning, came around to score when Paula's hit got by Irv Noren in left field. Afterward, Ford said that Paula had hit a low, inside curveball. "I pitched him there hoping to get a double play," said Whitey. "He grounded out to Martin on the same pitch the time before. But he golfed this one and hit it real good."[6] Paula raced around to third on the error by Noren and scored a second unearned Washington run on a ground out. The single by Paula was the only hit that Ford allowed, and after Elston Howard gave him an insurance run with an RBI triple in the eighth, Whitey completed the second one-hitter of his career. The 4–2 win kept the Yankees half a game behind the White Sox.

By the time Ford's turn came around again on September 7, the Yanks had moved a game ahead of Chicago but now trailed Cleveland by half a game. Boston was still in the race, only three games out of first. Only 18 games remained in the regular season. Ford squared off against Kansas City right-hander Arnie Portocarrero at the Stadium and neither pitcher allowed

Ford, Mantle and Martin celebrate after Ford pitched a one-hitter against Washington on September 2, 1955, to keep the Yankees within half a game of the White Sox. Ford threw another one-hitter five days later against Kansas City to become only the fifth pitcher in major league history to throw consecutive one-hitters. (National Baseball Hall of Fame Library, Cooperstown, N.Y.)

a hit through four innings. The closest either team had come to a hit was a line drive off the bat of Kansas City's Harry "Suitcase" Simpson that was backhanded nicely by Yankee shortstop Phil Rizzuto.

Ford continued his no-hitter through the fifth, and then Mantle singled to center in the bottom of the fifth for the first hit of the game. He was safe at second on a fielder's choice grounder by Noren but overran the bag. Though he was eventually tagged out in a rundown, he avoided the tag long enough for Noren to reach second, from where he scored on a two-out single by Martin.

Now nursing a 1–0 lead, Ford retired the Athletics without a hit in the sixth inning and retired the first two batters in the seventh. Then he walked Hector Lopez, and second baseman Jim Finigan followed with a flare down the right-field line that fell just beyond the reach of Hank Bauer and bounced into the stands for a ground-rule double. After intentionally walking Enos Slaughter, Ford uncorked a wild pitch and Lopez scored the tying run. Whitey worked out of the jam with no further scoring and the game remained tied 1–1 into the bottom of the ninth. With one out, Bauer doubled to left and went to third on an infield hit by Berra. Mantle was intentionally walked to load the bases, and then Portocarrero walked Noren to force home the winning run. The double by Finigan had been Kansas City's only hit, making Ford only the fifth pitcher in major league history to pitch back-to-back one-hitters.[7] With his record now 17–6 and with three starts remaining, Ford had an outside shot at 20 wins. Most importantly, the win allowed New York to keep pace with the other three teams in the race, all of whom won.

After crushing Kansas City 13–0 the following day and then splitting two games with Chicago, the Yanks played a double-header with the Indians on September 11 at Yankee Stadium, needing a sweep to move past the Indians into first place. New York won the first game 6–1 behind the four-hit pitching of Tommy Byrne and then Ford squared off against Herb Score in the nightcap. Ford outlasted the rookie and held a 2–1 lead in the eighth inning. With one out, Whitey allowed his fourth hit — a homer by Bobby Avila — and the game was suddenly tied. It didn't stay that way for long, as Hoot Evers doubled, moved to third on a ground-out and scored when Ford threw a wild pitch with Ralph Kiner at the plate. The Yanks had two more shots at reliever Don Mossi but came up empty, with Evers making a spectacular diving catch in deep left center with a man on to end the game. The 3–2 loss left the Yanks where they had been at the start of the day — a game and a half behind the Indians.

With 12 games remaining in the regular season, the Yanks finally made their move. Bob Turley started the streak with his sixth shutout of the season, a 6–0 whitewashing of the Tigers at the Stadium. Then Don Larsen beat the Tigers to keep New York within a game of Cleveland, and after an off day it was Ford's turn again, against Boston in the opener of a weekend series in New York. Whitey was opposed by 6'6" right-hander Frank Sullivan, gunning for his 19th win of the season. Boston had slipped out of the pennant race (trailing the Indians by seven games with 10 to play), but seven of those last 10 games would be against the Yankees, so they would play a major role in determining the AL pennant winner.

The Yanks opened the scoring in the second inning, but at great cost. Throughout his career, Mantle was the best drag bunter in baseball. Batting left-handed, he was very adept at dropping the ball down midway between the first-base line and the pitcher's mound, and he could get down the line faster than any man in baseball when he first came up — allegedly in 3.1 seconds. Gradually the accumulation of all of his leg injuries slowed him a bit, and each successive injury made his muscles more prone to pulls. As his career progressed, it seemed that a disproportionate number of his muscle pulls occurred when he dragged a bunt and accelerated into his highest gear, yet he never stopped dragging bunts. In this game against Boston, he beat out a drag bunt but pulled up lame with a pulled hamstring muscle in his right thigh. The injury would cause him to miss the last nine games of the regular season (except for two pinch-hitting appearances) and would have major ramifications for the World Series.

Mantle left the game for a pinch runner, who eventually scored on an RBI single by Martin. A Martin single and a Rizzuto double produced a second run off Sullivan in the fourth. Ford wriggled out of a bases-loaded jam in the top of the fifth by striking out Billy Klaus and Karl Olson, and then Berra slammed his 26th home run of the season in the bottom half of the inning to give Whitey a 3–0 lead. Ford gave back a run in the sixth but was cruising with one out in the eighth when three straight singles suddenly narrowed the gap to 3–2. Whitey bore down and fanned Grady Hatton for the second out, but Jimmy Piersall followed with a single to left to tie the game. After an error extended the inning, Ford was replaced by Jim Konstanty, who promptly yielded a double that gave the Red Sox a 4–3 lead.

Boston turned the game over to 41-year-old reliever Ellis Kinder, well past his prime but still a formidable pitcher for an inning or two. With one out in the bottom of the ninth, Bauer hit his 20th homer of the season into the left-field seats and the Yanks were even again. Then, with two down, Berra hit his second homer of the game well back into the right-field seats to give the Yanks a 5–4 win and a 2-percentage-point lead over the Indians, who lost to Detroit. It was the first time since August 29 that New York had been atop the American League standings. After sweeping the last two games of the Boston series while the Indians were losing two more to Detroit, the Yanks left on a season-ending seven-game road trip with a two-game lead in the standings.

The Yankees played a day-night double-header against Washington on the final Tuesday of the regular season and won their sixth straight game in the opener behind Tom Morgan's clutch relief pitching. With Ford on the mound for the night game, New York took a 3–1 lead in the third and then seemingly put the game out of reach with six runs in the seventh. Ford singled and scored in both rallies and yielded just four hits and one unearned run through seven innings. However, he tired in the eighth and was reached for a two-run pinch homer by Jim Lemon. When Whitey walked two batters with two out, Stengel replaced him with rookie south-paw Rip Coleman, who promptly yielded an RBI single to Mickey Vernon. It took a parade of four Yankee relievers to get the last four outs, but Tommy Byrne finally nailed down a 9–7 win, raising Ford's record to 18–7 and giving New York a three-game lead in the loss column with only five to play.

After Bob Turley stretched the Yankee winning streak to eight games by beating the Senators for his 17th win of the season, the Yanks had a chance to clinch by winning either end of a September 23 double-header against the Red Sox. Tommy Byrne started the first game but was routed in the third inning of an 8–4 loss, so Don Larsen went for the clincher in the nightcap. A first-inning homer by Gil McDougald got the Yanks off and running and they tacked on two more runs to give Larsen a 3–0 lead. He shut Boston out for six innings but ran out of gas in the seventh, yielding three singles and a run. With two on and one out, Stengel summoned Ford from the bullpen for his sixth relief appearance of the year. Whitey proceeded to walk Billy Klaus, loading the bases for Ted Williams, who hit .356 that year. Ford escaped when Ted grounded to Billy Martin, who started a 4–6–3 double play. Jackie Jensen cut the Yankee lead to 3–2 with a homer leading off the Boston eighth, but Ford retired the last six Red Sox batters in order (striking out three of them) to save the win for Larsen and clinch the Yankees' 21st American League pennant, Stengel's sixth in seven years as their manager. The final margins in the AL standings were three games over the Indians and five over the White Sox.

Ford's 18 wins tied him with Frank Sullivan and Bob Lemon for the league lead and his winning percentage of .720 was second in the AL to teammate Tommy Byrne, who had finished the season 16–5. Ford led the league in complete games with 18; his ERA in those 18 games was 1.17, but his two bad early season starts and his bad patch in the first three weeks of July inflated his overall ERA up to 2.63, which was still second-best in the AL behind Billy Pierce's 1.97 ERA. Only Bob Turley and Herb Score gave up fewer hits per nine innings, but what got Ford into trouble in most of his bad outings was wildness: his 113 walks (4.0 per nine innings) would be the most in his career. Although he was fourth in the league in strikeouts with 137, his ratio of strikeouts to walks was only 1.21, as compared to his eventual career ratio of 1.80. But all in all it was Ford's best season so far, highlighted by the consecutive one-hitters and the pair of two-hitters. There was no Cy Young Award yet (it was instituted the following year), but Whitey was named the American League Pitcher of the Year by *The Sporting News.*

Mantle batted .306 and led the league in homers (37), triples (11), walks (113), on base percentage (.433) and slugging percentage (.611). He also scored 121 runs and knocked in 99. Berra's statistics weren't quite as gaudy (.272, 27 HR, 108 RBI), but his leadership, clutch hitting and solid performance behind the plate earned him his second straight MVP Award and his third in five years. Only Jimmie Foxx, Joe DiMaggio and Stan Musial had ever won the award three times. Coincidentally, Yogi's cross-town counterpart, Roy Campanella, also won his third MVP Award that season. Mantle inexplicably finished fifth in the MVP balloting.

The Yankees' opponent in the 1955 World Series would be the Brooklyn Dodgers, who were 0-for-7 in their seven previous World Series appearances. No other team in baseball history had made that many trips to the Fall Classic and come up short every time. The first two losses (in 1916 to the Boston Red Sox and in 1920 to the Cleveland Indians) had been long forgotten by 1955, but the last five defeats had all come since 1940 and at the hands of the Yankees, their hated cross-town rivals. After each of those years, the Dodgers' adoring fans were left to console themselves with the constant refrain: "Wait 'til next year!"

The 1941 loss to the Yanks had been an especially tough one. Trailing two games to one, the Dodgers appeared to have evened the Series in Game 4 when Dodger reliever Hugh Casey struck out Tommy Henrich for what should have been the game-ending out. However, Dodger catcher Mickey Owen let the third strike get past him and Henrich reached first safely to keep Yankee hopes alive. Two doubles, a single, two walks and four runs later, the Yankees were up three games to one and they finished off the Dodgers the following day.

After losing the 1946 pennant to the Cardinals in the first playoff in major league history, Brooklyn signed Jackie Robinson prior to the 1947 season. With Robinson hitting .297, stealing a league-leading 29 bases and scoring 125 runs to win the first Rookie of the Year Award, the Dodgers won the pennant by five games over the Cardinals. The 1947 World Series between the Dodgers and the Yankees was a true classic and included two of the most memorable games in Series history. The Dodgers won both games, breaking up Bill Bevens' no-hitter with two out in the last of the ninth inning to win Game 4 and then evening the Series in Game 6 when Al Gionfriddo made a great catch to rob Joe DiMaggio of what would have been a game-tying home run. However, Joe Page shut the Dodgers down the following day and the Yanks won Game 7.

By the time the two teams met again in the 1949 World Series, the Dodgers had added center fielder Duke Snider, first baseman Gil Hodges and catcher Roy Campanella to a lineup that already included Robinson, shortstop Pee Wee Reese and right fielder Carl Furillo. These six players would form the nucleus of the great Dodgers teams of the 1950s, the team that Roger Kahn dubbed "The Boys of Summer." After splitting a pair of 1–0 games to open the Series, the two teams battled into the ninth inning of Game 3, tied 1–1. Then Johnny Mize belted a two-run pinch double off the right-field screen at Ebbets Field to propel New York to a 4–3 win and Brooklyn folded in five games.

After losing the 1950 pennant to the Phillies on the final day of the season and then losing the famous 1951 playoff to the Giants after blowing a mid-August lead of 13½ games, the Dodgers tried their luck against the Yanks again in 1952. New York rallied from a three-games-to-two deficit to win the last two games at Ebbets Field on home runs by Mantle, with Billy Martin making a spectacular catch of a windblown pop-up to save Game 7. Brooklyn's 1953 loss to the Yankees in six games was their fifth loss to New York in a 13-year period.

After finishing second to the Giants in 1954, the Dodgers destroyed the National League in 1955. With Campanella (.318, 32 HR, 107 RBI), Snider (.309, 42 HR, 136 RBI), Hodges (.289, 27 HR, 102 RBI), Furillo (.314, 26 HR, 95 RBI) and Newcombe (20–5) leading the way, the Dodgers got off to the best start in NL history. They won their first 10 games, had a nine-game lead when their record reached 22–2 and romped to the pennant by 13½ games over the Braves and 18½ games over the Giants. The Dodgers' only weakness was their pitching depth: the only pitcher on their staff other than Newcombe to win more than 11 games was reliever Clem Labine (13–5). The Yankee starting rotation of Ford (18–7), Turley (17–13), Byrne (16–5) and Larsen (9–2) was superior to that of the Dodgers. Therefore the Yanks were favored to beat the Dodgers for the sixth straight time, but they would have to do it without Mantle, who would be available only for limited duty because of his hamstring injury.

The two aces— Ford and Newcombe — opposed each other in the Series opener at Yankee Stadium. The Dodgers opened the scoring in the second inning when Carl Furillo sliced the first pitch down the right-field line, just inside the foul pole. The ball struck the top of the four-foot railing and bounced into the stands, about 300 feet from home plate. Then Jackie Robinson tripled and Don Zimmer singled him home, and Brooklyn had a quick 2–0 lead. But the Yanks responded with two runs of their own in the bottom half of the inning when Elston Howard hit a two-run homer in his first World Series at-bat. The Dodgers regained the lead in the third inning on a home run by Snider into the upper deck in right field, but the Yankees again responded immediately when Ford worked Newcombe for a walk and came around to score on a single by Bauer and two ground outs.

Ford poses with Brooklyn's Don Newcombe before Game 1 of the 1955 World Series. Ford beat the Dodgers 6–5 despite a disputed steal of home by Jackie Robinson. (National Baseball Hall of Fame Library, Cooperstown, N.Y.)

Then veteran Joe Collins (who had hit 13 homers during the regular season while platooning at first base with Bill Skowron) struck twice. Using a bat borrowed from Mickey Mantle, Collins hit a solo homer in the fourth and a two-run blast in the sixth to give the Yankees a 6–3 lead. When Billy Martin followed with a two-out triple, Newcombe was gone, not to return in the Series. After running up a record of 18–1 by July 31, Newcombe had been just 2–4 in August and September and his arm was clearly tired. Don Bessent came on in relief and got out of the inning when Martin tried unsuccessfully to steal home.

The Dodgers made one last comeback in the eighth, aided by a Yankee error. With one out and Furillo on first, Robinson hit a sharp grounder to Andy Carey at third. The potential double-play ball got through Carey and the runners ended up on second and third. A sacrifice fly by Zimmer plated one run, and then a dramatic steal of home by Jackie Robinson (only the ninth steal of home in Series history) brought the Dodgers within a run. Robinson was nearing the end of the line by then (he would retire after the following season), and age, injuries and incipient diabetes had significantly reduced Jackie's production that year. Yet the competitive fires still burned within him, and when Ford went into a windup with Robinson on third, Jackie took off for home. Ford threw the pitch low and Berra had the ball in his mitt on the ground in front of the plate when Robinson slid in. Jackie appeared to most of the 63,869 in attendance to be out, and the tape of the game bears that out. But umpire Bill Summers (standing in back of Yogi) ruled otherwise, which made Berra apoplectic. In *Slick,* Whitey said: "To this day, I still believe that Jackie was out. I've seen the films of that play maybe fifty times, and Robinson is out every time."[8]

Ford got the third out in the eighth, but Stengel opted to bring in right-hander Bob Grim (a Brooklyn native) to pitch the Dodgers' ninth. A one-out single by Snider gave Dodgers fans hope, but a home run bid by Campanella fell short and Grim struck out Furillo to end the game.

In Game 2, the Yanks chased Billy Loes with a four-run fourth and left-hander Tommy Byrne pitched a five-hitter and drove in the winning runs with a two-run single. The 4–2 Yankee win sent the Series over to Ebbets Field with the Dodgers down two games to none, and few of their own fans expected them to come back.

The Dodgers' pitcher in Game 3 was 23-year-old Johnny Podres, who had been 9–10 on the year with a 3.95 ERA. Hampered by a sore arm, Podres had won only two of his last 13 starts and had not completed a game since mid-June. Yankees right fielder Hank Bauer had pulled a muscle in Game 2 and couldn't play, so Mickey Mantle played right field, limping badly due to his torn hamstring muscle.

Roy Campanella hit a two-run homer in the first inning off Yankee starter Bob Turley, but Mantle led off the second with a shot into the center-field seats above the 393-foot sign and limped around the bases. Moose Skowron tied the score later in the inning when he knocked the ball out of Campanella's glove at the plate. But the Dodgers came right back in the bottom half of the inning, loading the bases for Jim "Junior" Gilliam. Jackie Robinson was the runner on third and he broke toward the plate on four straight pitches as if to repeat his Game 1 steal of home, so disconcerting Turley that he walked Gilliam, forcing in a run and sending Turley to the showers. After scoring another run that inning, the Dodgers cruised to an 8–3 victory.

Don Larsen opposed Carl Erskine (11–8) in Game 4. The Yanks knocked Erskine out in the fourth inning, but Larsen yielded homers to Campanella and Hodges before being relieved with nobody out in the Dodgers' fifth, trailing 4–3. The Yankees might have escaped further damage that inning had relief pitcher Johnny Kucks remembered to cover first base on a grounder to first baseman Joe Collins, but Pee Wee Reese beat him to the bag, and Snider followed with a tremendous three-run homer that was reported to have dented a car in a parking lot across the street from Ebbets Field.[9] The Dodgers won, 8–5, to even the Series at two games apiece.

Snider was the main man again in Game 5 at Ebbets Field, hitting two home runs off Bob Grim to become the first player to hit four home runs in two different World Series. His nine World Series homers extended his own National League record. Rookie Roger Craig held the Mantle-less Yankees to two runs on four hits in six innings, and Clem Labine (who had pitched the last 4⅓ innings to get the win the previous day) pitched the final three innings to get the save. Dodgers outfielder Sandy Amoros hit a two-run homer to offset solo clouts by Bob Cerv and Yogi Berra, and the 5–3 Brooklyn victory put the Yankees on the brink of the unthinkable — losing to the Dodgers— as the Series moved back to the Bronx.

That night, Ford appeared on the *Ed Sullivan Show* with Mantle and Byrne. When Sullivan asked Ford who would pitch the next day's game for the Yankees, Whitey replied innocently: "I am, and Tommy's pitching the seventh game."[10] It was simply an ingenuous answer from a player with the utmost confidence in himself and his teammates, but that response added to the perception around the country that Ford was cocky.

Newcombe was unable to come back against Ford in Game 6 because of his sore arm, so manager Walter Alston had to gamble on rookie left-hander Karl Spooner. In the final week of the 1954 season, Spooner had been brought up from the Texas League and had made one of the most spectacular debuts of any pitcher in history. He shut out the champion Giants on 3 hits in his first start, striking out 15. He followed that up with a four-hit shutout of the Pirates on the final day of the season, fanning 12 more to set a NL record of 27 strikeouts in two consecutive games. However, he hurt his arm in spring training in 1955 and was only 8–6 on the season.

The Yankees made it clear early that there would be a seventh game. Spooner faced six batters, five of whom scored, the last three on a home run by Moose Skowron. The five runs would be the extent of New York's scoring in the game but they were more than enough for Ford. Whitey had all four of his pitches working (fastball, curve, slider and changeup), and he dominated the potent Dodgers lineup. He was a little wild in the second inning, hitting Furillo and walking Hodges, but he induced Jackie Robinson to hit into a double play. Brooklyn got on the board in the fourth inning on an infield hit, a walk and a single by Furillo, but Ford snuffed out the threat by retiring Hodges and Robinson on ground balls.

The Dodgers mounted one last threat in the seventh when a single, a wild pitch and a walk put runners on the corners with two out, but first baseman Joe Collins made a nice play on a grounder in the hole by Reese to get the third out. Ford retired the Dodgers in order in the last two innings to finish off a four-hitter and post his second win of the Series, 5–1. He struck out eight and got 15 outs on ground balls. After the game, he said his plan had been to stay ahead of the Dodgers' hitters so they would have to swing at his breaking pitches low and away, resulting in one ground ball after another.[11] Hall of Famer Ty Cobb (owner of baseball's highest career batting average of .367) visited Ford in the Yankees' dressing room after the game and told him: "Son, that was a gorgeous game you pitched, just perfect. I'd hate to have been hitting against you myself."[12]

Stengel said that all hands would be on deck for the next day's finale. "My pitchers will have most of the winter to rest," he said. "If necessary, everybody works tomorrow. And that goes for Ford, too. He pitched a beautiful, smart game out there today but he's going to have to be ready overnight, if I should need him."[13] Ford said that was fine with him, and added: "I wished we could have started the seventh game immediately after the sixth today, with me continuing to pitch. I could have gone nine more innings."[14]

The home team had now won all six games, and 62,465 fans jammed Yankee Stadium on October 4 for Game 7 to see if the Yankees could keep that streak going. The pitching matchup was Tommy Byrne versus Johnny Podres. The two lefties matched zeros for the first three innings, although Podres needed a little luck to get out of the third. With runners on first and second and two out, Gil McDougald bounced an infield hit to third that would have loaded the bases for Berra, who hit .417 in the Series. But Phil Rizzuto, playing in his ninth and last World Series, slid into the batted ball and was automatically out to end the inning.

A double by Campanella and a single by Hodges gave the Dodgers a 1–0 lead in the fourth, and Hodges knocked in another run in the sixth with a sacrifice fly. Alston then made the move that decided the 1955 World Series. His normal practice was to switch Junior Gilliam (a switch hitter) back and forth between second base and left field, depending on whether the opposing pitcher was right-handed or left-handed. If he was right-handed, Gilliam played second and the left-hand-hitting Sandy Amoros played left field. If a left-hander was pitching, Junior played left field and Don Zimmer (who batted righty) started at second base. That was the lineup for Game 7 against the left-handed Byrne. But Alston had pinch-hit for Zimmer in the top of the sixth and had to move Gilliam to second base and insert Amoros in left field.

In the Yankees' sixth, Billy Martin drew a walk and Gil McDougald beat out a bunt to put runners on first and second with nobody out and red-hot Yogi Berra up next. The Dodgers outfield was swung way over toward right because you could count the number of times Berra hit the ball to left field during the course of a season on one hand. Yogi sliced a fly ball right down the left-field line, deep into the corner. If it stayed fair, it was a sure double and maybe a triple, and a tie game. Or so thought probably everybody in the ballpark and millions more watching on television. Starting from his position about 50 yards from the left-field line, the speedy Amoros sprinted into the corner trying to catch the ball. At the last instant, he slammed on the brakes to avoid crashing into the low railing of the stands that angled out almost to the foul line, and stuck out his glove. He caught the ball, one foot fair and two feet from the railing. The play was only possible for a left-handed outfielder, because had Gilliam or any other righty been out there, there is no way he could have reached across his body with his left (glove) hand to catch the ball. Not only did Amoros catch the ball, but he whirled and made a perfect throw to Reese, who relayed the ball to first to double up McDougald. Gil had been so sure the ball couldn't be caught that he was around second and heading for third when Amoros caught the ball. Instead of a tie game and a man on second or third with nobody out, the Yanks had only a runner on second with two out, and they failed to score.

The Yankees threatened once more in the eighth inning when singles by Rizzuto and McDougald put runners on the corners with one out, but Podres worked out of the jam, getting Berra on a pop-up to short right and striking out Bauer. In the ninth, Skowron grounded back to Podres, Cerv flied out to Amoros, and Howard grounded to short to end the game. At 3:43 p.m. (EDT) on October 4, 1955, "Next Year" finally arrived for the Dodgers. It was fitting that Pee Wee Reese made the final play, because he was the only one who had been with the Dodgers since 1941 and had suffered through all of the disappointments—five World Series losses to the Yankees, two NL playoff losses and a pennant lost on the final day of the season.

Sixteen major league teams played a total of 1,234 games in 1955 to decide who would play in the World Series, and then the Dodgers and Yanks played seven more games, and in the end, the championship came down to whether the Dodgers had a left-handed or right-handed left fielder in the game on one play. The Dodgers had been lucky and Mantle had been hurt, but the Boys of Summer were long overdue to win a championship. Johnny Podres was a deserving winner of the Babe Ruth Award and the *Sport Magazine* Corvette as Series MVP, but Ford had won two games in the Series as well, including the crucial sixth game. His performance in this World Series further established Ford's reputation as a big game pitcher.

FIVE

Chasing Twenty Wins

After two consecutive seasons without a world championship (not to mention a World Series winner's share, which was a significant part of their income back then), the Yankees went into the 1956 season determined to get back to the Series and recapture what they felt was theirs. As the acknowledged ace of the pitching staff, Ford knew that he would need to have a good year in order for New York to beat out Cleveland and Chicago again. As with any top pitcher, Whitey had an individual goal as well: to win 20 games. The Yanks would also need good years out of Mantle and Berra. The latter (who turned 31 during the season) was still in his prime, and Mantle had given notice in 1955 that he might be ready to achieve the superstardom that had been predicted for him back in the spring of 1951 when he first joined the Yankees. In fact, when asked before the start of the 1956 season whether he thought he could repeat as AL homer champ, Mickey answered: "I think that this year I'd rather lead the league in runs batted in, home runs and hitting, and that's my goal for this year."[1]

Mantle started the season with a bang on Opening Day, hitting two long home runs off Camilo Pascual of the Washington Senators at Griffith Stadium with President Eisenhower in attendance. Mickey loved to hit at Griffith Stadium (the site of his 565-footer in 1953), and Eisenhower seemed to be a good luck charm for him. (Mickey nearly always homered when Ike was in attendance.) While lots of players have hit two home runs on Opening Day before, the distance of these two blasts signaled that this year might be something special. The first one cleared the 31-foot-high center-field wall at the 408-foot mark and landed on the roof of a house across the street from the stadium, approximately 465 feet from home plate. The second one (with two men on base) cleared the same wall at the 438-foot mark and landed in a tree across the street.[2] Casey Stengel said later: "They tell me that the only other feller which hit that tree was Ruth. He shook some kids outta the tree when the ball landed. But the tree's gotten bigger in twenty-five years, and so, I guess, have the kids the Babe shook outta it."[3] Not to be outdone, Berra drove in five runs with a homer, a double and two singles as the Yanks won the game, 10–4.

Stengel held Ford out of the three-game Washington series so that he could start the home opener on April 20 against the Red Sox, who were expected to be a contender. Backed by a three-run homer by Mantle, Whitey spun a five-hitter to beat the Sox, 7–1. The news was not all good, however. After Ford doubled in the fifth and Bauer followed with a triple, Mantle strained his right hamstring again beating out a surprise two-out bunt that scored Bauer. Fortunately the strain was not as severe as the one that had sidelined him during the previous September. In fact, though limping perceptibly, the following day Mickey slammed his fourth homer in five days 20 rows back into the Stadium's third deck in right-center field. It struck a seat 415 feet from the plate and 100 feet above the ground.[4] The Yanks won that game as well, 14–10, with Berra and Bauer also homering.

The usually reliable Yankees infield made things tough for Ford in his second start of the season (committing three errors), but Whitey limited the damage to two unearned runs and nailed down a 4–2 win over the Orioles by striking out pinch hitter Tom Gastall with the tying runs on base.

Ford won his third straight start on May 1, beating Detroit 9–2 with a complete-game seven-hitter. Mantle homered in that game and then hit four more in the next four days, including two mammoth shots against Kansas City at Yankee Stadium on May 5 that powered a 5–2 Yankees victory. The first was a routine Mantle blast high into the upper deck in right. The second one allegedly hit the facade *atop* the third deck in right field.[5] Mantle now had nine homers in the first 16 games of the season.

The following day, Ford shut out the White Sox 4–0 at the Stadium, striking out six and not allowing a runner past second base. This time it was Berra who delivered the big blow, a two-run homer in the third inning. It was Yogi's eighth homer of the season, putting him right behind Mantle.

Ford improved to 5–0 with a 3–2 win over Baltimore on May 11 (his fifth complete game in five starts), but it wasn't easy. After spotting the Orioles single runs in the first and second, Whitey pitched shutout ball the rest of the way and also contributed a key fifth-inning double that led to the tying run. Baltimore nearly took the lead in the top of the ninth when Bobby Adams tried to score from second on a two-out single by Billy Gardner, but left fielder Elston Howard made a strong throw home and Berra blocked the plate like the Rock of Gibraltar. New York then won the game in the bottom of the ninth on a triple by Joe Collins and a single by Moose Skowron.

Ford made it 6-for-6 with a 10–3 complete-game win over the White Sox on May 17. All of the Chicago runs were unearned, the result of two throwing errors by Phil Rizzuto. Whitey had two hits and an RBI, but the batting highlight for the Yanks was Berra's 11th homer of the season.

It was Mantle's turn to lead the way the following day, and he switch-hit a pair of tape-measure homers into the left- and right-field upper decks at Chicago's Comiskey Park, the second one tying the game with two out in the ninth inning and completing a 4-for-4 day. Berra also went 4-for-4 (including a homer and two doubles) and the Yanks pulled the game out in the 10th inning, 8–7.

At this point in the season, the Yanks were in first place by two and a half games over Cleveland with a 19–10 record. They couldn't have asked for a better start from their three stars. Mantle was batting .409 with 15 homers and 32 RBIs, while Berra was batting .357 with 12 homers and 33 RBIs. The two of them were 1–2 in the American League in homers and RBIs. Ford was the first pitcher in either league to win six games, and with five earned runs allowed in six complete games, his ERA was a miserly 0.83.

Ford's winning streak came to an end on May 22 when he lost a tough 3–2 decision to the Tigers in Detroit. The Yanks scored two runs in the first inning off right-hander Frank Lary and Ford shut the Tigers out on three hits through seven innings. He yielded a run in the eighth on singles by Harvey Kuenn, Al Kaline and Bill Tuttle, but still seemed to have the game in hand. However, Charlie Maxwell doubled off Whitey in the ninth and light-hitting catcher Red Wilson followed with his first homer of the year to shock the Yanks. The win was just the second of the season for Lary, but both wins had come against the Yanks and he would beat New York three more times that season. With seven wins against New York in his first two years in the majors, Lary was starting to establish a reputation as a Yankee-killer.

Ford bounced back in his next start, blanking the Red Sox on five hits, 2–0. He struck out five and got his usual quota of ground-ball outs (17) as only two Boston runners reached second base. He completed the shutout in a tidy 1 hour and 49 minutes, although he did take the time to pick up a $2 bill that was blowing around out by the mound. It was Whitey's eighth complete game in eight starts, and the Yanks moved out to a four-and-a-half-game lead over Cleveland.

Two days later, Mantle *really* hit one. Two, actually: one in each game of a Memorial Day double-header against the Senators, against two of his favorite pitchers, Pedro Ramos and Camilo Pascual. In the first game of the Memorial Day double-header, Mantle hit "the best ball I ever hit left-handed" off the right-field facade at Yankee Stadium, 18 inches from the top. It was the closest anyone had come to hitting a fair ball out of the Stadium; the ball had appeared to be above the roof and going out, but had descended slightly at the last instant against a slight breeze and hit the facade 117 feet above the field, about 396 feet from home plate. It was estimated that this one would have traveled between 550 and 600 feet if it hadn't hit the roof.[6] Almost incidentally, the three-run shot was the key blow in a 4–3 win, just as his homer into the right-field upper deck off Pascual broke a 3–3 tie in the second game as the Yankees swept the double-header to open up a six-game lead in the AL pennant race. Mantle was now leading the majors in all three Triple Crown categories with a .425 batting average, 20 homers and 50 RBIs in 41 games. He was the first player ever to hit 20 homers before June, and he was now 11 games ahead of Babe Ruth's pace in 1927 when he hit 60.[7]

Ford's string of complete games came to an end on June 3 at the hands of the Tigers. He walked home a run in the fourth inning and then was knocked out in the fifth as Detroit southpaw Billy Hoeft went the distance to beat the Yanks, 6–3. Ford absorbed a second straight loss five days later when he was rocked for six runs in five innings of a 9–0 loss to Cleveland that brought the Indians within three and a half games of the Yanks. Five walks contributed to Whitey's demise, but the first run was all Early Wynn needed as he shut out the Yanks on just five hits.

Things returned to normal in Ford's next start as he no-hit the White Sox for the first six innings at the Stadium and led 4–0, thanks mainly to Andy Carey's three RBIs. Nellie Fox broke up the no-hitter leading off the seventh with a ground ball back up through the middle that Whitey couldn't get his glove on. With the spell broken, Chicago pushed across two runs, but Ford shut them down over the final two innings to complete a four-hitter. He struck out six and picked off his seventh runner of the season. The 4–2 win gave Whitey a 16–3 career record against the White Sox.

Ford's push for 20 wins was temporarily derailed in his next start when he was forced to leave a game against Cleveland in the second inning with sacroiliac trouble. The Yanks won the game, 9–4, but Whitey would be side-lined for a week.

Mantle went into a mild slump in the first half of June (hitting only one homer in the first 13 days of the month), but broke out of it with six homers in seven days. Homer number 25 on June 18 cleared the right-field roof of Detroit's Briggs Stadium (possibly bouncing on top of the roof) with two men on to beat the Tigers; only Ted Williams (in 1939) had ever cleared this roof previously.[8] Two days later, batting right-handed against Billy Hoeft, he hit two balls into the center-field upper deck in Detroit in a 4–1 Yankees win, giving him 27 homers as of June 20 and putting him 18 games ahead of Ruth's 1927 pace.

Ford's back was still bothering him when the Yanks moved on to Chicago and he lasted just one inning in the opener of a June 24 double-header against the White Sox, yielding a three-run homer to Larry Doby. Chicago won both games and moved within a game of the Yanks in the AL standings. Two days later, Whitey gave it another try and this time he went the route, allowing Kansas City seven hits in an 8–4 win that raised his record to 9–4.

On July 1 at Yankee Stadium, Ford and Mantle helped the Yanks stretch their lead to four games by taking two from the Senators. Whitey struggled somewhat in the opener but four double plays and two pickoffs helped keep the Yanks in the game until Joe Collins won it 3–2 with a two-run eighth-inning homer, with Tom Morgan getting the win in relief. Then Mantle homered from both sides of the plate in the same game for the second time in the 1956 season (and fourth time in his career) to power New York to an 8–6 win in the second game. First he tied the game 6–6 in the seventh inning with a right-handed shot into the third deck in left, and then he won it with a left-handed blast into the Yankees bullpen with a man on in the bottom of the ninth inning. The second one (his 29th of the season) was the 150th of his career, at the age of 24. Unfortunately, on July 4 Mickey strained the lateral ligaments in his bad knee trying to throw a runner out at the plate, missed four games entirely and hobbled around with a knee brace in a number of others. By the time he connected for his 30th homer on July 14, he had slipped several games behind Ruth's pace.

Ford got one more start before the All-Star break and picked up his 10th win, beating Boston 6–1 at Fenway Park with a complete-game seven-hitter. Gil McDougald's three-run homer into the net above the Green Monster in the third inning provided Whitey with all the support he needed. The Yanks went into the break with a six-and-a-half-game lead over both Chicago and Cleveland.

Ford pitched an inning in the All-Star Game and gave up a two-run homer to Willie Mays, who practically owned Whitey throughout their careers. Baseball's four biggest stars all homered in that game, which was won by the National League, 7–3. Stan Musial also homered for the NL, and Mantle and Ted Williams connected off Warren Spahn for the AL.

The second half of the season started well for Ford when he outdueled Billy Pierce at the Stadium in the first game of a July 15 double-header. Whitey was touched for a run in the first inning when Luis Aparicio tripled and scored on a sacrifice fly by Minnie Minoso, but he yielded only two hits thereafter as the Yanks won 2–1 on a two-run single by Andy Carey. He struck out seven and walked none in raising his record to 11–4. When the Yanks won the nightcap as well (their 10th straight win), they dropped the White Sox into third place, 11½ games back and a game behind the Indians. The pennant race was rapidly losing any semblance of suspense.

New York finally lost a couple of games but Ford stretched his personal winning streak to four with a 6–2 win over Kansas City on July 20 at the

Stadium. He tied an AL record by fanning six Athletics in succession, but missed a chance at the major league record of eight (set by Max Surkont of the Milwaukee Braves in 1953) when he hit Enos Slaughter with a pitch with two out in the fourth.[9] Whitey lost his shutout in the eighth inning when an error and three hits plated two runs for the A's, but he pitched another complete game to pick up his 12th win, 6–2. He struck out eight in total and picked off his 10th runner of the year.

Ford got two more starts in July and won both of them to improve to 14–4 on the season with two months to go. First he beat the White Sox in Chicago with a four-hitter, 10–1, his fifth win over the Pale Hose that season. Then the Yanks moved on to Cleveland, where Whitey beat the Indians 13–6 on July 30 in the opener of a four-game series. He struck out 10 but walked eight, four of them in the ninth inning when the Indians pushed across three runs to chase Whitey, one out short of another complete game. The game had long since been decided, thanks to Mantle. After hitting only three home runs in the previous four weeks, Mickey hit his 33rd with the bases loaded off Bob Lemon in the second inning and then hit his only career home run off the great Bob Feller with a man on in the fifth. The win was Ford's sixth in a row and restored New York's lead over Cleveland to 10 games. But the Indians bounced back to win the last three games of the series as Early Wynn, Lemon and Herb Score limited the Yanks to a total of one run in the three games.

The Yanks moved on to Detroit and lost three more games. Ford's August got off to a bad start when he suffered a bruised left hand deflecting a line drive hit right back at him by Ray Boone (the patriarch of the three-generation Boone baseball family) in the first inning of the series opener on August 3. He left the game immediately and would be sidelined for a week. Mantle hit two home runs the following day (the seventh time that season he hit two in the same game), but Al Kaline trumped him with two homers of his own, including a three-run shot in the eighth inning that won the game for Detroit, 5–4. Mickey hit another homer the next day off Jim Bunning (off the front of the roof of Briggs Stadium's right-field upper deck) to tie the game in the sixth inning, but the Yankees lost their sixth straight game. However, the Indians obliged by losing three straight to Boston, leaving them seven games behind the Yanks.

Ford returned to the mound on August 10, pitching seven innings against the Orioles in a game won by the Yanks in the bottom of the ninth on a 450-foot ground-rule double by Mantle into the center-field bleachers at the Stadium. The victim of Mantle's blast was Billy Loes, Whitey's old neighbor from Astoria. The next day, Mickey hit number 40 into the right-field upper deck, becoming the first Yankee to reach that mark since Joe DiMaggio hit 46 in 1937.

Ford's bad luck continued in his next start on August 15 when he was again forced to leave the game early with an injury. After pitching three hitless innings to start the game, Whitey's left shoulder stiffened up in the fourth inning and he exited after that inning with a 1–0 lead. The Yanks eventually won the game thanks to Berra's 21st homer of the season, but Ford's injury overshadowed the win. The game was also marred by a temper tantrum on the part of Jimmy Piersall, who was so upset at not getting credit for a hit on a bobbled grounder into the shortstop hole that he kicked up huge divots of turf when he returned to center field after Boston was retired. The 39,427 fans at Yankee Stadium (who always enjoyed Piersall's zany antics) got a big kick out of it, but it took several minutes for a groundskeeper and Mantle to repair the damage.

With Ford out of action for 10 days, the Yanks sputtered a bit, losing six out of 10 during that span. Mantle put on a show during one of those losses, blasting No. 43 right-handed about 20 rows deep into the left-field upper deck at the Stadium on August 23, along with a 460-foot triple to center field and a bunt single. Despite the 10-day slump, the Yanks remained comfortably ahead of both Cleveland and Chicago in the AL standings.

Ford tested his sore shoulder against Chicago on August 25. It was Old Timers' Day at the Stadium, but the day was marred by the unceremonious and insensitive release of Phil Rizzuto in front of his old teammates. The move was made in order to clear a roster spot for 40-year-old Enos Slaughter (a .300 lifetime hitter over 19 seasons), whom the Yankees picked up from Kansas City in order to bolster their lineup for the upcoming World Series. In the game itself, Ford took a line drive by Nellie Fox off his right leg in the first inning but stayed in the game. Mantle opened the scoring with a two-run homer (No. 44) in the fourth inning, but the game slipped away in the seventh inning. With the Yanks leading 2–1, Ford retired the first two batters but walked Fred Hatfield, Chicago's No. 8 hitter. Pitcher Dick Donovan then beat out an infield hit. A single to right center by Luis Aparicio knocked in the tying run, and Donovan came around to score as well when Mantle made a bad throw that eluded third baseman Andy Carey. A fielding lapse led to another Chicago run in the eighth, and Ford went down to his fifth defeat of the season, 4–2. Whitey was winless since July 30, and with only six starts left in the regular season, his quest for 20 wins was in serious jeopardy.

Ford finally picked up his 15th win on August 31, beating the Senators 6–4 in Washington with President Eisenhower in attendance. As usual when Ike was on hand, Mantle homered, his 47th of the season. It was his fifth of the year off Camilo Pascual, against whom he hit more homers in his career (11) than he did against all but two pitchers.[10] The Yanks needed that

Ford listening to some "Stengelese" from Yankee manager Casey Stengel. (National Baseball Hall of Fame Library, Cooperstown, N.Y.)

homer, because Jim Lemon of the Senators owned Ford the way Mantle owned Pascual, and he hit three home runs off Whitey that day to drive in four runs. (The only other player ever to hit three home runs in a game at Griffith Stadium was Joe DiMaggio.)[11] The Senators collected only two other hits off Whitey and the Yanks led 6–4 when Lemon came up for the fourth time with one out in the eighth and a man on. When Stengel came out to get him, Ford said: "Let me stay in, Case. I'll get him this time." Replied Stengel: "What are you, out of your damn mind? The guy already hit three home runs. You want to try for four?"[12] Tom Morgan fanned Lemon and closed out the win.

With 47 homers entering September, Mantle was four games ahead of Ruth's pace. However, since Ruth hit 17 in September back in 1927, Mickey knew that his chances of hitting 60 were slim and he began to focus on winning the Triple Crown. He had the homer crown locked up (he was 21 ahead of his nearest challenger), but Detroit's Al Kaline was only eleven RBIs behind him and Ted Williams still had a chance to catch him for the batting title.

Needing to win all of his remaining starts in order to win 20, Ford beat the Red Sox 5–3 at Fenway Park on September 5 and then outdueled Washington's Chuck Stobbs back home at the Stadium four days later, 2–1. The latter game was scoreless until the bottom of the seventh when Yankees shortstop Billy Hunter hit a two-run triple. Ford lost his shutout in the eighth on a triple and a sacrifice fly but went the distance, allowing just six hits and striking out 11 to gain his 17th win.

Meanwhile, Mantle was slumping. All hope of breaking Ruth's record disappeared when Mickey hit .152 in the first 10 games of September without either a homer or an RBI. Now he had both Kaline (RBIs) and Williams (batting title) breathing down his neck. He finally broke his drought with a solo shot off Kansas City right-hander Tom Gorman on September 13. It proved to be the winning run in a 3–2 Yankee win as Ford pitched a complete-game five-hitter for his 18th win, tying his career high.

The Yankees needed just one more win to clinch their 22nd American League pennant when Ford's turn came around again on September 18 in Chicago. He was opposed by White Sox ace Billy Pierce (20–7) in a match-up between two of the best lefties in baseball. Larry Doby gave Chicago a 1–0 lead with a first-inning home run and Pierce sailed through the first three innings without allowing a base runner. The Yanks tied it in the top of the fourth when Billy Martin reached second on an error by Nellie Fox and scored when Mantle ripped a single to left. The White Sox grabbed the lead again on Walt Dropo's solo homer in the bottom of the eighth, but the Yanks came right back in the top of the ninth when Martin tripled off the wall in right center and scored the tying run on a pop-fly single to left by Berra. The score was still knotted at two when Mantle batted with two down and the bases empty in the top of the 11th. He slammed Pierce's first pitch into the upper deck in left field for his 50th homer of the season, giving the Yanks a 3–2 lead. Only Babe Ruth (four times), Jimmie Foxx (twice), Ralph Kiner (twice), Hack Wilson, Hank Greenberg, Johnny Mize and Willie Mays had previously reached the 50 mark.

Ford still needed to retire the White Sox in the bottom of the 11th to nail down the pennant and he immediately ran into trouble, allowing a single and a walk to put runners on first and second with nobody out. Bob Grim replaced Whitey and quickly put out the fire, getting Sherman Lollar to hit into a double play and striking out Jim Rivera with the tying run on third. Ford's fifth straight win raised his record to 19–5 with one start remaining.

With the pennant clinched, attention was focused on Mantle's quest for the Triple Crown, as well as Ford's quest for 20 wins. The Yankees traveled to Boston next, where Mantle and Williams would go head-to-head for the batting title. By now, Williams had overtaken Mantle and led, .355 to .350. In the first game of the three-game series, Mantle blasted his 51st homer over the distant center-field fence at Fenway Park and went 3 for 5, but Williams went 2 for 4 and retained a three-point lead. This home run was the Yankees' 183rd of the season, breaking the American League record held by the 1936 Yankees of Lou Gehrig, Bill Dickey and Joe DiMaggio. Williams then went hitless in the next two games while Mantle collected three hits in four at-bats to take over the lead again, .356 to .350. However, he pulled a thigh muscle running out a double and would be hampered for the final week of the season. Kaline was right behind him in the RBI race, 127–123.

Ford went for his 20th win on September 26 in Baltimore. The game appeared to be the mismatch of the season: the first-place Yankees against the sixth-place Orioles, with Whitey Ford (19–5) opposed by Charlie Beamon, a 21-year-old right-hander just recently called up from the minor leagues who was making his major league debut. The Yanks had all of their regulars except the injured Mantle in the lineup because they really wanted to get Ford his 20th, but they were unable to figure Beamon out, managing just four hits in the game — two of them by Ford. Whitey fell behind 1–0 in the third inning when he yielded two-out singles to Tito Francona and Bob Nieman and then threw a wild pitch. The Yanks had a chance to draw even in the sixth when Beamon walked the bases full with two out, but Martin fanned to end the inning.

The Yanks had their best chance in the seventh inning. With one out, Ford singled and went to third on a single by Slaughter. Stengel then sent Mantle up to pinch-hit for Joe Collins, but all Mickey could manage was a pop fly to short right, with Ford holding at third. When Bob Cerv grounded out to end the inning, the opportunity was lost, and Beamon held on to complete a 1–0 masterpiece. Of the three wins that Beamon accumulated in his short career, this was by far the biggest. Ford went the distance for his 18th complete game but picked up his sixth loss instead of the win he desperately wanted. Mantle felt awful about failing to deliver the tying run, but his buddy's reaction after the game was typical of Ford: "Forget it, Mick, let's go get a beer." It would have been Ford's turn to pitch again on the last day of the regular season and Stengel gave him the option of going for his 20th win. According to Mantle: "Whitey said no, the World Series was more important than winning 20 games, which is what I would have expected him to say. Whitey always was a team player, more interested in winning championships than any personal glory."[13]

The batting title came down to the final weekend of the season. As luck would have it, Boston was the opponent at Yankee Stadium in the final three games of the season. In the first game, Mantle went 1 for 4, hitting his 52nd and final home run of the year off Bob Porterfield. Williams went 0 for 3 and dropped five points behind Mantle. Mickey led Kaline in RBIs, 128–124. At this point, Stengel decided to rest Mantle's injury for the World Series and only allowed him to pinch-hit in the final two games. Mickey picked up an RBI in each game to finish with 130. The door was still open for Williams, but he went 1 for 6 in the final two games to finish at .345 versus Mantle's .353.

Kaline got four RBIs in his last two games but came up short, 130–128. Mantle had his Triple Crown, becoming only the 10th player in history to win it and only the fourth to lead both leagues in all three categories. Only Rogers Hornsby (1925), Lou Gehrig (1934) and Ted Williams (1942) had previously accomplished that feat. Mantle also led the league in runs scored with 132. For that season, one of the best of all time, Mantle was paid $32,500. By contrast, the Yankees paid Alex Rodriguez $22 million in 2004, or $36,605 per *at-bat*.

Despite the disappointment of not winning 20 games, this was easily Ford's best year yet. His winning percentage of .760 and his earned run average of 2.47 both led the league. His 18 complete games tied his career high and his 141 strikeouts were a career high. His walks dropped to 3.35 per nine innings. These statistics are all the more impressive considering that they were achieved in only 30 starts. By comparison, Frank Lary led the AL in wins with 21 (against 13 lossses) but had eight more starts than Ford. While this difference was partly due to Ford's injuries, in large part it was due to the way in which Stengel used him, frequently holding him back to start a series against a contender. The Yankees played 43 percent of their games against the other three first-division teams (Cleveland, Chicago and Boston), but 53 percent of Ford's starts were against those teams. Frequently he was matched up against the other team's ace: nine of his starts were against 20-game winners. Whitey's career record was now 80–28, for a gaudy winning percentage of .741 that was by far the highest of any active player. He was definitely on track to surpass Lefty Grove's modern baseball record for lifetime winning percentage (.680).

The Cy Young Award was instituted that year but there was only one for both leagues and Brooklyn's Don Newcombe had a career year (27–7) to capture the award. (Ford received the only vote cast for an American League pitcher.) If there had been a separate Cy Young Award for AL pitchers, Ford might have won it, although he would have had stiff competition from Cleveland's Herb Score, who was 20–9 with a 2.53 ERA and led the league in shutouts (5), strikeouts (263) and opponents' batting average (.186). Tragically, Score would be struck in the right eye by a line drive off the bat of Gil McDougald the following May and would miss the rest of the season. He never regained his effectiveness after returning the following year and won only 17 more games before retiring in 1962.

Two other Yankees pitchers had good years: Johnny Kucks (18–9, 3.85 ERA) and Tom Sturdivant (16–8, 3.30 ERA). Stengel juggled four other pitchers in both starting and relieving roles: Don Larsen (11–5), Bob Turley (8–4), Tommy Byrne (7–3) and Bob Grim (6–1).

Mantle and Berra, the most feared one-two punch in the league, finished first and second in the American League MVP balloting, with Mantle garnering every first-place vote. Berra's season statistics (.298, 30 HR, 105 RBI) were impressive, and he not only tied his own American League single-season record for home runs by a catcher but also surpassed Gabby Hartnett's major league record of 236 career homers by a catcher. Moose Skowron put together a fine season (.308, 23 HR, 90 RBI) after wresting the first base job from Joe Collins, and Stengel also got good production out of Hank Bauer (26 HR) and Gil McDougald (.311).

Over in the National League, the Dodgers almost didn't get the chance to defend their world championship. They were in a three-team dogfight with the Braves and Reds during the entire month of September and trailed Milwaukee by half a game on the second-to-last day of the season. But they beat the Pirates twice that Saturday while the Braves were losing a 12-inning heartbreaker to the Cardinals, and Duke Snider and Sandy Amoros both homered twice on Sunday as Brooklyn held off Pittsburgh 8–6 to win the pennant by a game over Milwaukee and two games over Cincinnati.

The 1956 Brooklyn Dodgers were essentially the same team that had finally beaten the Yankees the previous year, but many of the "Boys of Summer" were getting a little long in the tooth. Duke Snider led the NL in homers with 43, but this was Jackie Robinson's last year and Reese, Campanella, Hodges and Furillo were all past their prime.

Don Newcombe won the National League MVP Award in addition to the Cy Young Award. Second in the balloting for both awards was Dodgers pitcher Sal Maglie (13–5, 2.87 ERA), who had won six games in September as the Dodgers had overtaken the Braves, including a no-hitter against the Phillies on September 25. Maglie had been the Dodgers' arch-enemy during his six years with the Giants, not only beating them most of the time but also knocking them down incessantly. His knockdown pitches had touched off more than one brawl between the two teams. But in May of 1956 the Dodgers were desperate for pitching after losing 1955 World Series hero Johnny Podres to military service, so they acquired the 39-year-old "Barber" (so-called because of the frequency with which he shaved batters' chins) from the Indians, who had purchased his contract from the Giants the previous season. Dodgers pitcher Carl Erskine said: "When I saw Maglie standing in *our* clubhouse, wearing *our* uniform, I knew nothing in this world would ever surprise me again."[14] It was the ultimate irony that the man most responsible for winning the 1956 NL pennant for the Dodgers had been the most hated man in Brooklyn just six months before.

The 1956 World Series would be the last Subway Series in New York for 44 years, as both the Giants and the Dodgers would move to California after the 1957 season. It represented the end of an era, and in many respects this would be one of the classic World Series of all time.

The Series opened at Ebbets Field. Stengel led with his ace, Whitey Ford, but Dodgers manager Walter Alston passed over Don Newcombe in favor of Maglie, a great clutch pitcher and fresh off his no-hitter just eight days before. As great a pitcher as Newk was (he finished his career 149–90 with three 20-win seasons), he always came up short in the big games. He was 0–3 in previous Series starts.

Ebbets Field was one of Ford's least-favorite ballparks in which to pitch. Although its dimensions weren't any shorter than those of Yankee Stadium right down the foul lines, the fences were significantly closer between the foul lines, particularly in center field and in the power alleys. To compound the problem for Ford, most of the Dodgers sluggers batted right-handed. Hodges, Campanella, Robinson, Furillo and Reese were all right-handed batters and Gilliam was a switch hitter. Only Snider and Amoros batted left-handed. Against this lineup, Ford was much more effective when he had Yankee Stadium's cavernous left field to work with. In his only previous start there in the 1953 World Series, he had lasted only one inning. However, Whitey was the clear ace of the staff, so he got the ball for Game 1.

President Eisenhower was on hand, which guaranteed that Mantle would hit a home run. It came in the first inning with Enos Slaughter on base and carried over the 40-foot screen on top of the right-field wall, over Bedford Avenue and into a parking lot to give New York a 2–0 lead. However, the Dodgers tied it in the bottom of the second on a homer by Robinson and a double by Furillo that scored Hodges, who had reached base when Mantle (still hobbled a bit by his pulled thigh muscle) couldn't quite get to his pop fly to short center. The very next inning, an infield single by Reese and a pop-fly single by Snider set the table for Hodges, who hit what turned out to be the game-winning home run, a three-run shot to left field. Ford departed after retiring the side. A home run by Billy Martin in the top of the fourth cut the lead to 5–3, but the Yanks couldn't manage any further scoring against Maglie, who went the distance and fanned 10 to win the game, 6–3. The loss was Whitey's second (against three wins) in Series play, both incurred at Ebbets Field.

Since Johnny Kucks (18–9) had been the Yankees' number two pitcher during the season, he had been expected to start Game 2. However, Casey had used him in relief of Ford in an attempt to salvage the opener, so he started Don Larsen in Game 2. Larsen was a hard thrower who had also established a reputation as a hard drinker. His manager in Baltimore (Jimmy Dykes) had said that Larsen "fears nothing in the world except a night's rest." In his book *My Favorite Summer 1956,* Mickey Mantle said: "Larsen was easily the greatest drinker I've known, and I've known some pretty good ones in my time.... [But] he was all business when he was on the mound; one of the best competitors I've ever known."[15] Larsen had won four straight games in September after adopting an unorthodox no-windup delivery.

The Dodgers went with Newcombe. The Yanks got on the board first with a run in the first inning and then knocked Newcombe out in the second inning on an RBI single by Larsen and a grand-slam homer by Yogi Berra, the fifth in Series history. That gave the Yanks a 6–0 lead, but Larsen couldn't stand prosperity and promptly got knocked out himself in the bottom half of the inning. He might have escaped unscathed, but an error by first baseman Joe Collins on an easy double-play ball set up a big inning for the Dodgers. A walk to Furillo loaded the bases, and Campanella followed with a sacrifice fly. When Larsen reloaded the bases with two out by walking Gilliam, Stengel gave him a quick hook even though the score was still 6–1 in New York's favor. Casey brought in Kucks for the second straight game, which was a little strange since Kucks had relieved only three times during the season. Reese greeted Kucks with a two-run single to left, and Stengel brought in the left-handed Tommy Byrne to pitch to Snider. The Duke hit one over the right-field wall and all of a sudden it was tied at 6–6. It was Snider's 10th World Series homer, extending his NL record and tying him with Lou Gehrig for second place overall behind Babe Ruth's 15.

The Dodgers kept on hammering a parade of Yankees pitchers (seven in all, a Series record), with Gil Hodges doing the major damage with a pair of two-run doubles. The 13–8 win sent the Series across town to the Stadium with the Yanks down two games to none.

Stengel came back with Ford in Game 3 on just two days' rest, since he'd pitched only three innings in the first game. Alston started Roger Craig, who had beaten the Yanks in Game 5 the previous year. A crowd of 73,977 paid $439,658 to see the game, an average of $5.94 per person.

The Dodgers scratched a run off Whitey in the second on a walk, an infield hit and two fly balls, but Billy Martin tied the game in the bottom half of the inning with his second homer of the Series. Martin was a .257 lifetime hitter with only 64 homers in his 11-year career, but in four World Series against the Dodgers, he hit .333 with five homers and 19 RBIs. He hated the Dodgers, and nearly always rose to the occasion against his better-known counterpart (Robinson), who hit just .234 in his six World Series against the Yanks.

Brooklyn took a 2–1 lead in the top of the sixth when Snider hit a sacrifice fly to deep center to score Reese, who had tripled. But the Yanks got themselves back in the Series in the bottom half of the inning when Bauer and Berra singled and Slaughter hit a two-out home run to give New York a 4–2 lead. (Slaughter had a previous World Series homer at Yankee Stadium in a different era, off Yankee ace Red Ruffing in the final game of the 1942 Series to help the Cardinals beat the Yanks.) Enos was seven for 12 in the first three games; this was what the Yankees had hoped for when they picked him up in late August.

The Dodgers got an unearned run off Ford in the seventh on a walk, an infield hit and an error by third baseman Andy Carey, but the Yanks added an insurance run in the eighth on an RBI double by Berra to make the score 5–3.

The Dodgers had one last shot in the ninth when Carl Furillo led off with a double into the gap in right center, but he committed the cardinal sin of trying to stretch it into a triple even though Brooklyn needed two runs to tie, and Hank Bauer made a perfect throw to Billy Martin, who gunned down Furillo at third. Ford then struck out Campanella and retired Charlie Neal on a grounder to third to secure his fourth Series victory and pull the Yanks back within a game.

After the game, Ford modestly pointed out that several of the balls hit off him that day (including Furillo's double in the ninth) might have been homers at Ebbets Field. He felt that he had pitched well enough to win at Yankee Stadium but not well enough to win at Ebbets Field.[16] He was certainly glad to be back home in the Bronx. As Mantle said: "Whitey was a master at using the whole ballpark, getting those big hitters to hit the ball to the warning track in left center and center."[17]

It was Tom Sturdivant versus Carl Erskine in Game 4. Three years earlier, Erskine had struck out a Series-record 14 Yanks in winning Game 3 of the 1953 Series. This time he wasn't as sharp. Duke Snider made a great catch in center field to rob Hank Bauer leading off the Yankees' first, but then Collins doubled and Berra singled him home to give the Yanks a 1–0 lead.

Snider doubled leading off the fourth for the Dodgers' first hit and Gil Hodges singled him home to tie the score. In the Yankees' fourth, Mantle walked, stole second and scored on Martin's single. McDougald's sacrifice fly made it 3–1.

Mantle came up again in the sixth, batting left-handed against Ed Roebuck (in relief of Erskine), and pounded a home run 15 rows deep into the right-center-field bleachers, above the 407-foot sign. It was Mickey's seventh World Series homer, and the Yanks led, 4–1.

Future great Don Drysdale made his first Series appearance for the Dodgers in the seventh inning and Bauer welcomed him with a two-run homer. Sturdivant finished with a six-hitter and a 6–2 win that squared the Series at two games apiece.

October 8, 1956, was a day that defied all the odds. Stengel surprised everybody by starting Larsen again instead of Kucks or Turley in Game 5 at Yankee Stadium; the Dodgers countered with Maglie. After both pitchers set down the side in order in the first, Jackie Robinson led off the second with a line shot to third. The ball glanced off Andy Carey's glove, right to McDougald at short, who threw out the aging Robinson by half a step. The younger Robinson would have beaten the throw easily.

Larsen set down the first 12 Dodgers, and Maglie matched him for the first 11 Yankees batters. But Mickey Mantle got the first hit of the game and gave Larsen a 1–0 lead with two out in the fourth when he wrapped a line drive around the right-field foul pole for his third homer of the Series.

In the Dodger half of the fifth, Larsen had three close calls in a row. Jackie Robinson led off with a deep drive to left that went foul, before flying out to Bauer in deep right. Gil Hodges then creamed a 2–2 fastball deep into the gap in left center, probably a home run at Ebbets Field but playable in Yankee Stadium's "Death Valley." Mantle raced back and made a beautiful back-handed stab of the ball on the dead run, the best catch of his career, according to him.[18] It was certainly his most important catch. Sandy Amoros followed with a drive into the right-field seats—foul—before grounding out to second.

After this inning, Larsen walked up to Mantle in the dugout and said: "Hey, Slick. Wouldn't it be funny if I pitched a no-hitter?"[19] One of baseball's oldest superstitions is that you never talk about a no-hitter in progress, for fear of jinxing the pitcher. For the rest of the game, Larsen kept talking about the no-hitter in the dugout between innings, and his teammates kept walking away from him because they didn't want to be the one to jinx him.

Larsen retired the Dodgers easily in the top of the sixth on two pop-ups and a strikeout and then contributed to an insurance run in the bottom of the sixth, sacrificing Carey (who had singled) to second, from where he scored on a single by Bauer. Hodges made a great play on a smash by Mantle to prevent further damage.

Leading off the Dodgers' seventh, Gilliam hit the ball sharply but right at McDougald. Reese hit a ball to deep center where Mantle hauled it in. Snider flied to left. Six outs to go.

Robinson led off the eighth with a bouncer back to Larsen. Hodges scared the crowd with a line drive right at Andy Carey at third. Amoros hit a drive to center that was no trouble for Mantle. Maglie then struck out the side in the Yankees' half of the eighth, and Larsen walked out to the mound to try to complete the fifth perfect game in modern baseball history and the first in Series play.

In the ninth, Larsen went to 1-and-2 on Furillo, who then flied out to Hank Bauer in right. Campanella fouled off the first pitch and then grounded out to Billy Martin at second. Maglie was due up; Alston sent Dale Mitchell up to pinch hit. Mitchell had been picked up late in the season by the Dodgers after a fine 11-year career with the Cleveland Indians in which he compiled a .312 lifetime average. (He would retire after the Series.)

The first pitch was outside for a ball. Then a called strike, followed by a swinging strike. Every one of the 64,519 in attendance was standing. Mitchell, a left-handed batter, then fouled a ball into the left-field stands. The next pitch was in the vicinity of the outside corner, a borderline strike. Mitchell started to swing and held up, but the right hand of veteran umpire Babe Pinelli (working the last game of his distinguished 22-year career) shot up, ending the game. Yogi Berra ran out and jumped into Larsen's arms, practically knocking him over. Within seconds Larsen was engulfed by his teammates, and his life was changed forever. As the *New York Daily News* stated the following day, the imperfect man had pitched the perfect game.

Ford missed the last four innings of Larsen's perfect game because pitching coach Jim Turner had him warming up from the sixth inning on, waiting for the bubble to burst.

Larsen's niche in baseball history is permanent. Fifty years later, there still has not been another no-hitter (much less a perfect game) in Series play. Larsen's perfect game remains perhaps the most famous baseball game ever played. While retiring 27 men in order is remarkable enough, what makes this game even more unbelievable is that in a World Series between two teams boasting five pitchers who won the Cy Young Award during their careers (plus Maglie, who probably would have won it in 1951 had the award existed then), it was a journeyman pitcher like Larsen (who retired nine years later with a career record of 81–91) who authored the only World Series no-hitter in history.

The Yanks now led, three games to two. Bob Turley followed Larsen's masterpiece with nine innings of three-hit shutout pitching the following day at Ebbets Field, notching 11 strikeouts, a Yankees Series record. Unfortunately for the Yanks, surprise starter Clem Labine (who had started only three games all season, appearing 59 times in relief) matched Turley, allowing just seven hits. Neither team got a runner as far as third base; it was only the second time in World Series history that a game was scoreless after nine innings. (The other time was in 1913, when Christy Mathewson of the Giants bested Eddie Plank of the Athletics in 10 innings, 3–0.)

The Yanks went in order in the 10th. With one out in the Dodger half, Gilliam worked Turley for a walk and was sacrificed to second by Reese. Snider was passed intentionally, bringing up Robinson with two out and the winning run on second. Jackie got the last big hit of his great career, hitting a ball over Slaughter's head in left that short-hopped the wall and sent the Series into a seventh game the following day at Ebbets Field.

Johnny Kucks finally got to start a game, opposed by Newcombe. Dodgers fans likely did not have a good feeling about this one, the way the Yankees owned Newk. After Bauer led off the game with a single and stole second, Newcombe bore down and fanned both Martin and Mantle. He got two quick strikes on Berra, but then Yogi swatted a high fastball over the wall in right field to give the Yankees a 2–0 lead before the Dodgers even came to bat.

Kucks breezed through the first couple of innings for the Yanks and then Billy Martin led off the Yankees' third with a single. After Newcombe struck out Mantle again, Berra did a "deja vu all over again" by hitting another two-run shot over the right-center-field wall. Yogi's 10 RBIs in the Series (eight of them against Newcombe) broke Lou Gehrig's record of nine.

The Yankee onslaught continued in the fourth when Elston Howard led off with an opposite-field home run, after which Newcombe departed for the final time in a World Series game, disappointed again. It remained 5–0 through six innings as Kucks cruised.

In the top of the seventh, Martin singled and Mantle walked. Alston decided not to take any more chances with Berra, so he had Roger Craig walk him intentionally. That brought up Moose Skowron, who was hitless in eight trips to the plate during the Series. He had been replaced for most of the Series by Joe Collins, but Billy Martin had talked Casey into putting Skowron back into the lineup for Game 7. Moose made both of them look good by belting the first pitch from Craig into the left-field seats for the sixth grand slammer in Series history. It was also the Yankees' 12th homer of the Series, a new record.

With the score now 9–0, the only remaining suspense was whether Kucks would pitch a shutout. He yielded his third hit with two out in the ninth, but struck out Robinson to end the game, the Series and Robinson's career.

Although the Yanks broke a number of slugging records in the Series, it was their pitching that won it for them. After losing the first two games, the Yanks got outstanding pitching performances from each of their five starters, who yielded only six runs in the last five games. Ford's Game 3 victory turned the Series around and started the Yankees on their way. Whitey now had three World Series rings in his five years in the majors.

Six

Ford vs. Spahn

By all objective measures, the two best pitchers of the 1950s were Whitey Ford and Warren Spahn. (Sandy Koufax didn't have his first good season until 1961.) If the two pitchers are compared up through the age of 36, a good case can be made that Ford was the better pitcher. However, injuries derailed Ford at that point while Spahn went on to enjoy seven more good seasons, including some of his best. On a career basis, Spahn ranks among the 10 best pitchers of all time, as evidenced by his inclusion among the nine pitchers selected for Major League Baseball's All-Century Team in 1999. Many consider him to have been the best left-hander in baseball history. But regardless of his rank among baseball's elite, he was one of the most *remarkable* pitchers of all time.

He made his major league debut for the Boston Braves in 1942, four days before his 21st birthday. However, he was almost immediately sent back down to the minors because Braves manager Casey Stengel ordered him to throw at Pee Wee Reese, and he refused.[1] He then lost three and a half years of his career to active duty in World War II and received the Purple Heart for shrapnel wounds suffered in a battle along the Rhine. As a result, he didn't win his first major league game until he was 25 years old, yet he still won more games than any other left-handed pitcher in history (363). He had *thirteen* 20-win seasons, a record for left-handers. Only Cy Young had more 20-win seasons (15), and nine of those seasons came before the turn of the century. (Christy Mathewson also had 13 20-win seasons.) For the 17-year period 1947 through 1963, Spahn *averaged* slightly more than 20 wins per season. He led the NL in wins eight times, and his 63 shutouts are sixth on the all-time list.

Spahn's durability was legendary: 12 times in his career he recorded seasons of 20 or more complete games, leading the league nine times, including seven straight *starting* at age 36. He completed 57.4 percent of his career starts. (As a comparison, the premier pitcher of the current era, seven-time Cy Young Award winner Roger Clemens, had completed only 17.6 percent of his career starts as of the end of the 2005 season.) It is unlikely that his

National League record for innings pitched (5,243.7) will ever be broken. He wasn't a bad hitter, either: he still holds the NL record for career homers by a pitcher (35).

It seemed as if Spahn got better with age. He threw his first no-hitter when he was 39 years old, striking out 15. He threw another no-hitter when he was 40. In 1963, at the age of 42, he was 23–7 with an ERA of 2.60 and seven shutouts. On July 2 of that season, four days after pitching a three-hit 1–0 shutout against Don Drysdale and the Dodgers (retiring the first 19 batters), he hooked up with San Francisco's Juan Marichal in one of the best pitching duels in baseball history. They matched zeros for 15 innings before Willie Mays finally homered in the 16th inning to win it for the Giants. Stan Musial summed Spahn up best when he said: "I don't think Spahn will ever get into the Hall of Fame. He'll never stop pitching."[2] He finally quit at the age of 44 and was inducted into the Hall of Fame in 1973.

Appendix F includes a comparison of the career statistics of Ford and Spahn, as well as those of the other six southpaws generally considered to be among the best in history. Spahn won 127 more games than Ford, but also had 139 more losses. His winning percentage of .597 was 93 percent-age points lower than Ford's modern baseball record of .690. A portion of that differential can be attributed to the fact that the Yanks were a better team than the Braves for most of those seasons: during Ford's career, the Yanks had a winning percentage of .587 in games in which Whitey was not involved in the decision, as compared to .526 for the Braves when Spahn was not involved in the decision. But Ford's winning percentage exceeded that of his team by 103 percentage points as compared to 71 for Spahn, so Whitey still had the edge in this regard. Ford also had the edge in career earned run average (2.75 to 3.09) and in ERA differential (his career ERA was 1.09 runs better than the league average versus 0.80 for Spahn).

These statistics highlight the difference between the two careers. On any given day, and for many entire seasons, Ford was more effective than Spahn and gave his team a bigger edge when he was on the mound. However, Spahn pitched much more frequently and therefore gave his team a bigger cumulative edge (in terms of pitcher wins and pitching runs)[3] over the course of most seasons and certainly over the course of his career. Whereas Ford was injured fairly frequently during his career, Spahn had 17 consecutive seasons with at least 32 starts. He answered the bell every fourth day, year after year, and piled up career statistical totals that are not likely to be approached again. Jim Murray of the *Los Angeles Times* once said of him: "The only way he could get a sore arm is by slamming a door on it."[4]

Ford and Spahn were similar in many respects. Neither had a 90-mph fastball, yet both could get a strikeout when they needed it. (Spahn led the league in strikeouts four straight seasons while Ford established a Yankees

Ford (left) and Warren Spahn clown around before a spring training exhibition game. Ford and Spahn opposed each other four times in the 1957 and 1958 World Series. (AP/Wide World Photos)

single-season record for left-handers that lasted until Ron Guidry broke it.) Both pitchers had an encyclopedic knowledge of the hitters' weaknesses and relied on intelligent pitch selection, good location and changes in speed to keep the hitters off balance. Dodgers great Maury Wills said of Spahn: "Just when you're edging up looking for the screwball, he busts that fast one in on you. A medium fastball when you're not looking for it is as good as a blazer anytime."[5] Ford held opposing batters to a lower batting average over the course of his career and had more strikeouts per nine innings (5.6 to 4.4), but Spahn walked fewer batters per nine innings. (They had identical career strikeout/walk ratios.) Both of them had great pick-off moves and could hit and field their position much better than the average pitcher. Both of them were great money pitchers. In the final analysis, Ford did it slightly better but Spahn did it more often and for more years.

The two of them went head to head for the first time in the 1957 World Series. That the Yankees would play in the '57 Series was a foregone conclusion; they were, after all, in the middle of a streak in which they won 14 pennants in 16 years. But their next challenger was in doubt at the start of the 1957 season. The Yanks had played Brooklyn in four of the previous five years, but the "Boys of Summer" were moving into the autumns of their careers and they were faced with a challenge from an unlikely city: Milwaukee.

The Braves franchise had been pretty dormant since their miracle 1914 season in Boston, in which they had started the season by losing 18 of their first 22 games, been in last place at the halfway point on July 4 (15 games behind John McGraw's defending NL champion Giants), and then come storming back in the second half of the season to catch the Giants, win the pennant, and sweep the powerful Philadelphia Athletics in the World Series. But during the next 38 years before their move to Milwaukee in 1953, the Boston Braves suffered the same fate as their crosstown rivals in Fenway Park: one solitary pennant and no world championships. By 1952 their attendance had dwindled to 281,000, so they moved to Milwaukee, where they were welcomed with open arms. The fans there had long supported a minor league team and they were hungry for major league baseball. During the Braves' first five years in Milwaukee, they drew an average of 2,045,000 fans per year, a National League record that certainly made the Brooklyn Dodgers and New York Giants owners sit up and take notice.

The team's fortunes improved on the field as well. Led by Spahn (23–7, 2.10 ERA) and 21-year-old third baseman Eddie Mathews (.302, 47 HR, 135 RBI), the Braves rose all the way from seventh place in 1952 to second place in 1953, 13 games behind the Dodgers. In an effort to close that gap further, they acquired Giants hero Bobby Thomson during the off-season. In a cruel twist of fate, Thomson broke his ankle so badly in spring training that he missed almost the entire season, and the player the Braves had traded to New York to get Thomson (Johnny Antonelli) pitched the Giants to the 1954 NL pennant by eight games over the Braves.

However, there were some positive ramifications of the Thomson trade. Two years before, the Braves had paid the Indianapolis Clowns (a black semi-pro team) $7,500 for the contract of a young prospect named Henry Aaron. He was not on the parent club's roster in the spring of 1954, but the day after Thomson's injury he was inserted into the vacant spot in the Braves' lineup, and he homered, tripled and singled in that day's exhibition game. The rest, as they say, is history.

The other eventual dividend from the Thomson trade was that he was traded back to the Giants in 1957 for second baseman Red Schoendienst, who would be a key player on their pennant-winning teams and was good enough to be voted into the Hall of Fame by the Veterans' Committee in 1989.

By 1955, Aaron and Mathews had developed into one of the best one-two punches in the league, but the Braves didn't yet have the pitching to seriously challenge the Dodgers, who finished 13½ games ahead of them. In 1956, however, it appeared as if Milwaukee might finally break through and win the pennant. Aaron won his first NL batting title with a .328 average, Mathews had 37 homers and first baseman Joe Adcock came into his own as a power hitter with 38 homers and 103 RBIs. Spahn won 20 games for the seventh time and had support from Lew Burdette (19–10) and Bob Buhl (18–8). After a slow start that had the team idling in fifth place in June, Fred Haney replaced Charlie Grimm as manager and the Braves won their first 11 games under Haney to move into contention. Spahn won 10 straight games in August and September, and his 20th win on September 25 moved the Braves in front of the Dodgers into first place with three games left against the fourth-place Cardinals. However, they dropped two out of three while the Dodgers were sweeping the Pirates to snatch the pennant from the Braves.

Finally in 1957 the Braves could not be denied. Aaron had an MVP year, batting .322 and leading the NL in homers (44), RBIs (132) and runs (118). Schoendienst came over from the Giants and led the NL with 200 hits (two more than Aaron). Adcock was hurt most of the season, but Mathews had a good year (.292, 32 HR, 94 RBI) and left fielder Wes Covington chipped in with 21 homers in only 96 games. Spahn was 21–11 with a 2.69 ERA and led the league in wins, complete games (18) and pitching runs (35.8).[6] He was a near-unanimous winner of the Cy Young Award, capturing all but one vote. Buhl (18–7, 2.74 ERA) and Burdette (17–9) both had excellent seasons. The Braves also had a secret weapon named Bob "Hurricane" Hazle who was called up from the minors in August to fill in for injured center fielder Billy Bruton. Hazle hit .403 in 41 games down the stretch before his coach turned back into a pumpkin the following season. Milwaukee pulled away in September to win the pennant by eight games over the Cardinals and 11 over the Dodgers, who were in their final season in Brooklyn.

For the Yanks, it was business as usual as they won the AL pennant by eight games over the White Sox. However, the pennant race was not a cakewalk and Ford suffered through a very trying season.

The season started normally enough with Ford going the distance at Yankee Stadium to beat the Senators on Opening Day 2–1 when Andy Carey singled home the winning run in the bottom of the ninth. Whitey beat the

Senators again six days later, but came out after seven innings with an 11–2 lead when his shoulder stiffened up a little. The shoulder stiffened up again in his next start against Boston, costing Whitey a win. He left the game after seven innings with a 2–0 lead, but Bob Grim blew the lead in the ninth inning before Berra won the game with a 10th-inning homer.

The shoulder stiffness occurred much earlier in his next start. After retiring the first five batters against Chicago on May 4, Ford removed himself from the game and the Yanks suddenly had their best pitcher on the shelf. He stayed there until May 21, when he tested his arm against the White Sox, who led the Yanks by two games in the AL standings. Whitey carried a 1–0 lead into the sixth inning before an error by Bobby Richardson opened the door for three unearned runs and a 3–1 Chicago win. When Ford's arm was again sore after this game, the Yankees put him on the disabled list in the hope that rest would cure the problem, which was diagnosed as a strained shoulder tendon. The injury short-circuited what might otherwise have been a very good season, because his ERA was a miniscule 0.88 when he went on the DL.

Ford's injury wasn't the major Yankees news item of the month. That distinction belonged to the famous Copacabana nightclub incident in which six Yankees became involved in an altercation with a drunken bowling team. The following day was Billy Martin's 29th birthday and Mantle and Ford had planned a birthday party for their pal. After a day game at home against Kansas City, a group consisting of Mantle, Ford, Berra, Bauer and Kucks (all of whom brought their wives) took Martin out to dinner at a New York City restaurant. After dinner, the group went to the Copacabana to see Sammy Davis Jr. and was seated near several bowling teams celebrating the end of their season. Some of the bowlers were making loud racist remarks about Sammy and Bauer asked them to stop it. A 42-year-old delicatessen owner took exception and the two headed for a back room, followed by other members of both parties. By the time the Yankees players (including Bauer) got there, the bowler was already stretched out, probably punched out by a bouncer.[7]

The players and their wives were hustled out of the club but unfortunately word got out and the incident was all over the newspapers the following morning. The players were called in and interrogated by ornery general manager George Weiss, who fined them each $1,000 (except for Kucks) for breaking curfew the night before a game. (Kucks was fined just $500 because his salary was only $15,000.) While these fines are insignificant by today's standards, at the time they were among the largest ever levied on a ballplayer, exceeded only by $5,000 fines assessed to Babe Ruth and Ted Williams. Mantle's 1957 salary was only $62,000, while Berra was making $60,000 and Ford, $35,000.[8]

The fallout from this incident continued for weeks and was a major distraction. The victim (who had suffered a broken jaw) pressed charges against Bauer and the case eventually went to a grand jury, which exonerated Hank after hearing testimony from the five other players and a number of other witnesses. Berra's succinct assessment of what had happened was: "Nobody never hit nobody nohow."[9]

Unfortunately there was a more permanent repercussion from the incident. George Weiss had long felt that Martin was a bad influence on Mantle and Ford and had been looking for an excuse to get rid of him. (Weiss also wanted to clear the way for Bobby Richardson, the Yankees' second baseman of the future.) Until then, Casey had been able to protect Martin (one of his all-time favorite players), but this incident gave Weiss the excuse he was looking for. The morning after the fight, Billy predicted that he was gone. Sure enough, a month later he was exiled to Kansas City as part of a seven-player deal that brought Harry "Suitcase" Simpson and Ryne Duren to New York, thereby breaking up the triumvirate of Mantle, Martin and Ford. In actuality, Mantle was never better than he was during Martin's last season and a half with the Yanks, belying Weiss's opinion about Billy's influence on Mantle. As for Ford, it was well known that he never went out drinking with Martin and Mantle the night before he pitched. "I always got to bed early on the night before I was scheduled to pitch," Ford said after he retired. "I was very serious about that. On the other nights, I might go out, but on the night before I pitched, I always made sure I got my proper rest, about seven or eight hours of sleep."[10] According to Mantle: "He'd never go out the night before he pitched.... I didn't ever ask him to go out with me those nights.... But when Whitey pitched, he always felt like unwinding that night after the ball game.... If he pitched a good game, I was always ready to celebrate with him. Lucky for both of us, he won 236 games when he was pitching for the Yankees."[11] Martin weighed in on the subject in his 1987 autobiography *Billyball:* "People say I was a bad influence on Mickey and Whitey. But both of them are in the Hall of Fame and I'm not. Maybe I was a better influence on them than they were on me."[12]

The soreness in Ford's pitching shoulder persisted despite injections and massage and Whitey missed the entire month of June. With their ace unavailable, the Yanks looked to Mantle and Berra to carry the team. They trailed Chicago by six games on June 8, but then Mickey got red-hot and the Yanks passed the Sox before the end of the month.

For a good part of the season it appeared that Mantle would match his great 1956 season and possibly win an unprecedented second straight Triple Crown. He had 19 homers by the middle of June and then almost hit a ball out of Yankee Stadium on June 23. Batting left-handed against Chicago's Dick Donovan, Mickey hit a ball deep into the upper deck in right field.

The Chicago center fielder that night, Jim Landis, said that he saw the ball hit the facade of the right-field roof before deflecting into the upper deck, and that "if it was a couple of feet more to the left, it would have gone clear out of Yankee Stadium. I also feel when it hit the facade it still wasn't on its downward flight."[13] However, there was uncertainty in the press box as to where the ball had hit, and in the absence of replays, this blast was not reported as one of Mantle's façade homers.

Ford made his first appearance in six weeks on July 1, pitching two innings in relief of Kucks and picking up the win when Mantle's 22nd homer in the 10th inning beat Baltimore, 3–2. The following day he picked up another extra-inning win with four fine innings of relief work. He went back into the starting rotation but was unable to complete more than six innings in any of his first four starts, though the Yanks won three of the four games. On July 30 he finally went the distance for the first time since Opening Day, beating Kansas City 10–4 in a game with an amusing subplot. This was the first time he had faced Kansas City since Billy Martin had been traded to the Athletics, and the story goes that Whitey told Billy that he would tell him what was coming if the Yanks were way ahead late in the game. Ford was supposed to stand straight up if a fastball was coming or bend over if it was a curve. The Yanks led 10–3 when Martin batted for the last time in the eighth inning with nobody on base. Ford tipped Martin that a slow curve was coming, and Billy wrapped it around the left-field foul pole for a home run. "I wanted him to hit it for a single or double," Ford said years later.[14]

Ford followed up that win with another complete game, a six-hit 5–2 win over the Indians. However, he experienced an ominous ache in his left shoulder early in the game. He lasted six innings in a 4–3 loss to Baltimore and then had to come out in the second inning of a game against Boston when the ache in his shoulder got worse. This time he took 12 days off to give the soreness a chance to subside.

While Ford was struggling, Mantle continued to pound American League pitching. He hit for the cycle in a July 23 win against Chicago that stretched the Yankees' lead over the White Sox to five and one half games. The home run landed in the next-to-last row of the right-center-field bleachers at Yankee Stadium, 465 feet from home plate. The triple came in the seventh inning with the bases loaded and won the game. For good measure, he also stole a base and threw out a base runner. Three days later he hit his 200th career homer off Detroit's Jim Bunning, reaching the milestone at the age of 25. When he homered against Boston on August 13, he was leading the AL in homers (32) and RBIs (83), and his batting average was .384, just four points behind Ted Williams, who at the age of 39 was making another run at .400. Unfortunately, a few days later Mickey's famous temper got the better of him and he suffered a self-inflicted injury that derailed his run at another Triple Crown. After losing a golf match to team-mate Tom Sturdivant, Mantle swung his putter at a tree limb overhead and the putter came down and gouged an ugly gash — down to the bone — in his left shin. The injury developed into a painful case of shin splints, and though he continued to play through the end of August, he could barely run.

On August 27 the White Sox came into Yankee Stadium for a three-game series, trailing New York by three and a half games. Not only did the Yanks win the first game of the series by a 12–6 score, but Ford tested his arm with a few innings of relief work and pronounced himself fit. Two days later, Whitey blanked the White Sox on one hit in a five-inning relief stint and picked up the win when the Yanks won the game on an Enos Slaugh-ter home run in the 11th inning to sweep the series and move six and one half games ahead of Chicago.

After a few more impressive relief stints indicated that Ford's shoul-der was sound again, Casey inserted him back into the rotation and Whitey won three consecutive starts as the Yanks won 10 out of 13 to clinch their 23rd American League pennant and their eighth in nine years under Casey Stengel. He went the distance in a 4–1 win over Washington, losing a shutout on a ninth-inning home run by Roy Sievers. He beat White Sox ace Billy Pierce 7–1 in a game that all but put the final nail in Chicago's coffin, and then survived ninth-inning homers by Ted Williams and Jackie Jensen to beat Boston, 7–4.

Ford lost his final World Series tune-up start to finish the season with an 11–5 record, his worst since joining the Yankees. He pitched only 129.3 innings and completed just five of his 17 starts. He didn't throw a single shutout and three of his 11 wins came in relief. Nevertheless, his ERA of 2.57 would have been the third best in the league behind teammates Bobby Shantz (2.45) and Tom Sturdivant (2.54) if Whitey had pitched enough innings to qualify. He had won two big games against the second-place White Sox coming down the stretch and finally seemed to have shaken his shoulder problems, just in time for the World Series.

Mantle had entered September tied with Williams at .376, tied with Washington's Roy Sievers with 90 RBIs, and leading the AL with 34 homers. At that point, his shin splints got so bad that he was hospitalized on Sep-tember 5 for four days and missed nearly the entire month of September. He finished with a .365 average, 34 homers and 94 RBIs; Williams won the batting crown with a .388 average and Sievers won the homer and RBI crowns. Even missing a month, Mantle led the AL in runs (121) and walks (146), and his on base percentage of .512 has been bettered by only three players since 1900: Babe Ruth, Ted Williams and Barry Bonds. He also had

Ford (left) with Bobby Richardson after Whitey won the opening game of the 1957 World Series against the Milwaukee Braves, besting Warren Spahn, 3–1. (National Baseball Hall of Fame Library, Cooperstown, N.Y.)

the second-best stolen base percentage in the league, with 16 steals in 19 attempts. Mickey won his second straight MVP Award (beating out Williams and Sievers), so the two MVPs would be meeting in the World Series.

Most baseball fans assumed that the Yankees would win the Series easily. However, looking back with the benefit of final career statistics, the 1957 Braves had three of the greatest players of all time in Spahn, Aaron and Mathews. Hammerin' Hank is No. 1 all-time in homers (755), RBIs (2,297), and total bases (6,856); No. 2 in runs (2,174); and No. 3 in hits (3,771). He was an All-Star in 21 of his 23 seasons, batted over .300 14 times, had eight seasons of 40+ homers and 11 seasons of 100+ RBIs. Mathews was an excellent fielder and his 512 career homers tie him with Ernie Banks for No. 17

all-time. In fact, Mathews and Aaron hit more homers together as teammates (863) than any other duo, more than Ruth and Gehrig (859), Mays
and McCovey (800), and Mantle and Berra (702).

The 1957 Series opened at Yankee Stadium, with Ford opposing Spahn
in front of a near-capacity crowd of 69,476 that paid an average of just over
$6 apiece to watch this matchup of future Hall of Famers. The game was
scoreless for four and a half innings, with both pitchers working out of several minor jams and looking fairly sharp. Then the Yanks broke through
against Spahn in the bottom of the fifth inning, taking a 1–0 lead on a single by Jerry Coleman and a double by Hank Bauer.

The key moment in the game occurred in the top of the sixth inning.
Ford suddenly lost control of his curveball and walked Johnny Logan and
Eddie Mathews to start the inning, with Aaron, Adcock and Andy Pafko
coming up. "I had considerable trouble with my control," he said after the
game. "On some deliveries my curve hung high. On others it broke too
low." But just as suddenly, his control came back. "While pitching to Hank
Aaron, my arm became strong," he said. "I struck him out on three straight
[curves], getting each one exactly where I wanted to get it."[15] Whitey then
retired Adcock on a grounder to first and fanned Pafko to end the inning.

The Yanks gave Ford a bit of a cushion in the bottom half of the inning,
scoring two runs on an RBI single by Andy Carey and a perfectly executed
squeeze bunt by Jerry Coleman. Ford lost his shutout with two out in the
seventh on a single up the middle by Red Schoendienst (scoring Wes Covington, who had doubled), but then retired the last seven batters to finish off
a neat five-hitter and pick up his fifth World Series win, 3–1. All five of his
Series wins had come at home, while his two losses had come at Ebbets Field.

Stengel had planned to start Bob Turley in Game 2, but strangely had
had him warm up several times during the opener and so switched to Bobby
Shantz. Though he was five years removed from his 24–7 MVP season of
1952, Shantz was still an effective pitcher, as evidenced by his league-leading ERA. He was only 5'6" and 142 pounds, but he was quick as a cat and
the best-fielding pitcher in baseball. Braves manager Fred Haney countered
with Lew Burdette, who was alleged throughout his career to throw a very
good spitter. Burdette had once been Yankees property and had been with
them for spring training in 1951, but the Yanks had traded him to the Braves
for Johnny Sain later that season when they needed a veteran pitcher for
the stretch drive. Burdette claimed that Stengel had never even known his
name, and he was highly motivated to prove to the Yanks that they had
made a mistake by trading him.

The Braves took a 1–0 lead in the second inning when Aaron hit a ball
over Mantle's head in dead center for a 450-foot triple and scored on a single by Joe Adcock. The Yanks tied it in their half of the second on a walk

and two singles; they almost broke the game open, but Covington made a great catch in left field to rob Shantz of an extra-base hit with two men on.

Johnny Logan and Hank Bauer traded solo homers in the third inning and then Shantz was undone by bad luck and bad fielding in the fourth. After singles by Adcock and Pafko, Covington hit a little dying quail that dropped into short left center to score Adcock, and Pafko followed him home when Slaughter threw wildly to third. Burdette made those two runs stand up by blanking New York over the final six innings for a 4–2 win that evened the Series at one game apiece.

Game 3 at Milwaukee's County Stadium pitted Bob Buhl against Bob Turley. Milwaukee native Tony Kubek (the American League's Rookie of the Year with a .297 batting average) gave the Yanks a 1–0 lead with a first-inning home run, and Buhl then walked both Mantle and Berra. The ensuing play was not only one of the four key plays that decided the Series but it also had a permanent negative impact on Mantle's career. Buhl tried to pick Mantle off second but threw wildly into center field. When Schoendienst leaped for the ball, he fell heavily on Mantle's right shoulder as Mickey scrambled back to the bag. Although Mantle jumped up and advanced to third (from where he scored the second Yankees run on a sacrifice fly by Gil McDougald), he had wrenched his shoulder badly and would never again throw or hit left-handed as well as he had before this injury. The extent of the damage from this harmless-looking collision was not immediately apparent; in fact, Mickey hit a two-run homer off Gene Conley later in the game to stretch the Yankees' lead to 7–1. However, the shoulder stiffened up overnight, and Mickey would be practically useless to the Yanks for the rest of the Series, missing two games entirely and getting only one more hit after batting .400 in the first three games. The shoulder required surgery during the off-season and was never again pain-free. The fact that the Yanks almost certainly lost the 1957 Series as a result of this injury paled in comparison to the negative impact of the injury on the last 11 years of Mickey's career.

After yielding a run in the second inning and loading the bases with two out, Turley got a quick hook from Stengel. Don Larsen came on in relief (his first World Series appearance since his perfect game the previous October), retired Aaron on a fly ball to end the threat and pitched the final seven innings to get the win, yielding only a two-run homer to Aaron. Kubek added his second homer of the game with two men on to make the final score 12–3.

Spahn got the ball for Milwaukee in Game 4 as they attempted to even the Series. Stengel decided to give Ford a fourth day of rest and went with Tom Sturdivant (16–6).

Sturdivant carried a 1–0 lead into the bottom of the fourth but then was rocked for a three-run homer by Aaron and a solo shot by Frank Torre

(Joe's older brother). Ahead 4–1, Spahn pitched beautifully until two were out (with no one on) in the ninth. Yogi Berra kept the Yankees' hopes alive with a single and McDougald followed with another single. Elston Howard then hit a 3-and-2 pitch into the left-field bleachers to tie the game, stunning the 45,804 Braves fans in attendance.

Reliever Tommy Byrne retired the Braves in the bottom of the ninth, and then New York took a 5–4 lead in the top of the 10th. Spahn retired the first two hitters, but Kubek beat out an infield hit and scored on a triple off the left-field fence by Bauer. After Spahn got the third out, Byrne tried to nail down the game (and most likely the Series) for the Yanks in the bottom of the 10th. That's when key play No. 2 occurred.

Pinch hitter Vernal "Nippy" Jones led off, batting for Spahn. Jones had been called up from the minors to back up Frank Torre at first base when regular first baseman Joe Adcock got hurt. He had been kicking around the minors for five years, having last appeared in the majors in 1952. Byrne's first pitch was low and inside and skipped past Berra. Umpire Augie Donatelli called it a ball, but Jones claimed to have been hit on the foot. To prove his point, he retrieved the ball and showed Donatelli a tiny black smudge on the ball that he claimed was shoe polish. Donatelli agreed and awarded him first base. Jones was promptly removed for a pinch runner, and never appeared in a major league game again.

Despite the fact that Jones was the first man to reach base against Byrne (who had come on in the eighth inning), Stengel pulled him in favor of Bob Grim, whose 19 saves during the season had led the AL. After Red Schoendienst sacrificed the runner over to second, Johnny Logan tied the game with a double to left field. Eddie Mathews then hit the only World Series home run of his great career, and the Series was tied at two games apiece.

Game 5 at County Stadium was a classic pitching duel between Ford and Burdette. The Yanks nearly scored in the fourth when Gil McDougald hit a ball over the left-field fence, but Wes Covington made a tremendous leaping catch to bring the ball back onto the field and keep the game scoreless. The Yanks then got two runners on base with one out, but Harry Simpson (who was playing first base in place of injured Moose Skowron) hit into a double play. The absence of Mantle and Skowron certainly made Burdette's task easier.

Ford matched zeros with Burdette until the bottom of the sixth and then was victimized by a mental error on the part of second baseman Jerry Coleman. With two out and nobody on, Mathews hit a routine grounder right at Coleman. Perhaps because it was his final year and his range had decreased, Coleman was playing all the way back on the outfield grass, and Mathews tore down the line and was called safe when he crossed first in a dead heat with the ball. Aaron followed with a little pop fly to short right center that fell in for a single between Coleman and Bauer, and when Joe Adcock singled to right for the only legitimate hit of the inning, the Braves scored the only run of the game. "Aaron never should have had the chance to bat in the inning," said Coleman after the game. "I blew the play and cost Ford the game after he had done such a great job.... I should have made that third out easily. I misjudged Mathews' speed. I should have charged the ball another step, rather than waited for it. If I had he would have been out."[16]

The Mathews gift was the third key play that swung the Series Milwaukee's way. Ford allowed only three other hits in the game, but Burdette picked up his second victory of the Series with a seven-hit shutout. This was one of four Series games in his career in which Ford pitched brilliantly but was denied victory either because of poor fielding or because a reliever failed to hold a lead. His record total of 10 World Series wins could easily have been 14.

The Series moved back to New York for Game 6, with Bob Turley going against Bob Buhl. This was Yogi Berra's 53rd World Series game, a new record, and Yogi hit his 10th Series homer with a man on in the third to give the Yanks an early 2–0 lead. After the Braves caught up on home runs by Torre and Aaron, Hank Bauer homered off the screen attached to the left-field foul pole in the bottom of the seventh, tying a World Series record by hitting in his 13th straight Series game. Turley made this run stand up, fanning Aaron in the ninth and then inducing Covington to hit into a game-ending double play to finish off a four-hitter.

For Game 7 at the Stadium, Haney bypassed Spahn (who was sick with a virus) and brought Burdette back on only two days' rest. He had other pitchers available but opted to go with the hot hand, and Burdette made him look like a genius.

Stengel had Sturdivant rested with Ford and Shantz in reserve, but instead he played one of his famous hunches and started Don Larsen. This particular hunch lasted only two and one third innings, although to be fair to Larsen, poor Yankee fielding contributed heavily to his demise.

Bauer led off the Yankees' first with a double to left (setting a new record by hitting in his 14th straight Series game) but the Yanks failed to score. From the Yankees' standpoint, the game went downhill from there. With one out and Bob Hazle on first in the Milwaukee third, Logan hit a double-play grounder to Tony Kubek at third base (key play No. 4). Kubek's throw to second pulled Coleman off the bag, and instead of reaching out and tagging Hazle to get the lead runner, Coleman threw on to first, just wide enough to allow Logan to beat the throw.

Giving the Braves five outs with Mathews and Aaron coming up was asking for trouble, and Mathews responded by dumping a soft liner into the right field corner, scoring two runs. Stengel pulled Larsen and brought in the left-handed Shantz to face the right-handed Aaron, who hit a grounder up the middle to score Mathews from second. When Covington blooped a single to left and Frank Torre followed with a weak grounder to Coleman for a force at second, the Braves had four gift-wrapped runs and the Series was essentially over, the way Burdette was pitching. Lou really had his good spitter that day, and he shut out the Yanks on four hits until the ninth inning, when the Yanks (trailing 5–0) made it mildly interesting. Singles by McDougald and Coleman and an infield hit by Byrne loaded the bases with two out. Moose Skowron hit a smash down the third-base line that might have cleared the bases and brought the tying run to the plate, but Eddie Mathews made a spectacular backhanded stab and stepped on third to give Milwaukee its first world championship. For the first time since 1948, the world championship left New York City.

Burdette joined a very select group of pitchers who have won three games in a World Series, and he became the first pitcher to throw two shutouts in the same Series since Christy Mathewson threw three in a span of six days for the Giants in 1905. The former Yankees reject certainly exacted his revenge. But while Burdette was clearly the MVP of the Series, Milwaukee's four future Hall-of-Famers all made significant contributions. Aaron hit .393 with three homers; Mathews had two game-winning hits plus the crucial leg hit in Game 5 and the game-saving play in Game 7; Spahn won Game 4; and Schoendienst hit .278, although disappointed Yankees fans felt that his most important contribution to the Braves' cause was accidentally knocking Mantle out of the Series.

In the head-to-head match-up between Ford and Spahn, Whitey had the edge. They were both 1–1 in the Series, but Whitey's ERA in his two starts was 1.13 while Spahn's was 4.70. Ford pitched what should have been a shutout in the key fifth game and lost because a routine play wasn't made behind him. But as always, he took it in stride. Years later, Jerry Coleman said of Whitey: "Nothing seemed to bother him in a game. If you blew a play, he'd say 'Give me the goddamned ball and we'll get them.' In the 1957 World Series, I blew the [fifth] game for him, and maybe the Series.... But Whitey never said a thing to me."[17]

SEVEN

A Great Season
Interrupted by Injuries

The 1958 season was historic in that it saw the introduction of major league baseball to the West Coast. The Dodgers and the Giants both broke their loyal fans' hearts and moved to California because their owners felt they could make more money in new stadiums in markets that weren't carved up into thirds. Both teams were tired of losing to the Yankees— both on the field and at the box office. Neither team fared particularly well on the field in their first year out west (the Giants finished third, the Dodgers seventh), but both teams got the desired increases in attendance despite playing in interim ballparks. The 1958 attendance in Los Angeles (1.85 million) was 79 percent higher than the final year's attendance at Ebbets Field (1.03 million), and the 1958 attendance in San Francisco (1.27 million) was nearly double that of the previous year's attendance at the Polo Grounds (653,923).

The Yankees now had New York all to themselves for a few years, but strangely their attendance did not increase; in fact, it decreased from 1.50 million to 1.43 million in 1958. (These figures are a far cry from the 2005 attendance figures: 4.09 million for the Yankees, 3.60 million for the Dodgers, and 3.14 million for the Giants.) Most die-hard Dodgers and Giants fans refused to convert to being Yankees fans, preferring to save their allegiance for the Mets, who were formed in 1962 specifically to fill the void left by the defection of the Dodgers and Giants.

The Yanks opened the 1958 season in Boston, but Stengel predictably held Ford out of the three-game series at Fenway Park in order to start him in the home opener against Baltimore on April 18. He was opposed by fellow Astoria native and former Dodger foe Billy Loes, who pitched well but not well enough to stop Ford from winning his fourth straight home opener. Whitey yielded a first-inning run on three successive singles after two were out but limited the Birds to just two hits thereafter to win, 3–1, with Mantle tagging up and dashing home from third on a pop fly to short center to score the winning run.

Ford (left) with former Astoria neighbor Billy Loes before the two opposed each other on April 18, 1958, in the Yankees' home opener, won by New York, 3–1. (AP/Wide World Photos)

The Orioles got another shot at Ford a week later in Baltimore and extended their scoreless streak against Whitey to 16 innings, managing just four hits through eight innings. However, the Yanks weren't doing much better against Orioles right-hander Connie Johnson, who allowed a first-inning run on a double by Mantle and a single by Skowron but held the Yanks at bay thereafter. The Orioles got a break when an error by Gil McDougald allowed the lead-off batter to reach base in the bottom of the ninth, but Whitey got two outs and was one out away from a 1–0 shutout. He proceeded to walk Jim Busby, and then former teammate Gene Woodling lined a ball inches fair down the right-field line to score both runners and shock the Yanks, 2–1.

After yielding just one earned run in his first two starts, Ford got hammered for five earned runs in a 10–1 Yankees loss to Frank Lary, who ran his career record against New York to 10–4. But he bounced back to beat Washington 8–0, though he was forced to leave the game after seven innings after being hit on his pitching arm by opposing pitcher Bob Wiesler. Whitey turned the game over to rookie closer Ryne Duren, who fanned five Senators in the final two innings to preserve the shutout. Duren petrified hitters, because he threw as hard as anyone in the league and had a reputation for wildness. He wore thick glasses and when he was called into a game he always threw his first warm-up pitch about 95 m.p.h. over the catcher's head and up against the screen in order to remind the hitters not to dig in against him.

Whitey's next three starts were on the road and he beat three pretty good pitchers: Washington's Camilo Pascual, Chicago's Billy Pierce and Cleveland's Ray Narleski, allowing a total of five runs while hurling three complete games. The first two of these wins came during a 10-game Yankees winning streak that pushed their season record to 23–5 and opened up an eight-and-a-half-game lead over the second-place Indians in the American League standings.

Ford was not the only Yankees pitcher off to a good start. Bob Turley was off to an amazing start: 7–0 with seven complete games (including four shutouts) in seven starts and an ERA of 0.86. Bobby Shantz had won all four of his starts, and Don Larsen, though troubled with a sore arm, was 3–0 with an ERA of 0.00 in three starts, including two shutouts. He also had two home runs. (He hit .306 with four homers that year and was sometimes used as a pinch hitter.) In all, Yankees pitchers had 17 complete games and seven shutouts in the first 30 games of the season, and Ford was just getting warmed up.

Mantle was off to a very slow start. His right shoulder had not fully recovered from the off-season surgery necessitated by his World Series injury and he was striking out left-handed at an alarming rate. He had only four homers at the end of May and the Yankee Stadium boo-birds were really letting him have it. He turned his season around on June 2 with Ford on the mound. Mickey's solo shot off Chicago right-hander Jim Wilson in the first inning staked Ford to a 1–0 lead, and then Whitey went on a strikeout binge. After fanning Sherman Lollar to end the third, he struck out the side in the fourth (Walt Dropo, Bubba Phillips and Tito Francona) and whiffed Jim Landis and Wilson for the first two outs of the fifth before Luis Aparicio ended the string by grounding out. The six consecutive strikeouts tied the American League record that Whitey shared with six others (including Walter Johnson and Bob Feller), and made him the first to do it twice.[1] (He had previously done it on July 20, 1956.) A sixth-inning homer by Bauer increased the Yankees' lead to 2–0, but the White Sox mounted a serious threat in the top of the eighth. An error by Andy Carey opened the door and an infield hit and a walk loaded the bases with one out. Walt Dropo made a bid for a game-tying hit with a hard grounder into the shortstop hole, but Tony Kubek snared it and started an inning-ending double play. Ford closed out the White Sox for his first shutout of the season, striking out 10 in all.

Starting with his homer against Chicago on June 2, Mantle hit seven homers in seven days, including a tape-measure blast on June 4. Batting right-handed against Chicago's Billy Pierce, Mickey hit a ball that broke a chair in the 19th row of the distant left-center-field bleachers at Yankee Stadium, 478 feet from home plate. It was the first of four times that he would reach this particular section of Yankee Stadium, which had been reached only seven previous times in the Stadium's history, including twice by Joe DiMaggio and once each by Jimmie Foxx and Hank Greenberg.[2] The following day he hit a ball off Early Wynn that landed at the base of the wall in dead-center field (just below the 461-foot sign) and he legged it out for his third inside-the-park home run of the season.

It was Berra's turn to supply the offense when Ford went for his sixth straight win on June 7 versus the Indians at Yankee Stadium. After a homer by Cleveland center fielder Roger Maris tied the game at two in the fifth inning, Yogi smacked a three-run homer in the sixth that provided the winning runs in Ford's 6–3 complete-game win. Five days later, Moose Skowron hit a ball into the same section of the Stadium's left-center-field bleachers that Mantle had reached the previous week (the ninth time it had been done and the first of three times for Skowron in his career), but Ford was gone by the time the Yankees won the game in the 12th inning, having been relieved by Duren in the 11th inning with the score knotted at two.[3]

The Tigers were the next visitors to Yankee Stadium and they swept a four-game series from New York, with Frank Lary and Jim Bunning throwing back-to-back shutouts. New York's lead in the American League was pared to seven games over the second-place Red Sox, with the surprising Kansas City Athletics just a half game further back. The Yanks counted on Ford to break the losing streak when they opened a three-game series against the Indians in Cleveland, and he came through with a three-hit 4–0 shutout, striking out 10. No Indians runner reached second base until two were out in the ninth, and 42-year-old Enos Slaughter preserved the shutout with a game-ending diving catch of a sinking liner.

Ford's seven-game winning streak came to an end on June 23 in Chicago when Sox right-hander Ray Moore shut out the Yanks on three hits, 2–0. Whitey went the route but lost on a two-run homer by Sherman Lollar as the Yanks were shut out for the fourth time in nine games. They were starting to show some cracks in the foundation (having lost 16 of their last 30 games), yet they still led the AL by seven and a half games. Mantle had aggravated his bad shoulder and his weak right knee two weeks earlier and was slumping badly; with his bat silent, the Yankees were vulnerable.

The Yanks bounced back to win their next three games and then Ford took the mound on June 28 against the second-place Athletics in Kansas City. The result was his third shutout of the month, a nifty three-hitter in which he faced only 30 batters. Whitey struck out eight and allowed just one Kansas City runner to reach second base as the Yanks hit three homers and cruised, 8–0. It was Ford's 100th major league win, and he reached the century mark with only 36 losses, the fewest of any pitcher in major league history. The only pitcher who has even come close to this record has been Dwight Gooden, who reached 100 wins in 1989 with only 37 losses. The difference is that Ford kept on winning at that rate while Gooden was 94–75 for the remainder of his career. Whitey's career winning percentage of .735 was still tracking well above Lefty Grove's modern baseball record of .680.

At the end of June, Mantle was nine homers behind Boston's Jackie Jensen in the AL homer race, 23–14. But then he exploded for seven homers in the first six days of July to close the gap. After homering in both games of a July 1 double-header against the Orioles, Mickey hit two long home runs against Washington on June 3 to help Ford win his 10th game of the season, 11–3. Not even a two-run homer by nemesis Jim Lemon could keep Whitey from beating the Senators for the 12th straight time, dating back to the start of the 1955 season.

The Yanks reached the halfway point of their season with a record of 51–26, which was good for an 11-game lead over the second-place Red Sox. With a 10–4 record at this point, Ford was once again in good position to make a run at 20 wins. He started the second half of the season with one of the finest stretches of pitching of his career.

Ford's first victims were the White Sox. After the two teams split a double-header on July 13, Whitey squared off against Early Wynn in the rubber match the following day. Ford was nearly untouchable, allowing just three hits and walking none as he posted his fourth shutout of the season, 5–0. He even drove in a run himself with a single. Mantle homered off Wynn for the third time that season; he hit more homers off the Hall of Famer in his career (13) than he did against any other pitcher.[4] However, while the homers were starting to pile up (23), the strikeouts were piling up as well. He had already fanned 75 times, which matched his total for the entire 1957 season.

Ford kept the zeros coming in his next start six days later as he whitewashed the Athletics at the Stadium, 8–0. He allowed five hits and again walked none, and four of the five base runners were immediately erased by double plays. Whitey was now 12–4 on the season and gaining momentum.

Ford's consecutive scoreless innings streak grew to 27 in his next start as he tossed his third straight shutout, blanking the Indians on four hits at Municipal Stadium, 6–0. A two-run homer in the sixth inning by Ford's

Ford with sons Tommy (left) and Eddie, and Mickey Mantle Jr. (holding the bat) during spring training in 1958. (National Baseball Hall of Fame Library, Cooperstown, N.Y.)

batterymate, Elston Howard, provided all the support Whitey needed. His ERA was now down to an amazing 1.68.

Mantle switch-hit homers for the sixth time in his career on July 28, giving him 14 homers in July and moving him to within one of Jensen, 29–28. Unfortunately, his buddy's shutout string ended at 28 the following day when the Athletics pushed across a run in the second inning on two infield singles. Ford gave up a more legitimate run (a homer by Hal Smith) in the fourth and then left the game for a pinch hitter in the eighth inning with the score tied at two. With Ryne Duren sidelined by a fractured cheekbone (courtesy of a Paul Foytack pitch), Stengel turned the game over to Art Ditmar and the game was soon lost, 7–3. Ford was denied a win in his next start as well, yielding just two runs in seven innings but picking up his fifth loss as Chicago right-hander Dick Donovan beat the Yanks with a three-hitter.

The Yanks, and Ford, reached the high point of their regular season on August 8 in front of a Yankee Stadium crowd of 43,606. Whitey scattered three Boston hits in hurling his seventh shutout of the season, 2–0. It was his fourth three-hitter of the season and he was now within one of the Yankees' record for shutouts in a season set by Russ Ford in 1910. He was also within two of the American League record for shutouts by a left-hander held by none other than Babe Ruth. The Babe had tossed nine shutouts in 1916 when he was still with the Red Sox. Had it not been for the two shutouts Ford had lost early in the season (one due to a ninth-inning error and the other one finished by Duren after Whitey was hit on his left arm by a pitch), he would already have been tied with Ruth, who made 41 starts in his record-setting year. Ford had accumulated his shutouts in only 22 starts and his ERA was a miniscule 1.67. With possibly 10 starts remaining in the regular season, Whitey (14–5) appeared to be a lock to win 20 the way he was pitching.

The Yanks were now a season-high 35 games over .500 and led the second-place Red Sox by 16½ games in the AL standings. Turley's record was a remarkable 17–4, though his ERA was much higher than Ford's. Mantle had 30 homers and his batting average was climbing toward the .300 mark. Nobody could have anticipated that the Yanks would stagger to the end of the season, going 21–26 and having their AL margin whittled down to 10 games.

One significant reason for the decline was a sore left elbow that beset Ford in his next start and plagued him for the rest of the season. His elbow suddenly started hurting when he threw his curveball, and when he tried to get by on just his fastball, he was hit hard. He stayed in the rotation despite the sore elbow, but after struggling in three straight outings, he took himself out of a game on August 29 after facing just two batters (both of which he retired) and rested the elbow for 16 days before giving it another try.

With the pennant already clinched and with any chance of winning 20 games long gone, Ford's sole objective when he returned to the mound was to regain his effectiveness in time for the World Series rematch with the Milwaukee Braves, who had all but clinched the National League pennant.

Without Ford, the Yankees wouldn't have much of a chance, so they collectively held their breath when Whitey tested his elbow on September 14 against Kansas City. The elbow was fine, even when he threw curves, and he left the game for precautionary reasons after five innings with a 6–1 lead. "I threw hard all the way," said Whitey, "and mixed in about a dozen curves. I stopped after five innings because that was as far as I intended to go."[5] Unfortunately the Yankee bullpen blew the lead, so although the Yanks eventually won the game in extra innings, Ford was denied his elusive 15th win of the season.

Ford was even sharper in his last two tune-up starts. He threw seven shutout innings against Baltimore at Memorial Stadium, yielding just five hits and departing with a 4–0 lead rather than risk reinjuring the elbow going for the Yankees' shutout record. Once again the Yankees' bullpen squandered the lead, as the Orioles scored five runs in the bottom of the ninth to win the game. He faced the Orioles again a week later at the Stadium, opposed by Hoyt Wilhelm, who just six days before had inflicted the ultimate indignity on the sputtering Yanks by no-hitting them 1–0. Wilhelm was a 35-year-old knuckleballer who had been a reliever his entire career and pitched his no-hitter in only the ninth start of his career. He was nearly as good in his encore performance against New York, but Ford was better. Whitey retired 18 of the 19 batters he faced, allowing only a first-inning inside-the-park homer by Joe Taylor. Unfortunately the Yanks managed just a single run off Wilhelm, and both pitchers were long gone by the time the sixth-place Orioles pulled out their fourth straight win over New York.

Ford finished the season with a 14–7 record, somewhat disappointing after having been 14–5 on August 8. However, he led the majors in ERA (2.01), shutouts (seven) and opponents' on-base percentage (.276). He allowed fewer base runners per nine innings than any pitcher in either league, and his strikeouts-to-walks ratio of 2.34 was his best yet. He had 15 complete games in only 29 starts, and with a little luck and better support might have won 20 despite missing nearly a month of the season. Despite the modest win total, Ford did some of the best pitching of his career in 1958. If the three August games that he pitched with his sore elbow are excluded from his season statistics, his ERA was 1.60, which would have been the lowest ERA in either league since Walter Johnson's 1.49 mark in 1919.[6]

Turley finished the season 21–7 with an ERA of 2.97. He led the league in numerous categories, including wins, winning percentage (.750), complete games (19), opponents' batting average (.206), and hits per nine innings (6.53). His six shutouts were second behind Ford's seven, and he was third in the AL in strikeouts. It was definitely a career year — one that he would never come close to matching. (He never won more than nine games in a season after 1958.) He won the Cy Young Award, beating out upcoming World Series rivals Warren Spahn (second) and Lew Burdette (third). Other than Turley and Ford, the Yanks had no starter who reached double figures in wins. At least they had found a new closer during the season, as rookie Ryne Duren led the AL with 20 saves and posted a 2.02 ERA in his 76 innings, allowing just 40 hits and striking out 87.

Mantle waged an exciting battle in September for the AL home run crown with Jensen, Cleveland's Rocky Colavito, Washington's Roy Sievers and Kansas City's Bob Cerv. Colavito was right on his heels when the Yanks played the Tigers in Detroit on September 17. Batting left-handed against Jim Bunning, Mantle cleared the right-field roof of Briggs Stadium with a blast that struck a building across the street on the fly, more than 500 feet from home plate. In 1956 Mickey had hit a ball out of Briggs Stadium but the ball reportedly had bounced on top of the roof on the way out. This one *definitely* cleared the roof on the fly; the only other person ever to do this was Ted Williams in 1939.[7] The homer was Mickey's 41st of the season, and when he hit No. 42 a week later, he had his third home run crown in four years, edging Colavito by one.

Though Mantle's 1958 season was not as good as his previous two, it was still better than that of any other player in the American League that year. Besides home runs, he led the league in runs (127), runs produced (182), total bases (307) and walks (129). Although he batted "only" .304, that was only 24 points behind the batting champion (Ted Williams), and his on-base percentage of .445 was second in the AL behind Williams. He even finished fourth in the league in stolen bases with 18 in only 21 attempts. However, the MVP voters gave the award to Boston's Jackie Jensen and dropped Mantle all the way to fifth (behind Turley, Colavito and Cerv), even though Mantle's statistics were better in every important offensive category except RBIs and the Yanks finished 13 games ahead of the Red Sox. Unfortunately, after his two spectacular MVP years of 1956–57, Mickey was no longer judged against his peers, but rather against his Triple Crown stats of 1956. Ironically, both Jensen and Cerv had been teammates of Mantle's back in 1951 and had been his competition for the Yankee center field position after DiMaggio retired.

Although Mantle's season had been productive, it had become clear that Mickey would never again be as good a hitter from the left side of the plate as he had been before Red Schoendienst fell on his shoulder in the '57 Series. He would still hit the majority of his home runs left-handed because he batted so much more often from that side, but he would never again hit well for average from the left side and he struck out much more often left-handed. In 1958 he struck out once every 5.4 plate appearances, as compared to once every 8.3 plate appearances the previous season.

Several other Yankee sluggers had less productive seasons than usual. Yogi Berra missed 33 games with injuries and his power totals (22 HR, 90

RBI) reflected that. Bill Skowron also had an injury-plagued subpar year (14 HR, 73 RBI), and he was spelled at first base from time to time by rookie Marv (not yet Marvelous) Throneberry, who hit seven homers. Some of the slack was picked up by Elston Howard (who hit .314 splitting time between catcher and left field) and by Norm Siebern, who was brought up from the minors, hit .300 and won the Gold Glove for AL left fielders.

The Braves coasted to the National League pennant by eight games over the Pirates, with the Giants another four games back. Hank Aaron's production (.326, 30 HR, 95 RBI) was down significantly from his 1957 MVP season and Eddie Mathews and Joe Adcock had off years as well. But Spahn recorded his ninth 20-win season (22–11) and Burdette his first (20–10), and they carried a Braves pitching staff that had no one else with more than 10 wins. The old refrain of "Spahn and Sain, then pray for rain" became "Spahn and Burdette, then hope for wet." (Ironically, it had been Sain whom the Braves had traded to the Yankees in 1951 to get Burdette.) Combined, they had more Cy Young Award votes than Turley but they cost each other the award by splitting the vote.

The much-anticipated World Series rematch between the Yanks and the Braves got underway on October 1 at Milwaukee's County Stadium. Once again, it was Whitey Ford for the Yanks versus Warren Spahn for the Braves. Hank Bauer led off the Series with a single, extending his record hitting streak in Series play to 15 games.

New York got on the board first when Moose Skowron lined a solo home run into the left-field seats with two out in the top of the fourth. But the Braves replied with two runs in the bottom of the fourth after two were out, with the second run scoring on a single by Spahn, who had hit an incredible .333 during the season (36 for 108).

The Yanks came right back in the top of the fifth when Ford walked and Bauer followed with a homer to give New York a 3–2 lead. That's how it stayed through seven innings.

In the Milwaukee eighth, Ford walked Mathews and then Aaron doubled off the fence in right, just beyond the leaping Bauer's glove. With runners on second and third and nobody out, Ford departed in favor of Ryne Duren, who only recently had created quite a furor by getting into a shoving match with Ralph Houk during the Yankees' pennant celebration. Apparently Ryne had a bit too much to drink and squashed Houk's unlit cigar in his face, to which the Major took exception. At any rate, Duren did a nice job (limiting the Braves to just one run on a sacrifice fly), but the game was now tied. Once again, Ford had pitched well in a World Series game but not gotten a win.

Spahn retired the Yanks in the ninth and 10th, and the Braves pecked away successfully against Duren in the bottom of the 10th. Successive singles by Adcock, Del Crandall and Billy Bruton sent the crowd of 46,367 home happy and made Spahn a winner for the third time in five Series decisions, with a complete game, as usual.

Game 2 matched '57 Series hero Burdette against Turley. After the Yanks scored a run in the top of the first, the Braves exploded for seven runs in the bottom half of the inning, the biggest first inning in Series history. Bruton led off with a homer into the right-field bleachers, and Red Schoendienst followed with a double. After a one-out walk to Aaron, Wes Covington singled in the second run and Stengel got out his quick hook, replacing Turley with Duke Maas (11–8, 3.85 ERA). After walking Crandall and giving up a two-run single to Logan, Maas served up a gopher ball to Burdette, who rubbed salt in the wound by homering for the final three runs of the inning. Yankees fans were really starting to hate Burdette. They also wondered why Casey would pull the Cy Young Award winner in the first inning when the score was still only 2–1.

The rest of the game was essentially garbage time as the Braves pounded five Yankees pitchers for 15 hits and a 13–5 victory. The only Yankee to really solve Burdette was Mantle, who hit two long homers to pass Gehrig and Berra on the all-time World Series home run list and tie Duke Snider for second with 11. Ever gracious in victory, Burdette told reporters after the game that he wished the Yankees were in the National League. "They would be lucky to finish fifth," he said.[8] Apparently he was not worried about the old saying that "what goes around, comes around."

Having lost the first two games with their two best pitchers, the Yanks returned to the Stadium with the odds heavily against them. Fortunately, there were no rainouts that would have allowed Milwaukee to come right back with Spahn and Burdette again, and the Yanks got a shot at right-hander Bob Rush. Stengel went with Don Larsen, who had pitched pretty well during the season with a 9–6 record and an ERA of 3.07.

Surprisingly, the game remained scoreless for four and one half innings. Then Rush walked the bases full in the Yankees' fifth and Bauer delivered a two-run single to give the Yanks the lead and extend his record hitting streak to 17 games. For good measure, Hank followed a seventh-inning walk to Slaughter with his third home run in three games, and Larsen and Duren combined on a six-hit shutout as the Yankees climbed back into the Series, 4–0.

The 71,563 fans who packed Yankee Stadium for Game 4 were treated to another great Spahn-Ford duel. The Yankees wasted what turned out to be their only scoring opportunity in the fourth inning. Mantle tripled with one out but Skowron failed to get him home (bouncing back to Spahn), and then Berra ripped a bullet toward right field that Schoendienst was able to get just enough of his glove on to knock down. He pounced on the ball and barely nipped Yogi at first.

After five scoreless innings, the Braves got a gift in the top of the sixth when Yankee Gold Glove left-fielder Norm Siebern lost a routine fly ball by Schoendienst in the late-afternoon October sun. "I should have caught it," Siebern said later. "I flipped down my sunglasses and, as I dashed toward center, had a good line on it. But when the ball got up over the stands, I suddenly saw nothing. I had completely lost sight of it."[9] Mantle couldn't get there in time to make the play and the ball went between them for a triple. Logan then hit a routine grounder that went right through Kubek's legs.

Spahn knocked in another run with a bloop single to left in the seventh after Siebern ignored Stengel's waves for him to move in closer. Then Siebern completed a nightmare of an afternoon by losing another routine fly ball in the sun in the eighth inning, allowing it to bounce right in front of him for a double that led to a run and a 3–0 Milwaukee lead. No wonder Yogi once said about left field at the Stadium: "It gets late early out there."

Regardless of Siebern's problems in left field, the bottom line is that the only run Spahn needed that day was the one he himself knocked in. He pitched the finest World Series game of his career, shutting out the Yanks on just two hits (Mantle's triple and a seventh-inning single by Skowron). It was Spahn's fourth World Series win, three of which had come at the Yanks' expense. Bauer's hitting streak ended at 17 games, which was still the World Series record as of the end of the 2005 season. Typically, though victimized once again in a World Series game by poor fielding, Ford refused to blame Siebern. "I'm always sore when the opposition scores a run, but more so when it happens in the World Series," he said. "But I feel sorry for Siebern. He tried."[10]

Down three games to one and facing a pitcher in Game 5 who had beaten them four straight times, the Yanks appeared to have no chance. Then up stepped Bob Turley.

New York took a 1–0 lead off Burdette in the bottom of the third when McDougald tomahawked a high fastball right down the left-field line and off the screen attached to the inside of the foul pole. That was all the scoring through five innings.

Yankees fans got a scare in the top of the sixth when Bruton led off with a single and Schoendienst followed with a blooper to left that looked like a sure hit. But Elston Howard (playing left field in place of shell-shocked Norm Siebern) came sprinting in to make a diving catch and then doubled Bruton off first, rendering a subsequent hit by Mathews harmless.

Burdette finally cracked in the bottom of the sixth. Bauer led off with a single and Mantle singled him to third. Berra then doubled to right field, scoring Bauer to make it 2–0 and sending Mantle to third. After Howard was intentionally walked (loading the bases), Skowron ripped a single to right to score another run and send Burdette to the showers. Juan Pizarro tried to stop the bleeding, but McDougald whacked a ground-rule double to score two more and then Turley emulated Spahn and Burdette by driving in two runs with a single to make the score 7–0.

Turley completed the shutout (a five-hitter), striking out Aaron in the ninth to join Walter Johnson as the only men to twice strike out 10 or more batters in a World Series game. The Series would at least return to Milwaukee.

Hindsight is 20/20. It's always easier to say what a manager *should* have done after you see how what he *did* do turns out. Nevertheless, I think Fred Haney made a mistake by bringing Spahn back in Game 6 on two days' rest instead of pitching Bob Rush (who had pitched well in Game 3) and saving Spahn for Game 7, with Burdette in reserve. Spahn was so dominant in Game 4 that if Haney had stuck to the traditional 1–4-7 rotation for his ace, I think he would have won. It is said that the first question Fidel Castro asked American reporters after his takeover of Cuba in 1959 was: "Why did Fred Haney pitch Spahn in the sixth game?"

With his back to the wall, Casey brought Ford back on two days' rest as well. Both teams scored single runs in the first, with Bauer hitting his fourth homer of the Series (tying the record held by Ruth, Gehrig and Snider) and Aaron driving in the Milwaukee run. Then Ford got into trouble in the second, with a little help from the umpire. With one out, Covington hit a sinking liner to center that Mantle appeared to have caught before it hit the grass, but the umpire ruled that he trapped it. "I caught it," said Mantle after the game. "There's no question about it. I caught the ball."[11] The way things had been going for Ford in the Series, somehow it wasn't surprising that he got another bad break. Andy Pafko singled Covington to third, and then Spahn completed a trifecta — singling in a run off Ford for the third game in a row. It was obvious that Whitey didn't have his best stuff, pitching on short rest. When he walked Schoendienst to load the bases, Stengel brought in Art Ditmar.

Johnny Logan was the first batter to face Ditmar, and he hit a fly ball to shallow left. Elston Howard made the catch and then fired a perfect throw to Berra to nail Pafko trying to score. The Yanks felt lucky to be down by only 2–1 at that point.

Facing elimination, the Yanks broke through against Spahn in the sixth to tie the score. Mantle singled, raced around to third when Bruton fumbled Howard's single to center, and scored on a sacrifice fly by Berra. Duren replaced Ditmar in the bottom half of the inning and fanned the side. The Yanks couldn't score off Spahn in the seventh, eighth or ninth, but fortunately Duren kept mowing the Braves down, allowing just one hit and striking out seven in four innings. It was nerve-wracking for Yankees fans knowing that one swing of the bat in the bottom of the ninth could win the Series for Milwaukee, but Duren came through. It was his finest hour as a Yankee.

Spahn labored on into the 10th inning. He had now pitched 28 tough innings (more than three full games) in just eight days, allowing only five runs. If Howard hadn't nailed Pafko at the plate back in the second inning, Spahn would have had his third win and a new Corvette from *SPORT Magazine* as Series MVP. But it wasn't to be for the 37-year-old warrior as he finally tired in the tenth. Gil McDougald tagged him for a lead-off homer to give the Yanks a 3–2 lead. After Howard and Berra singled with two out, Haney finally pulled Spahn, but Moose Skowron greeted reliever Don McMahon with a single that scored Howard with an insurance run. (Berra's two hits in the game gave him 60 in Series play, breaking the record held by Frankie Frisch.)

Duren came back out for the bottom of the 10th but he, too, ran out of gas. He notched his eighth strikeout and got two outs, but with Logan on first via a walk he took a full windup and Logan stole second. Aaron came through with an RBI single, narrowing the lead to 4–3. Then Adcock singled up the middle and all of a sudden the tying run was on third and the Series-winning run was on first.

Stengel went out to get Duren and signaled for Bob Turley, who had pitched nine innings just 48 hours before. Frank Torre (who had hit .300 with two homers in the previous year's Series filling in for the injured Adcock) was sent up to pinch-hit. He hit a soft liner toward right field and McDougald leaped up and gloved it to send the Series to another climactic seventh game.

Having used Spahn in Game 6, Haney had little choice but to use Burdette on two days' rest, as he had done with success the previous year. It was Ford's turn to pitch for the Yanks, but since he had been wasted the previous day, Stengel countered with Larsen, who had pitched seven shutout innings in Game 3 and was well rested.

The Braves scored in the first inning but left the bases loaded. The Yanks came back with two runs in the top of the second without getting a hit, thanks to two throwing errors by Torre at first base. Larsen blanked the Braves in the bottom of the second, but when he gave up two singles with one out in the third inning, Stengel pulled him and brought in Turley for the third straight game. Bullet Bob pitched out of a bases-loaded jam and blanked the Braves until two were out in the bottom of the sixth, when Del Crandall hit a solo homer to left field to tie the score at two apiece.

Burdette was pitching his heart out, using (as Mantle said in his book *All My Octobers*) "all the tools nature gave him, his arm and head and heart and tongue."[12] Through seven innings, he had given up just four hits and only the two unearned runs. But with two out in the eighth, Berra hammered a double off the right-field wall and Elston Howard singled him home with what proved to be the winning run. After Andy Carey reached on an infield hit, Skowron put the game out of reach with a three-run homer into the left-center-field bleachers.

Turley finished strong, allowing just two hits in his six and two-thirds innings. When Mantle gloved Red Schoendienst's fly ball for the final out, the Yanks had both their revenge and their 18th world championship. Elston Howard was voted Series MVP for his clutch hitting, fielding and throwing in the final three games, although either Turley or Hank Bauer (who led all hitters with 10 hits, four homers and eight RBIs) would have been worthy winners as well.

After battling for 14 games in 1957–58, the Yanks and Braves were about as even as they could be: seven wins apiece, with 54 runs on 106 hits for the Yanks and 48 runs on 107 hits for the Braves. The result of these two classic World Series was a draw.

For Ford, the end of the season was somewhat bittersweet. On the plus side, he had won his fourth World Series ring and had reached 100 career wins with the highest winning percentage of anyone who had ever done so. His career ERA of 2.61 was not only the lowest of any active pitcher but was also the lowest of any pitcher since Walter Johnson, who retired in 1927 with a career ERA of 2.17. He had done some of the finest pitching of his career. On the other hand, he had made 10 starts after August 8 (including the World Series) and had not won any of them, going 0–3 with seven no-decisions despite pitching well enough to win half of them. This would be the longest such streak of his career. Most frustrating to Whitey was his failure to win any of his three World Series starts against Spahn, his southpaw rival. Ford had pitched well in two of those games, but Spahn had been a little better and had gotten the breaks. Unfortunately, the two future Hall of Famers would never face each other again, except in the 1961 All-Star Game.

EIGHT

A Disappointing Season

The 1959 baseball season was an aberration, one of only two seasons during the 16-year period 1949–1964 in which the Yankees didn't win the American League pennant. Since they won 103 games during their other nonpennant season (1954), this was their only bad season during that entire stretch. There was a saying in those years that "as Mantle goes, so go the Yankees," and Mantle had a bad year in 1959, hitting only 31 homers and knocking in only 75 runs. But the Yankees' problems that year went far deeper than Mantle's off year. Production fell off up and down the Yankees' lineup, as evidenced by the fact that Mantle's 75 RBIs led the team. Bob Turley slipped badly from his 1958 Cy Young Award performance, all the way to 8–11 with a 4.32 ERA. Ford had a respectable year (16–10), but only two other pitchers reached double figures in wins. The Yanks fell eight games below .500 on May 22 and didn't climb above .500 to stay until September 10, eventually finishing third with a 79–75 record, 15 games behind the "Go-Go" White Sox of Nellie Fox and Luis Aparicio.

The highlight of this dismal season occurred on April 22, when Ford turned in one of the best pitching performances of his career. After beating the Orioles 3–1 in his first start of the season, Whitey faced the Washington Senators at Griffith Stadium in front of 7,337 shivering fans on a raw April night. For 10 innings, Ford and Senators right-hander Bill Fischer matched zeroes. But Washington manager Cookie Lavagetto pinch-hit for Fischer in the bottom of the 10th inning with a runner on second and one out and the move backfired when Ford pitched out of the jam. Ironically, Fischer (who would yield Mantle's 1963 "façade" home run that came within a few feet of becoming the first fair ball ever hit out of Yankee Stadium) was replaced by left-hander Chuck Stobbs, best known for yielding another of Mantle's memorable home runs—his 565-footer at Griffith Stadium in 1953. But on this night, Mantle was unable to get a hit off either of them.

Stobbs shut out the Yanks for three innings and Ford put three more zeroes up on the scoreboard. Finally, in the top of the 14th inning, Moose Skowron blasted a home run off Stobbs to give the Yankees a 1–0 lead and

Whitey blanked the Senators in the bottom of the 14th to complete a seven-hit shutout. He struck out 15, tying the Yankees' record set by Bob Shawkey in 1919 and setting a major league record for strikeouts in a night game. (The previous record of 14 had been shared by Johnny Vander Meer, Bob Feller, Bob Turley and Sam Jones, all of whom accomplished the feat in nine-inning games.[1]) No Senator even got as far as third base, and only three reached second. Remarkably, the game took only three hours and 40 minutes, which is no more than many of today's nine-inning games.

That win gave the Yankees a 6–3 record and the status quo seemed to be holding in the American League. However, the Yanks lost nine of their next 10 games to fall all the way to seventh place. They rallied briefly a few days later when they swept a Sunday double-header from the Senators, led by their three cornerstone players. A long homer by Mantle off Stobbs helped Ford win the opener, and then Berra homered and broke a major league record in the nightcap. (The second game was Yogi's 148th consecutive game without an error as a catcher, breaking the record held by Buddy Rosar of the 1947 Philadelphia Athletics.[2] The streak came to an end in the Yankees' very next game after 950 consecutive errorless chances, also a major league record.) But then the Yanks resumed their free fall, losing six of their next seven. When they were pounded 13–6 by the last-place Tigers on May 20, they fell into the American League cellar for the first time since 1940. As if that wasn't ignominious enough, in their very next game the Yanks were held to one hit by Baltimore's Hoyt Wilhelm as the Orioles routed Turley in the first inning en route to a 5–0 triumph. Wilhelm had pitched a no-hitter against New York the previous September, and only an eighth-inning single by Jerry Lumpe prevented another no-hitter. Mantle even tried batting right-handed against the right-handed knuckleballer, without success.

The Yanks bounced back to beat Baltimore in their next two games, with Mantle driving in six runs with five hits (including two homers) and Ford pitching a two-hit shutout. Two hits by Bob Nieman were the only blemishes on Ford's 9–0 masterpiece, and Whitey knocked in the first run himself with a fifth-inning single. He beat Baltimore again five days later, 5–2, going the distance and scoring New York's fifth run after lining a double into the right-field corner. He continued his hot hitting in his next start, driving in three runs with a double and his second career home run while pitching his third straight complete game to beat Detroit, 14–3. (Whitey's batting average that season was a very respectable .231, the second highest of his career.)

The Yanks actually made a run at the league leaders in June. Mantle started the run with a ninth-inning game-winning homer against Detroit on June 3 and New York won seven out of eight to reach the .500 mark for the first time since April 29. The following week the league-leading White

Sox invaded Yankee Stadium and the resurgent Yanks swept a three-game series, thanks in large part to Mantle. After he tripled and scored the winning run in the first game of the series, he hit a tape-measure three-run homer to spark New York to a 7–3 win in the second game. The ball landed deep in the right-field upper deck, just missing the façade. "It was the best one I've hit in two years," said Mantle. "I really hit the hell out of it."[3] He followed that up with a game-winning 10th-inning homer the following day as the Yanks completed the sweep, knocking Chicago out of first place.

The Indians were now atop the AL standings and they were the next visitors to the Stadium. Although Ford had to leave the series opener in the sixth inning after spraining an ankle running the bases, the Yanks prevailed 3–2 and then routed the Tribe 10–2 the following day behind two homers, a triple and five RBIs by Moose Skowron. Amazingly, New York had now crept within a game and a half of the league lead and most Yankee fans figured it was just a matter of time before the Yanks assumed their usual spot at the top of the standings. They dropped the last two games of the Cleveland series to fall back again, but then Mantle erupted for two homers and a triple against Kansas City on June 22 (driving in six runs in an 11–6 Yankees win) and Ford pitched a five-hitter the following day to beat the Athletics, 10–2, aided by Mantle's ninth homer in three weeks. When Ryne Duren shut down the White Sox with eight strikeouts in three scoreless innings of relief a few days later, the Yanks were a season-high four games over .500 at 36–32 and trailed Cleveland by just two games.

This proved to be the high-water mark of the Yankees' season, as they played .500 baseball (43–43) the rest of the way and tumbled further and further off the pace. Mantle injured his right ankle in late June and his right shoulder (injured in the 1957 World Series) began hurting again, as a result of which he began to strike out at an alarming rate batting left-handed. He hit only two home runs during the entire month of July. Rest might have helped, but he knew the Yanks had no chance to stay in the race without him in the lineup. In addition, he had almost no protection behind him in the lineup. Berra's production was falling off as he neared the end of his career, and Moose Skowron, after hitting 15 home runs before the All-Star break and being voted the starting first baseman for the AL in the All-Star Game, missed almost the entire second half of the season with a back injury and a broken left wrist. Pitchers began to pitch around Mantle even more than usual, so he began to expand the strike zone in an effort to drive in runs. As a result, he struck out more times that season (126) than in any other season of his career.

As the Yanks fell out of the race, Mantle became the lightning rod for the fans' displeasure. During one 20-game stretch he knocked in only one run, and Yankee fans booed him mercilessly after every strikeout. He had certainly heard the boos before; after the unprecedented buildup he had received as a rookie, anything less than his Triple Crown season of 1956 was viewed by some as a failure. But the booing of Mantle reached a crescendo during the 1959 season.

The fans' negative attitude toward Mantle during those years was fed partly by the press. During the first half of his career, Mickey was not very good at handling the press and he could be curt, uncooperative and downright surly with reporters after a bad game, sometimes even seeking refuge in the trainer's room to avoid the endless barrage of questions. His relationships with the regular beat reporters who knew him best were not too bad, but many of the other reporters ripped him frequently, portraying him as an aloof prima donna who refused to sign autographs for kids. The truth of the matter was that he signed countless autographs, but there were always more kids waiting and he was besieged by autograph-seekers wherever he went. He couldn't go out to dinner with his wife without a constant stream of people coming to his table looking for autographs, and many people were rude when he declined to sign, to the point of flipping ink on him. He eventually became less and less cooperative, which added to his negative image.

Ford, on the other hand, was never treated poorly by the New York press, even when he pitched poorly. The reporters loved him because he would always sit and patiently answer their questions, even after a bad game. His demeanor changed very little, regardless of whether he had just thrown a shutout or been knocked out in the first inning. After a bad game, the reporters might write that Whitey hadn't had his best stuff that day, but they would never criticize him.

Another reason Ford's image was more positive than Mantle's during the 1950s was his comportment on the field. While his competitive fires burned just as hotly as Mantle's, Ford rarely showed emotion on the field, regardless of what happened. He seldom argued with umpires and he never threw at the hitters. He had the total respect of everybody: teammates, opponents, umpires, the press and the fans. He was one of the most popular Yankees in franchise history.

Like Ford, Mantle was revered by teammates and opponents alike, many of whom admired him for playing in constant pain. However, Mickey would frequently argue balls and strikes with the umpires and he was famous for his temper tantrums when he struck out, which only increased the booing. When he homered, he showed almost no emotion, not wanting to show up the pitcher. He would run around the bases with his head down, almost like he was embarrassed. When he struck out, however, he would fling his batting helmet and then kick the water cooler. "Son," Casey would say, "it ain't the water cooler that's striking you out." In his later seasons, even as his skills were being eroded by constant injuries, Mantle's behavior and attitude became more and more like Ford's, with the result that he could do no wrong in the eyes of the press and most Yankee fans. But in 1959, Mantle bore the brunt of the Yankees fans' displeasure at having to endure a baseball season without a World Series.

Although the Yankees floundered during the second half of the season, Ford pitched well at times despite suffering a recurrence of the left elbow pain that had plagued him in both of the previous two years. After completing seven of his first 14 starts, Whitey went 13 starts without a complete game and was forced to skip a few starts. Stengel used him in relief a number of times, sometimes on short rest, which probably didn't help him any. During this period when he couldn't pitch nine innings, Ford was frequently relieved by Ryne Duren, who was one of the few bright spots of the season for the Yankees with a 1.88 ERA in 41 appearances. Duren saved a win for Ford just before the All-Star break, retiring all nine batters he faced, six of them on strikes. (Ford again helped out on offense, scoring the winning run on Tony Kubek's sixth-inning single after reaching base with a solid double.) Both Ford and Duren were selected for the All-Star Game and Ryne pitched superbly, allowing just one hit in three scoreless innings and striking out four. Ford fared less well, taking the loss when Willie Mays tripled in the winning run off him in the eighth inning.

Duren came to Ford's rescue again on July 14, saving a 1–0 victory over the Indians by striking out the side in the ninth inning. At that point, Duren hadn't allowed a run since April 30, a span of 31 1/3 innings covering 17 relief appearances. (The streak would come to an end in his next outing when shortstop Gil McDougald collided with left fielder Tony Kubek on a pop fly.) Duren saved Ford yet again five days later, striking out five in two scoreless innings as Whitey picked up his 10th win of the season against the White Sox, 6–2.

In late July, Ford's elbow problem flared up and he was forced to make a few early exits and miss a start, but when he returned he combined with Duren for two more shutouts. Whitey fanned 10 Kansas City Athletics in the first of these games before Duren struck out the side in the ninth, and then they combined to blank Baltimore 5–0 on September 1. In between, Ford turned in one of the best relief performances of his career, pitching five and two-thirds scoreless innings to beat the Tigers and Yankee-killer Frank Lary, who had won 12 of 13 decisions against the Yankees since the start of the previous season.

Ford was 14–7 after his win against Baltimore on September 1, but then lost three straight games (one in relief) to establish a career high for losses in a season. He finished strong, winning his last two starts. First he beat Boston 3–1 with a four-hitter for his first complete game since June 23, losing a shutout because of an eighth-inning Yankees error. Then he beat Baltimore with another complete game to finish the season with a 16–10 record. Although his winning percentage of .615 was the lowest he had recorded in his eight seasons in the majors, it was still among the top 10 in the league, as were his win total and his ERA (3.04). For the third straight season, Whitey's intermittent arm problems had limited him to fewer than 30 starts. Unfortunately, these arm problems were becoming a recurring theme.

Mantle also finished with subpar statistics—his worst since his rookie year. However, he provided a few highlights to an otherwise dreary last two months of the season. In an August 16 double-header at the Stadium, he hit two long home runs and a double that hit the center-field wall on the fly, just to the right of the 461-foot sign. Then he went on a nine-day tear during the first half of September. After a homer at Fenway Park on September 7, he went five-for-six with a homer on September 10 at home against Kansas City. On September 13 at the Stadium, the Yanks fell behind 1–0 in the top of the 11th against Cleveland but Mantle hit a two-run homer in the bottom half of the inning to win the game. He finished the hot streak by switch-hitting home runs in the same game for the seventh time in his career on September 15, driving in all of the Yankees' runs in a 4–3 loss to the White Sox at Yankee Stadium. His final total of 31 home runs was his lowest in five years, but it was still tied for fourth in the AL and his 104 runs ranked second. Although Mickey's production at the plate was off, he partially made up for it in other areas, leading all American League outfielders in fielding with a .995 average and stealing 21 bases in 24 attempts to edge Willie Mays for the best stolen base percentage in the majors (.875).

Berra hit only 19 homers and his 69 RBIs were his lowest total since his rookie year. However, he led all American League catchers with a .997 fielding average and he had many clutch hits. In an extra-inning win over Kansas City at Yankee Stadium on August 9, he hit his 300th career home run in dramatic fashion, pinch-hitting a game-tying home run with two outs in the bottom of the ninth. Yankees fans and management showered him with gifts on "Yogi Berra Day" at the Stadium on September 19.

The Yankees knew they had to retool and reload for the 1960 season. It was time to give Elston Howard the everyday catcher job and use Berra as part-time catcher, part-time left fielder. They needed pitching help, part of which they hoped to get from right-hander Ralph Terry, acquired from Kansas City during the 1959 season. Most of all, they needed a left-handed power hitter to protect Mantle in the lineup, preferably a right fielder to replace Hank Bauer, who was nearing the end of his fine career.

NINE

Pirates Steal Series, with Help from Stengel

In some respects, 1960 was another disappointing season for Ford, both from a team standpoint and from an individual standpoint. Of course, for the Yankees of that era, any season that didn't end with a world championship was a disappointment. But Whitey also struggled with shoulder problems during the first half of the season and had what was for him a subpar season. However, when the money was on the line during the most important regular-season games and the World Series, Whitey was at his very best.

The season started much like any other Yankees season of that era, with Ford winning the home opener for the fifth time in five tries. He beat the Baltimore Orioles (one of the teams expected to challenge the Yankees for the AL pennant), pitching seven strong innings and combining with Ralph Terry on a 5–0 shutout. Whitey drove in the first run himself with a third-inning RBI single and then Mantle hit a ball off the facing of the upper deck in right field leading off the fourth to give New York a 2–0 lead. After Ford pitched out of a jam in the top of the sixth, the Yanks put the game away with two runs in the bottom half of the inning and the outcome was never in doubt after that. Whitey probably could have finished the shutout himself, but Stengel didn't want him pitching more than seven innings in his first start of the season.

Despite the precautionary move by Casey, Whitey began experiencing shoulder problems shortly thereafter and didn't win his second game of the season until May 26, picking up two losses and two no-decisions in the interim and missing several starts. Mantle was off to a slow start as well, having missed part of spring training holding out because stingy general manager George Weiss had tried to cut his salary from $72,000 to $55,000. After a bitter 10-day holdout, Mantle settled for a $7,000 cut to $65,000. But he was not 100 percent healthy and had only four home runs on May 26. Fortunately the Yanks had made an excellent acquisition the previous

December, acquiring right fielder Roger Maris in a trade with the Kansas City Athletics. Maris had played three seasons in the majors, compiling a batting average of .249 and averaging 19 home runs and 68 RBIs. He was a left-handed pull-hitter with a stroke tailor-made for Yankee Stadium and the Yanks were counting on him to increase his homer output and strengthen their defense in right field. He certainly did the former, hitting 11 home runs in April and May and carrying the Yanks while Mantle and Ford were struggling. Even so, the Yanks were languishing in fourth place (tied with Detroit and trailing Baltimore, Cleveland and Chicago) when Ford returned to the hill on May 26 against the Orioles and they badly needed a win.

Whitey responded with a three-hit shutout of the Birds, a textbook 2–0 win in which the Yankees infield (including Ford) had an amazing 22 assists. Sixteen ground balls were gobbled up by shortstop Tony Kubek and third baseman Gil McDougald. When Whitey was really on his game, keeping the ball low and moving it around with his pinpoint control, he induced one ground ball after another. This was one of those games, and he made the two runs the Yankees gave him stand up. One of the reasons the Yankee players loved playing behind him (other than the fact that he usually won) was that he kept the game moving. He didn't walk many batters and he wasn't constantly going deep into the count. He didn't waste time between pitches and he threw strikes. The infielders were usually busy when he pitched and the games seldom took much more than two hours.

After this win over Baltimore, Mantle broke out of his slump, hitting 16 home runs between May 28 and July 4. (The homer on July 4 was his 300th.) The Yanks went on a 23–5 tear and surged into first place. With Yogi Berra and Moose Skowron following Mantle and Maris in the batting order, the Yanks once again had the most feared lineup in baseball. In a game on June 18 at Comiskey Park in Chicago, Mantle homered over the center-field fence, Maris followed with a shot into the upper deck in right, and Skowron belted one into the upper deck in left three innings later as the Yanks rained 19 hits on the White Sox in a 12–5 rout.

Although the Yanks as a team took off, Whitey lost a couple of 3–2 heartbreakers and was only 2–5 in mid-June, by far the worst start of his career. With the Yanks clinging to a precarious half-game lead in the AL standings, Ford was matched up against Yankee-killer Frank Lary on June 21 in the first game of a three-game series in Detroit. Once again he responded with a shutout (a four-hitter), beating the Tigers 6–0 with the help of two homers by Mantle and a triple by Maris. The homers were Mickey's 15th and 16th of the season, but he still trailed Maris by four in the home run race.

Ford followed up that win with another four-hitter five days later, a 6–2 win over the Indians in the first game of a double-header in Cleveland.

However, the Yanks dropped the nightcap despite two homers by Maris (No. 21 and No. 22) and dropped into second place, one game behind the Orioles. New York had regained the lead by the time Whitey beat the Orioles 5–2 in Baltimore in his last start before the All-Star Game, outpitching Hal "Skinny" Brown with a complete-game seven-hitter. The win evened his record at 5–5, certainly not the record he was used to having at the All-Star break. The following morning, the *New York Times* noted that Maris was six games ahead of Ruth's 1927 home run pace.

By Whitey's next start on July 18 in Cleveland, the Indians had slipped past the Orioles into second place in the standings, just a game and a half in back of the Yanks. Whitey gave them the same treatment he had given the Orioles, spacing out eight hits and going the route in a 9–2 win. Maris and Mantle both homered, with Roger retaining the seasonal lead, 29–22.

After having his four-game winning streak stopped by the White Sox, Whitey beat the Indians again, combining with Bobby Shantz on a seven-hit shutout and riding homers by Kubek, Mantle and Clete Boyer to a 4–0 win.

Next it was the Chicago White Sox who made a run at the Yanks, briefly surging into first place. But New York beat Detroit twice on August 2 to regain the lead. Whitey pitched beautifully in the nightcap (yielding just five hits in eight innings) but left the game trailing 1–0 on an unearned run. After reliever Duke Maas served up a home run to Norm Cash in the top of the ninth, the Yanks were in a 2–0 hole when they batted in the bottom of the ninth against Jim Bunning, who had allowed just two hits. Detroit manager Jimmy Dykes did the Yanks a favor by pulling Bunning after a lead-off walk to Bobby Richardson, and Maris deposited his 32nd home run of the year deep into the right-field seats off Bill Fischer to tie the game at 2. Bob Cerv won the game for New York with a 10th-inning pinch-hit homer.

After another loss to the White Sox evened his record again at 7–7, Ford turned in back-to-back gems. On August 13 at the Stadium, Whitey had a no-hitter going for five and two-thirds innings against the Washington Senators. He had walked one batter but had proceeded to pick him off first base, so he had faced the minimum number of batters when Washington pitcher Don Lee batted with two out in the sixth and the game still scoreless. Whitey walked Lee, and then Bob Allison singled to break up the no-hitter and put Ford in a jam. However, he retired Reno Bertoia on a pop to short to end the inning.

The Yanks broke through against Lee in the bottom of the seventh when Maris tripled and Mantle drove him home with a sacrifice fly. The Senators mounted a final threat against Whitey in the ninth when Allison led off with a double and Harmon Killebrew drew a one-out walk. That brought up Jim Lemon, who had once hit three home runs in one game off Ford. But this time Whitey struck him out, and then got Billy Gardner on a bouncer to first to complete a three-hit 1–0 shutout.

The following day was perhaps the low point of the season for the Yanks as they lost both games of a double-header to the Senators in excruciating fashion. Bob Turley blew the first game 5–4 by walking in a run in the sixth inning and then allowing a grand slam home run off the right-field foul pole by the opposing pitcher, Camilo Pascual. Then Ralph Terry walked in the winning run in the 15th inning of the second game to drop New York into third place, one-half game behind both Baltimore and Chicago. The two teams had battled for a total of eight hours, and the Yanks had come away empty. To make matters worse, Roger Maris had bruised his ribs trying to break up a double play in the sixth inning of the second game and had to be taken to Lenox Hill Hospital for x-rays. Although the x-rays were negative, Roger would be sidelined for 18 games. He had 35 homers at the time and had been exactly even with Ruth's 1927 pace at the start of the day's play, but he would hit only four more home runs during the last seven weeks of the season.

When the Orioles invaded the Stadium the following night for the first game of a two-game series, Mickey Mantle had something to prove. Stengel had pulled him from the second game of the previous day's double-header for not running out a double-play grounder — the same play on which the hustling Maris had been injured. After hearing some boos his first time up, he turned the boos to cheers with a pair of two-run homers, one in the fourth inning and another in the eighth inning to win the game, 4–3, behind the five-hit pitching of Art Ditmar. The win put the Yanks back into first place by half a game over both Baltimore and Chicago, and the two homers moved Mickey within six of Maris for the AL lead, 35–29.

Stengel faced a dilemma the following night. He had used practically every pitcher he had in the two previous days and he needed a starting pitcher for the second Baltimore game. Though he had never before pitched on only two days of rest in a regular season game, Ford volunteered. Once again, the Yanks made his task difficult by getting him only one run, delivered by a Johnny Blanchard single in the fourth inning. But Ford was sharp, mixing fastballs and curves with pinpoint control. His only anxious moment came when Jackie Brandt doubled leading off the game, but Whitey stranded him there and Brandt was the only Oriole to reach second base in the game. Two hits (one of them an infield hit) were all Whitey allowed from then on, and he struck out six in recording his second successive three-hit 1–0 shutout. He needed only 106 pitches to polish off the Birds, against whom he had now thrown 25 consecutive scoreless innings at Yankee Stadium in winning all three of his starts.

After a couple of no-decisions, Whitey faced the Orioles again on September 2 at Memorial Stadium in Baltimore. This time it was the opposing hurler who pitched a three-hit shutout, as Milt Pappas fanned 11 Yankees in shutting them down 5–0. The win moved the Birds into a virtual tie with the Yankees for the American League lead, and Baltimore proceeded to sweep the three-game series to take a two-game lead over New York, with Chicago a game and a half further back.

The Yanks still trailed the Orioles by half a game when they played the Tigers in Detroit on September 10. With the Yanks clinging to a 2–1 lead with two on and two out in the seventh inning, Mantle faced right-hander Paul Foytack. Back in 1956, Mickey had become the second player to hit a ball over the right-field roof at Briggs Stadium (Ted Williams had been the first in 1939). The pitcher had been Paul Foytack. Two years later, Mantle had cleared the roof again off Jim Bunning. Another two years had passed, and it was Foytack's turn again. Mickey launched his 33rd home run of the season over the roof to give the Yanks a 5–1 lead. It was the fourth ball hit over the right-field roof in the 48 years since the stadium had been built, and Mantle had hit three of them.[1] The Yanks won that game and then swept a double-header in Cleveland the following day (winning the second game on a Mantle homer in the 11th inning) to take a one-game lead over the Orioles and a three-game lead over the White Sox. But by the time the Orioles came into the Stadium on September 16 for a four-game series, they had pulled back into a tie with the Yanks, with Chicago two games back.

As usual, Whitey got the ball for the most important game of the year, and as usual he came through. The Yanks jumped out to a 1–0 lead in the fourth on a homer by Hector Lopez, added two more in the fifth on Maris's 39th homer of the season and tacked on a fourth run in the sixth. Meanwhile Ford pitched shutout ball for eight innings, which stretched his string of consecutive scoreless innings against Baltimore at Yankee Stadium to 33, dating back to the home opener. After retiring the first two Orioles in the ninth, another shutout seemed certain, but a single by Walt Dropo and a double by Ron Hansen put runners on second and third. When Whitey walked Gus Triandos to load the bases, Stengel opted to bring in Bobby Shantz to get the final out. Shantz succeeded, but not before yielding a two-run single to Jim Busby that ended Whitey's shutout streak. The 4–2 win opened up a one-game lead over Baltimore and ignited not only a series sweep but also a 15-game winning streak that carried right through the end of the season. New York won the pennant by eight games over Baltimore and by 10 over the White Sox. Since each head-to-head win resulted in a two-game difference, the five times Whitey beat the Orioles were the difference in the final AL standings.

Whitey won his last two starts, beating Washington twice to finish the season with a 12–9 record. In the second of these two games, Mantle hit two home runs off Chuck Stobbs (who had served up Mickey's 565-footer back in 1953) to pass Maris for the league lead, 40–39. When neither of them homered in the final weekend series against Boston, Mantle had his fourth home run title. As a team, the Yanks hit 193 home runs that season to break their own American League record, set in 1956. Maris led the AL in RBIs with 112 and edged Mantle in the second-closest MVP balloting ever, 225–222. (In his 1947 Triple Crown year, Ted Williams had lost the MVP to Joe DiMaggio by a single vote.)

Over in the National League, the Pirates had pulled away from the Braves, Cardinals and Dodgers in August to win their first pennant in 33 years, but the Yankees were heavily favored in the World Series. Only the most blindly fanatical fan would suggest that the Pirates were a better team that year. Not that they were a bad team; in fact, they were an excellent team. They had two future Hall of Famers: Roberto Clemente in right field and Bill Mazeroski at second base; they had the National League batting champion and MVP (Dick Groat) at shortstop and the MVP runner-up (Don Hoak) at third base; and they had excellent pitching, headed up by Cy Young Award-winner Vernon Law (20–9) and the best relief pitcher in baseball, Elroy Face. However, the 1960 Yankees were essentially the same team as the 1961 version, which is generally considered to be (along with the 1927 and 1998 Yankees) one of the three best teams in the history of baseball. Coincidentally, the last Pirates team to play in the World Series had been swept by the 1927 Yankees. No one would have been surprised if the result had been the same in 1960. The Yankees had hit 73 more home runs than the Pirates during the regular season. "We were expected to win," Mickey Mantle said later. "In this case, we should have."

The statistics of that Series are an accurate measure of the two teams. The Yankees outscored the Pirates (55–27), outhit them (91–60) and out-homered them (10–4). They had a team batting average of .338, a new Series record (as were the runs and hits totals). Two Yankees (Bobby Richardson and Mickey Mantle) broke the World Series record for RBIs. They also had the best pitcher in the Series, Whitey Ford, who threw two masterful shutouts. How could they possibly have lost? Aside from the Pirates playing over their heads, I believe the Yanks lost because of three things: a terrible managerial decision by Casey Stengel; several bad umpiring calls in Game 4; and a bad break at a critical point in Game 7. There's an old axiom in sports that says if you let an inferior team hang around until the end, anything can happen. In this case, it did.

Most Yankees fans believe that Casey Stengel blew that Series before a pitch was even thrown by not pitching Ford in Game 1. Most managers pitch their ace in Game 1 so that he can pitch three times if the Series goes seven games. The Yankees' ace was indisputably Whitey Ford. Though he had won only 12 games during the season, he had tied for the league lead in shutouts with four and had been among the top five in the AL in earned run average (3.08). He had won his last three starts and was fine for the Series. He had pitched the opening game of the Yankees' last four World Series (1955–58) and his teammates assumed that Whitey would get the nod once again. However, the Series started in Pittsburgh, and Stengel had an obsession about pitching Ford in Yankee Stadium with its cavernous outfield, so he held him out until the Series shifted to the Stadium for Game 3. Stengel himself had often said of Ford: "If you had one game to win and your life depended on it, you'd want him to pitch it." Unfortunately, when the Series came down to Game 7 and Stengel's job depended on the outcome, he didn't have Ford to pitch it. "Whitey was our best pitcher," said Mantle. "We needed him in a seventh game."

Pirates manager Danny Murtaugh picked his Cy Young Award winner, Vernon Law, to open the Series. Stengel picked Art Ditmar (15–9), who failed to last the first inning. After the Yanks took a 1–0 lead in the top of the first on a Roger Maris home run into the right-field upper deck, the Bucs struck for three in their half of the inning. Bill Virdon walked, stole second and scored when Groat lined a double to right. Bob Skinner bounced a single up the middle to score Groat and promptly stole second. Roberto Clemente then bounced a single up the middle to give the Pirates a 3–1 lead, and that was all for Ditmar. Jim Coates came on and retired the side.

Maris singled and Mantle walked leading off the Yankees' fourth, but a big inning was averted when Virdon made a great running catch of Berra's drive to the warning track in right center. Skowron followed with a single to narrow the margin to 3–2, but the Pirates came right back against Coates in the bottom of the fourth with a walk to Don Hoak and a preview home run by Mazeroski over the scoreboard in left and into the trees behind the wall. Maz had hit only 11 homers all season, but this would be a Series in which both second basemen exceeded their usual offensive output.

Law kept the Yankees at bay but finally tired in the eighth. Leading 6–2, he surrendered singles to Hector Lopez and Maris with nobody out and Mantle due up. Murtaugh brought in Elroy Face, who had won his first 17 decisions in 1959 and 22 straight dating back to his last five decisions of 1958, missing Carl Hubbell's record by two. The little forkballer struck out Mantle, got Berra on a fly to Clemente, and struck out Skowron.

The Yanks made it 6–4 in the ninth when Elston Howard pinch-hit an opposite field homer over the right-field screen with Bobby Richardson on base. Tony Kubek then singled to bring the tying run to the plate, but Lopez grounded sharply to Mazeroski for a game-ending double play.

Game 2 was a complete rout. In the fifth inning with the Yanks ahead 3–1 and left-hander Fred Green on in relief of starter Bob Friend, Mantle

Ford in action in the third game of the 1960 World Series against the Pittsburgh Pirates. Whitey pitched a four-hit shutout to beat the Bucs 10–0. (AP/Wide World Photos).

lined a homer to right center with Maris on base to increase the lead to 5–1. It was Mickey's 12th Series homer, putting him ahead of Duke Snider into second place behind Babe Ruth's record of 15.

The floodgates opened in the sixth inning. A triple by Howard and a double by Richardson kayoed Green and brought on ex-Dodger Clem Labine. Berra's bases-loaded single scored two more and Skowron's single made it 10–1. By the time the Pirates finally retired the side, the score was 12–1. Howard and Richardson both had two hits in the inning.

By now the Yanks were treating every Pirates pitcher as though he were batting practice pitcher Spud Murray, and in the seventh inning, Mantle put the icing on the cake. Batting right-handed against Joe Gibbon with two men on, Mickey hit a ball into the trees behind the 15-foot center-field wall at the 436-foot mark. It was the first ball ever hit over the center-field wall by a right-handed batter, and the distance to the landing spot was 478 feet. Pirates center fielder Bill Virdon said: "The ball got there more quickly than any ball I've ever seen.... It looked as though he shot it out of a gun."[2] Mickey's five RBIs in the game tied a Series record that would be broken 48 hours later. Bullet Bob Turley cruised to a 16–3 win, with a ninth-inning assist from Bobby Shantz.

It was more of the same two days later at Yankee Stadium. Ford finally got to pitch, and he retired the first nine men he faced. Meanwhile, the Yanks teed off immediately on future congressman Wilmer "Vinegar Bend" Mizell, chasing him in the first inning with three hits and a walk, including an RBI single by Skowron. With the bases loaded and one out, Murtaugh replaced Mizell with Clem Labine. After Elston Howard's infield single scored the second run, little Bobby Richardson (whose only home run of the season had come way back in April) stroked a line drive inside the left-field foul pole for the seventh grand slammer in Series history. (Players on that Yankees team had the last five of them: McDougald in 1951, Mantle in 1953, Berra and Skowron in 1956, and Richardson.)

Staked to a 6–0 lead, Ford allowed a lead-off double to Virdon in the fourth but stranded him there, retiring the heart of the Pirates' order (Groat, Clemente and Dick Stuart) in order. Whitey then matched the Pirates' output with a hit in the bottom of the fourth and was on base when Mantle launched another home run off Fred Green over the Pirates' bullpen in left center, about 10 rows in back of the 402-foot sign. It was Mickey's fourteenth Series homer, putting him only one behind Ruth. Later in the inning, Bobby Richardson came up with the bases loaded again and singled in two more runs to make the score 10–0 and set a new Series record for RBIs in one game with six.

Ford allowed his second base runner in the sixth when Mazeroski led off with a single, but three ground balls quickly retired the side. A single and a walk in the Pirates' seventh were neutralized by a double-play grounder, and Clemente singled for the Pirates' fourth hit with two out in the ninth. An error by shortstop Tony Kubek put runners on first and second, but Ford preserved his shutout by striking out Gino Cimoli to end the game. The Yanks had now pounded the Pirates' pitching for 35 hits in the last two games, while Ford faced only 31 batters in recording his sixth World Series win. At this point, the Series certainly looked like a mismatch.

It was Vernon Law versus Ralph Terry in Game 4. The Deacon got into trouble right away, yielding a single to Cerv and a double to Kubek on his first three pitches. After retiring Maris, he walked Mantle intentionally. Berra then hit a grounder to Hoak, who stepped on third and fired across to Dick Stuart at first to try to double Berra. The video slow motion shows that Berra clearly beat the throw, with Cerv scoring. Unfortunately for the Yanks, the umpire blew the call and the inning was over with no runs.

Terry held the Bucs hitless through four and then Moose Skowron belted his fifth World Series homer in the bottom of the fourth to give the Yanks a 1–0 lead. But the Pirates came back with three in the top of the fifth, with some more help from the umpires. Cimoli singled to right, and then Skowron fielded Smoky Burgess's grounder and fired to Kubek to try to

Ford before Game 6 of the 1960 World Series against the Pirates. The Yankees needed a win to stay alive in the Series. (National Baseball Hall of Fame Library, Cooperstown, N.Y.)

force Cimoli. The slow-motion replay shows that Cimoli beat the throw but then came off the bag for a second as Kubek tagged him. The second base umpire called him safe. Terry almost got out of the jam, retiring Hoak and Maz, but then Law helped his own cause with a double to left for one run and Virdon singled in two more to give the Pirates a 3–1 lead.

Law lasted until the seventh. Skowron led off with a double to right and advanced to third on a single by Gil McDougald. Richardson forced McDougald at second, scoring Skowron to make the score 3–2. Pinch hitter Johnny Blanchard singled to right, knocking out Law and bringing in Face. Bob Cerv hit a shot to right center that would have hit the wall at the 407-foot mark, but Virdon raced over and made a leaping catch against the wall to preserve Pittsburgh's one-run lead.

In the top of the ninth, it was Mantle's turn to make a great catch in the exact same spot. That kept it a 3–2 game as the Yanks came up in the bottom of the ninth. Skowron led off with a shot down the third-base line, but Don Hoak (who had been on the '55 Dodgers team that beat the Yanks) made a spectacular backhanded grab to rob him of a sure double. Face closed out the Yanks, getting Dale Long (batting for Richardson) to pop out to end the game. It had to be the only time in World Series history that a guy batting .438 with nine RBIs got pinch-hit for, the day after breaking the record for RBIs in a Series game. Stengel was famous for his hunches (like pitching Don Larsen in Game 5 in 1956), but in this Series, very few of his hunches panned out. The Yankees were left wondering how they could have outscored the Pirates 32–12 in the first four games and gotten only a split.

Ditmar got another chance in Game 5 at Yankee Stadium, against left-hander Harvey Haddix. Haddix was a pretty good pitcher (136–113 lifetime), but like Larsen is remembered mostly for one game. On May 26, 1959, he had pitched 12 perfect innings (the only man ever to do so) against the Milwaukee Braves, only to lose 1–0 in the 13th inning when Joe Adcock doubled and scored on a hit by Henry Aaron.

This time Ditmar lasted until the second inning. After a single, a double, an error and a bad-hop single over McDougald's head at third scored three Pirates runs, Ditmar got the hook and Luis Arroyo came on. Ditmar would win only two more major league games (against 10 losses) before quitting baseball in 1962, while the man over whom he had been selected to pitch the opener (Ford) would be the best pitcher in baseball the following year.

After the Yanks scored a run in the bottom of the second, Clemente restored the Pirates' three-run lead with an RBI single in the third. Maris narrowed the lead to 4–2 with a homer into the third deck in right field, but Face came on with two on and one out in the seventh and snuffed the rally, fanning Maris for the third out. He blanked the Yankees the rest of the way to record his third save; the 5–2 win sent the Series back to Pittsburgh with the Pirates ahead, three games to two.

Ford evened the Series in Game 6, proving that he could in fact pitch well at Forbes Field by throwing another shutout, a neat seven-hitter in which he faced only five batters over the minimum. While Whitey was toying with the Pirates, the Yanks pounded six Pirates pitchers for 17 hits and a 12–0 win. They broke the game open in the third with five runs on a two-run single by Mantle, a sacrifice fly by Skowron and a two-run triple by Richardson, giving him 11 RBIs in the Series, breaking by one the record held jointly by Yogi Berra (1956) and Ted Kluszewski (1959). He added another RBI triple later in the game to stretch the record to 12, which was nearly half of the 26 RBIs he had accumulated in 150 regular-season games. Even Ford had two RBIs. Some Yankees fans wondered why Stengel left Ford in to pitch the entire game, since the score was 8–0 after six innings. Had he exited at that point, he might have been available to pitch to a few batters in the seventh game. As it turned out, they sure could have used him.

The two shutouts in a single Series put Whitey in select company. Only

Ford pitching his second shutout of the 1960 World Series, beating the Pirates 12–0 in Game 6 to force a seventh game that ended on a walk-off home run by Pittsburgh's Bill Mazeroski. (AP/Wide World Photos)

two other pitchers had accomplished this feat since the World Series adopted a best-of-seven format in 1905: Christy Mathewson in 1905 and Lew Burdette (against the Yanks) in 1957. Mathewson had actually thrown *three* shutouts in the 1905 Series, and Yankees fans would always wonder if Whitey could have matched Matty if Stengel had given him the chance.

In the climactic seventh game at Forbes Field, Stengel gave the ball to Bob Turley, the hero of Game 7 two years before. Murtaugh countered with Law, who already had two wins in the Series. The Pirates drew first blood when Turley walked Skinner with two out in the first and Rocky Nelson followed with a home run over the right-field wall. After Hoak robbed Berra with another great play in the top of the second, the Pirates scored two more in the bottom half. Burgess led off the inning with a line-drive single down the right-field line. Stengel came out and gave Turley a quick hook, bringing in rookie Bill Stafford, who had been called up from the minors in mid-August and had pitched well down the stretch, going 3–1 with a 2.25 ERA. After a walk and an infield hit loaded the bases with nobody out, Stafford got Law to hit into a 1–2–3 double play and was nearly out of the inning. But Bill Virdon's clutch two-run single to right gave Law a four-run lead as he attempted to join the select group of pitchers who have won three games in a World Series.

Moose Skowron hit an opposite-field homer off Law in the fifth to get the Yanks on the board. When Richardson led off the sixth with a single and Kubek followed with a walk, Law departed in favor of Elroy Face. After retiring Maris for the first out, Face yielded a run-scoring single to center by Mantle and then Berra slammed a ball into the upper deck in right field to give the Yankees a 5–4 lead. They made it 7–4 in the eighth on an RBI single by Johnny Blanchard and a double by Clete Boyer.

Bobby Shantz (in the twilight of a career that included a 24–7 MVP year with the Philadelphia Athletics) had taken over from Stafford in the third inning and pitched five shutout innings. It should have been six, but Lady Luck smiled on the Pirates again in the bottom of the eighth, in a big way. Cimoli (batting for Face) led off with a single, but then Shantz induced Virdon to hit an easy double-play grounder to Kubek. On the last bounce before it got to Kubek, the ball hit a pebble and took a wicked hop, right into his Adam's apple. Kubek was taken to the hospital and was replaced by Joe DeMaestri. Twice before in the Series when the Yankees were protecting a lead in the late innings, Kubek had moved to left field to replace Berra and DeMaestri had gone in at shortstop. Before the inning had started, Kubek had asked Stengel if he should switch to left field and Casey had said no, because he didn't want to remove Berra. Maybe the bad hop would have handcuffed DeMaestri as well, but the nonmove left Stengel open for second-guessing again. Still, even after this terrible luck, the Yanks should have gotten out of the inning.

Groat singled to left to score Cimoli, making the score 7–5. Coates replaced Shantz and got the next two men out, bringing up Clemente. Roberto topped an easy dribbler to Skowron wide of the bag at first. Moose fielded it cleanly, but when he went to throw the ball to Coates covering, no one was there. Coates moved off the mound to try to field the ball, but when it got by him, he forgot to cover first. Maybe he figured Moose would take it himself, but Clemente was too fast. A run scored to make it 7–6.

Stengel should have yanked Coates right then and there, but he had lost confidence in right-handed closer Ryne Duren. Reserve catcher Hal Smith (a former Yankees farmhand and a right-handed batter) was up next and Casey opted to stay with Coates. Smith was in the game only because Murtaugh had pinch-run for Burgess in the seventh inning. He came through with the biggest hit of his life, a three-run homer over the left-center-field wall. Just like that the score was 9–7, Pirates. Ralph Terry relieved the shell-shocked Coates and got the final out of the inning.

Since Face had been hit for, Murtaugh summoned Bob Friend (0–2 in the Series) to pitch the ninth. Richardson led off with a single, and when Dale Long (batting for DeMaestri) followed with a single to right, the Yanks were very much alive. Murtaugh brought in the left-handed Haddix to pitch to Maris, who made the first out, but this also turned Mantle around, and he had hit much better right-handed during the Series (all three homers). Mickey promptly singled to right center, scoring Richardson and sending McDougald (running for Long) to third.

Mantle then made one of the smartest instinctive plays ever seen. Berra lashed a one-hopper down the first-base line, and Rocky Nelson, who was at first base instead of Dick "Dr. Strangeglove" Stuart, made a great grab of the ball, stepped on first for the second out and whirled to throw to second for the Series-ending out. But Mantle, knowing that he would be a dead duck at second and also realizing that the force was now off, made a split-second decision and dove back to first base, eluding Nelson's tag as McDougald scored the tying run. On a baseball field, Mickey was as smart as anyone.

Stengel left Terry in to pitch the Pittsburgh ninth. He had warmed up on and off since the first inning and was tired. His first pitch to Mazeroski was a ball. His second pitch was a hanging slider, and Maz drove it deep to left. Yogi ran back like he had a chance; then he ran out of room and backed off, hoping for a rebound off the wall. The ball barely cleared the ivy-covered wall and disappeared into the trees beyond.

Maz danced around the bases waving his cap and Pittsburgh celebrated its first World Series win since 1925. It was the first time the World Series had ever ended on a homer.

Mantle cried openly in the clubhouse. He had hit .400 in the Series with three homers and 11 RBIs, and had reached base 18 times in 33 trips to the plate. (The Series MVP went to Richardson, who hit .367 with 12 RBIs, but either Mantle or Ford should have won the award.) In *All My Octobers* (the last book that he collaborated on, in 1994), Mickey said: "The worst disappointment of my baseball career, and one that hurts to this day, was our loss to the Pittsburgh Pirates in the 1960 World Series. The better team lost, the only time I truly felt that way. It wasn't even close.... Just then, except for someone close to me dying, I felt as bad as I had ever felt in my life."[3]

Ford was upset as well. In *Slick,* Whitey said: "I felt I should have started the first game, so that I could pitch three times if it became necessary. Stengel had other ideas.... He said he wanted to save me for the first game at Yankee Stadium, which really ticked me off. It was the only time I ever got mad at Casey.... And the way I was pitching, I know I would have beaten them three times and we would have been world champs again.... I was so annoyed at Stengel, I wouldn't talk to him on the plane ride back to New York."[4]

Five days after the Series ended, the Yankees fired Casey Stengel and hired Ralph Houk as manager. The Yankees tried to dress the firing up as a retirement, but when the reporters asked Casey for the true story, he said: "I was told my services were no longer required. I know this. I'll never make the mistake of being seventy again."[5] A year later he came out of retirement to manage the 1962 Amazing Mets. Stengel left behind an unsurpassed record as manager of the Yankees: 10 pennants in 12 years. He also won seven World Series. It should have been eight.

TEN

Ford Finally Wins Twenty

The summer of 1961 was one of the great seasons in baseball history, particularly for Yankees fans. The Yanks were so good that year that it has generally been considered a toss-up as to whether the 1927 Yankees or the 1961 Yankees were the greatest team of all time (although now the 1998 Yankees can make that claim as well). Roger Maris hit 61 homers to break Babe Ruth's record and Mickey Mantle hit 54 homers. As a team, the Yanks smashed the all-time major league record with 240 homers. And Whitey Ford finally won 20 games (25, in fact) as he turned in one of the greatest pitching seasons in franchise history.

The seed for Whitey's great season was planted in January at Madison Square Garden. Whitey was there to see a college basketball game between St. John's and Kansas and ran into Ralph Houk, who had been named to replace Casey Stengel as the Yankees' manager. Houk asked him if he wanted to pitch every fourth day and Whitey eagerly agreed to try it. The idea had come from new pitching coach Johnny Sain, who had pitched on three days' rest during his heyday with the Boston Braves ("Spahn and Sain, then pray for rain") and believed in it. Whitey had started more than 30 games in a season only once under Stengel, but under Houk would start 39 games in 1961, the most in the AL. (Ironically, that was the same number of starts that Sain had made in 1948 when he had won 24 games to lead the Braves to the NL pennant.)

Houk also had an important preseason talk with Mantle. During spring training, Ralph took Mickey aside and talked to him about assuming a leadership role on the team. Mickey had always led by example but had never tried to exert any influence on the others in the locker room. In fact, he had once said: "There are two kinds of people. There are leaders and there are followers. And I'm a follower." But Mickey was flattered by Houk's request and agreed to give it a shot. Whereas Stengel had constantly criticized Mantle for his shortcomings, Houk treated Mickey with tremendous respect and praised him incessantly. Mantle responded well to this nurturing and became exactly the leader Houk wanted him to be. He had always inspired his teammates by playing all-out despite his physical pain, but now he was also urging his teammates on in the dugout, and they responded because they didn't want to let him down.

Houk made a decision in spring training that would have a major bearing on the home run race: he announced that Maris would bat third in the order, and Mantle fourth. This gave Roger a huge advantage because pitchers were never able to pitch around him, and thus he got better pitches to hit. If a pitcher fell behind on Roger 3-and-0 or 3-and-1, Roger knew he was likely to see a strike because the pitcher didn't want to walk him with Mantle up next. On the other hand, when Mickey was in the same situation, the pitcher was much less likely to "give in" and throw him a good pitch, because there were no more "M" boys coming up next to deal with. As a result, Mantle led the league in walks that year with 126 and ended up with 76 fewer official at-bats than Maris.

The season started inauspiciously with the Yanks losing the season opener 6–0 to the newly transplanted Minnesota Twins (the old Washington Senators) at Yankee Stadium. Whitey matched Twins pitcher Pedro Ramos for six innings but was lifted after yielding three runs in the seventh. It was his first loss in a home opener after five wins. But Whitey rebounded with a three-hit shutout of the Kansas City Athletics, striking out eight as the Yanks won 3–0, with Mantle knocking in all three runs with a homer and two singles. Houk was pitching Ford every fourth day regardless of whose turn it was, so Whitey pitched again in the Yankees' sixth game of the season and beat the Orioles 4–2, backed by Mantle's fourth homer of the young season. The following day, the *New York Times* pointed out that Mickey was "eight games ahead of the pace set by Babe Ruth when he hit sixty homers in 1927 for the major league record."[1]

Ford's next outing was a painful one, as he took a line drive off his kneecap in the second inning of a wild game in Detroit played in 40-degree weather. The ball was hit so hard it caromed into foul territory, and the batter and two other base runners scored when catcher Elston Howard retrieved the ball and then threw it into right field. Whitey stayed in the game but was hit hard, and four unearned runs and ineffective relief pitching helped give the Tigers an 11–8 lead. Only the heroics of Mantle, who tied the game in the eighth inning with a two-run homer batting left-handed and then won the game in the 10th inning with a two-run homer batting right-handed, got Ford off the hook and prevented the first-place Tigers from extending their lead over the Yanks to four games. Mickey already had seven homers, four of them when Ford was pitching. He always seemed to hit well for Whitey.

Whitey then beat the new Washington Senators on the last day of April. He trailed 2–1 when he was removed for a pinch hitter in the seventh inning, but the Yanks rallied that inning and the bullpen hung on for a 4–3 win. This was the first of his wins that was saved by left-handed reliever Luis Arroyo, who had joined the Yanks in the latter part of the 1960 season. After an undistinguished four-year stint in the National League pitching for three different teams, Arroyo had been demoted to the minor leagues. The Yankees bought him from the Havana Sugar Kings, a Cincinnati farm team in the International League temporarily playing in Jersey City, just across the Hudson River from Yankee Stadium. He had developed a good screwball while in Jersey City and had won five games and saved seven others for the Yanks down the stretch in 1960. He would be a key man for the Yanks in 1961 and it became customary for him to finish up many of Whitey's games, whether Whitey needed help or not. Now that Ford was pitching every fourth day, Houk wanted to minimize the wear and tear on his arm whenever possible.

On May 4, Ford beat the Minnesota Twins 5–2 to complete a three-game sweep and keep the Yankees even with the red-hot Tigers. Mantle again provided the support with his ninth homer and an RBI single. His homer landed deep in the right-field bleachers despite a gale-force wind blowing in from right field. But muscle pulls in his calf, groin and thigh followed, and Mickey would hit only one home run in the Yankees' next 20 games.

While Mantle was injured and slumping, Maris suddenly got hot and carried the team for a while, hitting six homers in 10 games to close to within one of Mantle, 10 to nine. Ford continued to pitch well but the bullpen blew two straight wins for him. After Arroyo inherited a 4–2 lead from Whitey against Kansas City and gave up a game-tying single to old friend Hank Bauer in a game the Yanks eventually lost, Whitey turned a 4–1 lead and one base runner over to Tex Clevenger in the ninth inning of a game against the league-leading Tigers and watched that lead get frittered away as well, although the Yanks eventually won the game in the 11th inning on a pinch single by Yogi Berra. Houk didn't take any chances in Whitey's next start, allowing him to pitch all nine innings of a 4–2 win over Baltimore in front of 47,890 at Yankee Stadium. Although a homer by Maris was the big blow for New York, Ford helped his own cause with an RBI single. He then improved his record to 6–1 by beating Boston 6–4 at the Stadium, although he needed Arroyo to save this one after a three-run homer by Jackie Jensen in the seventh inning broke up Whitey's shutout.

Trailing the Tigers by four and one half games and the Indians by a game, the Yanks traveled to Boston for a four-game series with the Red Sox. Whitey pitched the first game of the series on May 29 in a cold drizzle, opposed by journeyman Ike Delock, who would finish the season with a 6–9 record. It should have been a walkover for the Yanks, but Delock pitched his best game of the season and took a 1–0 lead into the seventh. Then Mantle broke out of his slump and got his buddy even again with a solo shot into the right-field bullpen, but the Sox scratched out another run against Whitey in the bottom half of the inning on two walks and a single by Vic Wertz, and the Yanks trailed 2–1 when Mantle came up with two out and a man on in the ninth. He drove a ball that looked like a carbon copy of his seventh-inning homer but was caught by Jackie Jenson at the bullpen wall. The loss dropped New York five games behind Detroit in the AL standings.

The Yanks rebounded the following day with seven homers (two each by Mantle, Maris and Skowron and one by Berra) to bury the Red Sox 12–3. Homers by Mantle and Maris keyed another win the following day, but suddenly ineffective Bob Turley got hammered in the series finale.

After the Boston series, Houk dropped Turley and Art Ditmar (a 15-game-winner the previous year) from the starting rotation, replacing them with young right-handers Bill Stafford and Rollie Sheldon. The Yanks proceeded to go on a tear, winning 14 of their next 17 games to pull into a virtual tie for the AL lead with Detroit and Cleveland. Mantle hit four homers during that span but Maris hit 10 to take over the lead in the home run race, 22 to 18. Ford chipped in with four consecutive victories during the streak to raise his record to 10–2. After beating Chicago 6–2 on a complete-game seven-hitter, four days later he took a one-hit shutout into the eighth inning against Minnesota at the Stadium. However, he yielded a two-run single to old nemesis Jim Lemon in the eighth and Arroyo came on to get the last five outs to nail down a 7–2 win. Whitey followed that up with a complete-game 5–3 win over Kansas City (backed by a homer and triple by Mantle) and an 11–5 win over the Indians in Cleveland, aided by two innings of hitless relief from Arroyo and a homer by Maris.

After finally catching the Tigers and Indians, the Yanks traveled to Detroit for an important three-game series and promptly lost the first two games to drop back into third place. They counted on Ford to salvage the final game of the series and Whitey responded with a masterful performance, allowing just three hits in eight shutout innings and striking out 12. The Yanks jumped all over Yankee-killer Frank Lary (previously 25–8 against them in his career), pounding out 15 hits for a 9–0 win. Included in the carnage were two home runs by Johnny Blanchard and one each by Moose Skowron and Roger Maris (No. 24). Whitey certainly could have finished the game himself but he was developing a blister on the index finger of his pitching hand, so Houk called on Arroyo to finish the shutout.

The Yanks moved on to Kansas City where they split the first two games of a four-game series. Then Mantle almost single-handedly beat the Athletics with two of the longest home runs ever hit in Municipal Stadium, accounting for all of the Yankees' runs in a 5–3 win and giving him 22 for the season. (The first homer hit the very top of a large scoreboard well in back of the right-center-field wall, and the second left the ballpark entirely, clearing a 40-foot outer wall in back of the right-field fence and traveling an estimated 500 feet.)[2] The following day, Ford won the series finale 8–3 for his sixth straight win in June. He had a shutout into the eighth inning before weakening and yielding once again to Arroyo. Maris drove in half of the runs with four hits, including his 27th home run. The homer was Roger's 15th in June and completed what was then the greatest home run binge in history: 24 home runs in 38 games, starting on May 17 and ending on June 22. (Ruth hit his last 24 homers in a 41-game stretch to reach 60 in 1927.)

Mantle homered again in Whitey's next start on June 26 but it was a three-run homer by Skowron in the ninth inning that beat the Los Angeles Angels 8–6 to give Whitey his 13th win of the season. Ford closed out June for the Yankees with a complete-game 5–1 win over Washington at Yankee Stadium, yielding just five hits and an unearned run as he raised his record to 14–2. It was his eighth win in eight starts in June, making him the first major league pitcher to win eight games in a month since Schoolboy Rowe of Detroit in 1934 and the first American League left-hander ever to do it. (Rube Marquard of the 1912 Giants was the only other lefty ever to do it.[3]) The M & M boys knocked in all of the Yankees' runs, with the big blow an inside-the-park home run by Mantle that hit the center-field wall on the fly, 461 feet from home plate. The Yanks were now a season-high 18 games over .500, but they still trailed the Tigers by two games in the standings. Mantle trailed Maris in the home run race, 27 to 25. (Ruth had 26 after the same number of games in 1927.)

The Yanks started July off the same way they had finished June, getting two home runs from Mantle and one from Maris to beat Washington at the Stadium, 7–6. Mantle's first homer landed 10 rows deep in the left-center-field bleachers above the 457-foot sign for his 1,000th career RBI. The second one tied him with Maris at 27, but the tie lasted about half an hour as Maris wrapped No. 28 around the right-field foul pole in the bottom of the ninth to win the game.

The following day, the Senators walked Mickey his first four times up but finally pitched to him in the eighth inning. Mickey hit his fifth homer in four games (well into the third tier in right field at Yankee Stadium), but Maris hit two himself (No. 29 and No. 30) to go two up on Mantle (and four homers up on the Babe) after 75 games. Roger homered again on July 4 and July 5, giving him five homers in the first five days of July.

Ford, too, picked up where he had left off at the end of June as he beat Detroit 6–2 in the first game of a July 4 double-header at Yankee Stadium, pitching a complete-game five-hitter and fanning 11 in front of the largest

Stadium crowd (74,246) since 1947. The win put the Yanks a few percent-age points ahead of the Tigers, but Detroit regained first place by winning the nightcap. Ford then won his 10th straight start on July 8, beating Boston 8–5 with help from Arroyo to reach the halfway point of the season with a record of 16–2. Mantle hit his 29th homer of the season (his 10th with Ford pitching), but by now Maris had 32. Roger hit No. 33 the following day as the Yanks split a double-header with the Red Sox and broke for the All-Star Game half a game behind the first-place Tigers.

The All-Star Game was played at Candlestick Park on July 11. Mantle and Ford went out to San Francisco a day early so that they could get in a round of golf. Giants' owner Horace Stoneham arranged for them to play at his club, where they ran up a $400 tab. When they tried to pay Stone-ham that evening, Horace suggested a wager of double or nothing on whether Mays would get a hit the next day off Ford, who was scheduled to start the game for the American League. Mays had owned Ford in previous All-Star Games, going 6 for 6 with two homers and a triple. Much to Man-tle's chagrin, Ford accepted the bet.

The following day, Mays came to the plate in the first inning with two out and nobody on base. Whitey threw him two curveballs and Willie hit two tremendous drives down the left-field line, both foul. With two strikes, Whitey decided to load up a spitter. He had learned the pitch from Joe Page when he first came up but never used it because he couldn't control it. This one went straight at Willie until suddenly dropping three feet and swerv-ing over the plate for strike three. Mantle came running in from center field jumping up and down and clapping like the Yankees had just won the World Series. Mays asked Ford: "What the hell is he so happy about?" The only people in the park who knew were Mantle, Ford and Stoneham.[4]

When the season resumed after the All-Star break, Mantle went on a rampage, hitting eight home runs in the next nine games to temporarily wrest the homer lead from Maris, 37–36. One of Mickey's homers helped Ford win his 11th consecutive start, a 5–0 shutout of Baltimore in the first game of a double-header on July 17. Whitey yielded six hits and struck out nine; Arroyo got the day off. Both of the M & M boys homered in the night-cap, but the homers were washed away when the game was rained out with the Yankees leading 4–1 in the fifth inning, half an inning short of being an official game.

The washed-out homers were not the only bad news on July 17. That was the day that Commissioner Ford Frick (an old pal of Ruth's) made his ridiculous ruling that Ruth's record could not be "officially broken" unless it was done within 154 games, the length of the schedule back in 1927. Any record set in the extra eight games would be listed separately and tainted by an asterisk. Although this ruling never had much credibility among baseball fans and was reversed 30 years later by Commissioner Fay Vincent, back then it caused a big stir and much debate.

Ford's winning streak nearly came to an end on July 21 at Fenway Park, a graveyard for left-handers. Mantle and Maris hit back-to-back homers in the first inning and Berra connected with a man on in the third, but Whitey was uncharacteristically wild and was knocked out in the fifth inning when the Red Sox reached him for three hits and four walks. It took a pinch-hit grand-slam homer by Johnny Blanchard with two out in the ninth inning to win the game 11–8 and get Ford off the hook.

Whitey rebounded in his next game, pitching seven shutout innings on a hot and humid night in the Bronx before letting Arroyo finish the 5–1 win over the White Sox in the first game of a twilight double-header. Mickey hit No. 38 in the opener but Maris hit two in each game to regain the home run lead, 40–38. The Yankees' 12–0 win in the nightcap moved them half a game ahead of Detroit in the AL standings. Four days later, Whitey pitched the Yanks into a two-game lead over the Tigers with a complete-game 5–4 win over the Orioles, thanks to an eighth-inning home run by Yogi Berra. The win was Ford's 13th in a row and raised his record to 19–2. For the second time in his career, he was one victory shy of the coveted 20 mark. But unlike in 1956 when he got only one crack at a 20th win, it was only July 29 and he still had 14 scheduled starts. At this point, 20 wins was a foregone conclusion and the only question was whether Whitey could reach 30 wins.

Whitey came up short in his first attempt at No. 20 against Kansas City on August 2 at the Stadium. He gave himself a 5–3 lead in the bottom of the eighth with a two-out, two-run single but couldn't hold the lead in the ninth. He gave up a two-run homer to pinch hitter Haywood Sullivan and Houk brought in Arroyo, two batters too late. Little Looey picked up the win when the Yanks won the game in the bottom of the ninth on a single by Maris, a double by Mantle and a ground ball by Bob Cerv.

Ford was denied victory No. 20 yet again in the first game of an August 6 double-header against Minnesota at Yankee Stadium despite pitching 10 innings. Mantle hit two homers off Pedro Ramos (No. 41 and No. 42) in an effort to get Whitey his milestone win, but homers by Bob Allison and Zoilo Versalles offset Mickey's blasts and the score was tied at 5 after nine innings. Ford yielded another homer in the top of the 10th (a solo shot by Bill Tuttle), but Johnny Blanchard matched that homer in the bottom of the 10th to get Whitey of the hook and keep his winning streak intact. The Yanks eventually won the game in the 15th inning but Whitey was long gone by then. Mantle hit No. 43 in the nightcap to help the Yanks to a 3–2 win that moved them two and one half games ahead of the Tigers. The three homers by Mantle put him two ahead of Maris and also moved him past Joe DiMaggio on the all-time home run list, 363–361. Considering that he had been compared against DiMaggio (frequently unfavorably) since the day he took over Joe's spot in center field at the Stadium, this milestone must have been very satisfying for Mickey.

By this time, the dual challenge to Ruth's record by the M & M boys was dominating the sports pages across the country. In the New York papers, the M & M score usually preceded the game score in the sports headlines, despite the closeness of the AL race. When neither homered, it was news, as in "Maris & Mantle Fail to Connect; Yanks Win." Before and after every game, there were dozens of reporters crowding around Mantle and Maris, asking the same dumb questions over and over. Mickey was used to it by now and handled it fairly well, but Maris, a small-town boy from North Dakota, was ill-prepared for the circus that followed him around for much of that season. Mantle had become the favorite of the writers as well as the fans, and most people were rooting for Mickey to break the record. He was starting his second decade as the Yankees' main man in 1961, whereas Maris was in only his second season with New York. Moreover, many people felt that Mantle was the one who *deserved* to break the record. After all, he had made a run at it in 1956, and thereafter one always had the feeling that it was just a matter of time before he would stay healthy for a full season and break Ruth's record. Maris, on the other hand, had never hit more than 28 homers in a season until the previous year, when he had hit 39 to finish one behind Mantle in the home run race.

A curious phenomenon that had begun in 1960 accelerated in 1961. Before Maris arrived in New York to challenge Mantle for home run supremacy, Mickey had been the whipping boy of the Yankees fans and press, especially during his subpar 1959 season when the Yanks slipped to third place. No matter how well he played, it was never enough for the fans. Mantle's 1956 Triple Crown season had raised expectations that he would always perform at that level; anything less was considered a failure. Then Maris arrived and Yankees fans had to decide which of the two sluggers to root for in the '60 and '61 home run races. Most of them picked Mantle. They began to cheer his every move, and for the rest of his career he was the most popular player in baseball, both at home and on the road. Maris was viewed as an interloper. As he told *Sports Illustrated* in a 1977 article: "What's funny is that when I first came to the Yankees everybody was giving Mantle a hard time. Why, I don't know. But when I got there, all that stuff just sort of slid off him and came onto me.... That's when Mickey got to be the golden boy."[5]

In *All My Octobers*, Mantle explained: "In a curious way, Maris made me more popular in New York than I had ever been. They wouldn't forgive Roger for not being Babe Ruth. They finally forgave me for not being Joe DiMaggio."[6]

Ford in action while beating Kansas City for his 22nd win of the 1961 season. (National Baseball Hall of Fame Library, Cooperstown, N.Y.)

The Los Angeles Angels followed Minnesota into Yankee Stadium and Ford finally got his 20th win on August 10. He went seven innings as the Yanks won 3–1 on homers by Richardson, Berra and Skowron. Fittingly, Arroyo saved the win for Whitey with two innings of scoreless relief; he had now finished 10 of Ford's 20 wins. The victory was Whitey's 14th in a row, tying the Yankees' record set by Jack Chesbro in 1904, the year he set the all-time season record for wins with 41. Had Mantle's ninth-inning drive in Boston back on May 29 been a few feet longer, Ford would have had 21 straight wins, which would have broken the major league record of 19 held by Rube Marquard of the 1912 New York Giants. Whitey was now 20–2; only Marquard had ever gotten to 20 wins with just two losses. (Ron Guidry of the Yankees duplicated the feat in 1978 and Roger Clemens became the first pitcher ever to open a season 20–1 in 2001 with the Yankees.)

The White Sox ended Ford's streak in his next start on August 15 when Juan Pizarro out pitched Whitey 2–1. Maris homered for the Yankees' only run; it was the fifth straight game in which he had homered and he moved ahead of Mantle to stay, 46–45. He hit two more off Billy Pierce in a 5–4 Yankee win the following day and then Ford beat the Indians 3–2 three days later in Cleveland to give the Yanks a three-game lead in the AL standings. He had to work hard for this win, since the Yanks didn't win the game until the 10th inning. Whitey had driven in a run with a fourth-inning single and held a 2–1 lead in the last of the eighth inning, but he wild-pitched in the tying run after two infield hits put him in a jam. After Elston Howard singled in the go-ahead run for the Yanks in the top of the 10th, Whitey recorded the first two outs in the bottom of the 10th before yielding a double to Ken Aspromonte and handing the ball over to Arroyo, who got the final out on a ground-out by Jimmy Piersall.

The Yanks moved on to Los Angeles where Maris hit his 50th home run on August 22, the earliest this had ever been done by nearly two weeks. (Ruth hit his 50th on September 4 in 1927 and Jimmie Foxx equaled that feat in 1932, the year he hit 58.) Ford lasted only four innings the following day but escaped with a no-decision when the Yanks won in extra innings. Whitey made another early exit in his next start against Kansas City (pitching just five innings and giving up three runs), but Elston Howard and Yogi Berra homered and Rollie Sheldon and Luis Arroyo held off the Athletics to give Whitey his 22nd win.

The Yanks finished up their long road trip with three games in Minnesota, winning only one of the games despite two home runs by Mantle, who joked: "I caught my man. Now Roger has to catch his."[7] Lou Gehrig hit 47 homers the year Ruth hit 60 to establish a record of 107 for teammates. Mantle now had 48, beating Gehrig. Maris was temporarily stalled at 51.

On September 1, the Detroit Tigers came to Yankee Stadium for a crucial three-game series, trailing the Yanks by only a game and a half. The home run race took a back seat for a few days while the Yanks attempted to put the Tigers away. A crowd of 65,566 turned out on Friday night to watch Ford oppose Detroit left-hander Don Mossi. Whitey pitched shutout ball for four and two-third innings before straining a muscle in his right hip and removing himself from the game, not wanting to jeopardize the Yankees' chances by staying in to try to add to his victory total. Mossi had matched him zero for zero. Bud Daley replaced Ford, and the scoreless duel continued into the ninth inning, with the Tigers hoping to close to within half a game. Luis Arroyo retired the Tigers in the top of the ninth and the Yanks had Maris and Mantle due up in the bottom half. Mossi retired the M & M boys, but then Howard and Berra both singled and Moose Skowron delivered a big two-out base hit to win the game and increase the Yankee lead to two and one half games. Arroyo got the win, his 10th in a row and fifth in relief of Ford.

Another huge crowd turned out on Saturday to watch the Yanks face their old nemesis, "Yankee-killer" Frank Lary. In addition to the fact that Lary was always tough on the Yankees, he was having the best year of his

Roger Maris and Mickey Mantle during the 1961 season when they set a season record for homers by two teammates (115), a record that still stands. (Miles Coverdale collection)

career (23–9); he finished second in the AL in wins behind Ford. Ralph Terry pitched for the Yanks.

In the bottom of the fourth with Maris on third and the Yanks trailing 2–1, Mantle showed what his priorities were by passing up a chance to gain ground on Maris and dragging a bunt single to score Maris with the tying run. With two out in the Yankee sixth, Maris hit his 52nd to give the Yanks a 3–2 lead and he added his 53rd in the eighth inning as the Yanks scored four runs to ice the game, 7–2, and increase their lead to three and one half games. Mantle pulled a muscle in his left forearm trying to check his swing in the sixth inning and it appeared unlikely that he would be able to play on Sunday.

After extensive heat treatments, Mantle asked Houk to play him in the third game on Sunday. Though he couldn't swing the bat properly, he swung it well enough, taking Jim Bunning deep in the first inning with Maris on base to give the Yanks a 2–0 lead. However, Houk lifted Yankee pitcher Bill Stafford for a pinch-hitter after seven innings and Arroyo was unable to hold the lead. The Yanks trailed 5–4 when they came to bat in the bottom of the ninth.

Facing right-hander Gerry Staley, Mantle tied the score with a 450-foot shot into the right-center-field bleachers. Elston Howard won the game with a home run a few minutes later, and the Tigers left town with their tails between their legs. In addition to tying the game, Mantle's ninth-inning homer was his 50th of the season, making him only the fourth man in baseball history to hit 50 twice. (Ruth, Foxx and Kiner were the others, and Mays, McGwire, Griffey, Sosa and Alex Rodriguez have subsequently accomplished it.) It was also the first time that teammates had hit 50 homers apiece in the same season. Mickey was now back in the race, trailing by 53–50 (with Ruth at 49).

Unfortunately, the batting on Sunday had aggravated Mantle's forearm injury enough that he had to sit out both ends of a Labor Day doubleheader the following day. When the Yanks beat Washington twice and Detroit lost again, suddenly the Tigers were six games behind and fading fast. When Ford shut out Washington 8–0 on five hits in the series finale two days later, the lead was eight games and the race was essentially over, just five days after the Tigers had come into the Stadium with the race still very much in doubt. The Yanks had five homers in that game (including two by Blanchard and No. 54 by Maris) to set a new American League record for homers in a season with 210.

Now all attention was refocused on the homer race. The Indians were next to try their luck at the Stadium and the red-hot Yanks swept five straight. The M & M boys hit two apiece in the series to make the score 56–53 for Maris, and they had now broken Ruth and Gehrig's record for homers by teammates.

During the Cleveland series, the Yankees held a "Whitey Ford Day" in appreciation of his spectacular season. They felt that he had been overshadowed by the home run race and deserved some recognition. Years later, Ford said: "It was the damndest thing. I'd been with the Yankees for ten years and for ten years I'd been hoping to win 20 games. Now I win 25, and all anybody asked me about was home runs."[8] Whitey was showered with all kinds of gifts, including a car, an electric golf cart, golf clubs, several nice vacations and numerous appliances, but the gift that was the highlight of the ceremony was the six-foot package of Life Savers that was wheeled in from the bullpen. When it got to the mound, out popped Luis Arroyo.

While this stunt was purely a joke and was taken in good humor by Whitey, there were some people that year who tried to belittle Ford's victory total by pointing out that Arroyo finished many of his wins. Arroyo was definitely a lifesaver for the Yanks that year with a record of 15–5 (including 12 wins in a row), 29 saves and a 2.19 ERA in a league-leading 65 appearances. But Whitey had always finished a high percentage of his games; in fact, he had led the AL in complete games in 1955 with 18 and completed 18 more the following year. It simply made no sense to let him finish every game when the Yanks were often way ahead. As it was, he still led the AL in innings pitched that year with 283 and averaged nearly seven and one-third innings per start. "I was more interested in winning games than finishing them," Ford has said, looking back. "Looey was having such a great year, I was glad to turn my game over to him in the eighth or ninth inning and conserve my energy for my next start.... I wasn't looking to bail out of there, but if Houk came to the mound and asked me how I felt, I'd try to be honest with him. If I was tired, I'd tell him I was tired because I knew he had Looey ready to come in."⁹ Whitey completed 11 games that year, and although Arroyo finished 13 of his wins, many of them were more of the mop-up variety than true saves. (The rules concerning saves were much more lenient then.) If he'd had to, Whitey could have completed many of those games himself.

The Yanks then traveled to Chicago, where they won their 13th straight game before finally losing. The win was their 100th of the season against only 45 losses, which meant they had played .740 baseball (77–27) since June 5. Their lead over the Tigers was now a bloated 11 1/2 games.

Whitey upped his record to 24–3 with a complete-game 11–1 win over the reeling Tigers on September 15. The Yankees broke the major league record for homers in a season (previously held by the 1947 Giants and the 1956 Reds) in this game, with Berra hitting a two-run shot to tie the record and Skowron breaking the record with a three-run blast.

The following night Maris hit his 57th off Frank Lary, bouncing the ball off the facing of the right-field roof at Tiger Stadium and back onto the field, where Al Kaline of the Tigers picked it up and tossed it into the Yankees' dugout so Roger could keep it. The next day, after narrowly missing a homer on an RBI triple off the top of the right-field fence, he hit his 58th into the upper deck in right-center field off Detroit's Terry Fox to win the game in the 12th inning. He was now tied with Jimmie Foxx and Hank Greenberg for the No. 2 spot on the all-time homer list (although Ruth also hit 59 in 1921), but he now had just three more games before Frick's deadline for breaking the record. They would be played at Memorial Stadium in Baltimore, a tough park in which to hit home runs.

At this point, Mantle's season essentially came to an end. He came down with a terrible cold that persisted despite antibiotics, and he would be unable to play in the Baltimore series except for one pinch-hitting appearance.

Maris went 0-for-8 in a twilight double-header on September 19, leaving him with just one game left to "officially" tie or break the record. Neither was it a good night for Ford, who saw a potential American League record go by the boards despite pitching beautifully. He hooked up with Baltimore's ace southpaw, Steve Barber, in the opener and yielded just one

Ford going for his 25th win of the 1961 season against Baltimore on September 19. Instead he picked up his fourth loss of the season, 1–0, preventing him from breaking Lefty Grove's record for the highest winning percentage in a season. (AP/Wide World Photos)

run, which was helped along by a Yankees error. Unfortunately Barber was even better, allowing just four hits in recording his league-leading eighth shutout of the season, 1–0. The all-time AL record for winning percentage in a season was Lefty Grove's mark of .886 in 1931 when he was 31–4. A 25–3 record for Whitey would have broken that record, but considering that the Yanks had taken him off the hook a few times during the season and had scored an average of 5.67 runs per game when he was pitching, he couldn't complain about the Yanks getting shut out for the second time when he was pitching. Besides, he was the last person who would have complained, no matter how many times they were shut out with him pitching.

On the night of September 20 in Baltimore (Ruth's birthplace), Maris made one of the most courageous efforts anyone who witnessed it is ever likely to see, under probably the most intense pressure and scrutiny that any athlete has ever endured. His first time up, he lined hard to right but didn't get under it enough and it was caught. In the third inning, he hit No. 59 off Milt Pappas, a line drive over the right-field fence at the 380-foot mark. After hitting a deep foul to right and then striking out in the fifth, Maris hit what looked like No. 60 off Baltimore reliever Dick Hall in the seventh, but the ball curved foul by 10 feet. He then hit a long fly, but he didn't pull it enough and it was caught against the wall in deep right center. His final at-bat was against Hoyt Wilhelm, whose knuckleball was very difficult to hit for a home run. He topped a little check-swing grounder down the first-base line, and phase one of the chase (the Frick phase) was over. Had Roger not lost a home run because of the rainout back in July, he would have tied Ruth in the same number of games that the Yankees played in 1927. (Ruth lost no homers to rainouts that year.) The pennant chase also ended that night as the Yanks clinched their 26th AL flag.

Determined to play despite still being sick, Mantle hit his 54th and last home run of the season on September 23, a three-run shot into the right-field bullpen at Fenway Park to help Ford win his 25th game of the year against the Red Sox, 8–3. Only Ruth, Maris, Foxx, Greenberg and Hack Wilson (56) had ever hit more in a season. Whitey again had trouble at Fenway Park, lasting only five innings, but Jim Coates pitched three scoreless innings and Arroyo came on to pitch a perfect ninth inning. It was Little Looey's 61st appearance of the season, breaking the Yankee record set by Joe Page in 1949.

When the Yanks returned home from Boston, Mantle went to see a New York doctor in a desperate attempt to get healthy and stay in the race. The doctor gave him a shot in the hip, but it just made things worse. "I don't think he injected me where he should have," said Mantle. "I think the needle hit me in the hipbone.... I don't know what he did, but it got infected. I woke up in the morning with a 104-degree temperature, and I couldn't move my leg."[10] Mickey was admitted to Lenox Hill Hospital, where a huge abscess resulting from the injection was surgically drained, leaving a hole in Mantle's hip the size of a golf ball. He watched the final games of the regular season from a hospital bed.

After going homerless in the last game in Baltimore and in two games in Boston, Roger needed two homers in the final five-game home stand at the Stadium to break Ruth's record in the eyes of everyone but Ford Frick. He got No. 60 on the night of September 26 against Baltimore's Jack Fisher, a tremendous drive that hit the front of the third deck in right field and bounced back onto the field. It was the second famous homer given up by Fisher in a year: on the exact same day in 1960, he had given up the dramatic home run that Ted Williams hit in his final time at bat.

After sitting out the second Baltimore game to rest and escape the pressure for a day, Maris returned for the final weekend series with the Red Sox. Ford made his final start of the regular season on Friday night, a tune-up for the first game of the World Series the following Wednesday. He was opposed by Red Sox ace Bill Monbouquette, who didn't want to go down in history as the man who surrendered the record-breaking homer and gave

Roger very few decent pitches to swing at all night. Ford pitched beautifully, striking out nine while shutting Boston out on four hits through six
innings. At that point, the Yanks led 1–0 on a Blanchard home run and
Houk pulled Whitey to rest him for the Series opener. On came Arroyo to
try to preserve win No. 26, a total not reached in the American League since
Bob Feller and Hal Newhouser did it in 1946. But this time Looey was not
equal to the task and blew the save, yielding a run in the seventh inning.
The Yanks won the game in the bottom of the ninth when Maris walked
for the second time and eventually scored on a single by Blanchard, but
Rollie Sheldon got the win.

Rookie of the Year Don Schwall was the Boston pitcher on Saturday and
he pitched Maris the same way Monbouquette had, forcing him to swing at
bad pitches if he wanted to swing at all. Roger went one for three, a single.

A crowd of 23,154 packed the Stadium for the final game on Sunday,
October 1. Most of them jammed the right-field stands hoping to catch the
61st home run ball, which had a $5,000 bounty on it from a California
restaurant owner. (It was a safe bet that it wouldn't be hit to left field, since
Maris hit only one homer into the left-field stands at Yankee Stadium in
the seven years that he played there.) Ford watched the game from the
bullpen because he knew Roger frequently hit the ball there and he wanted
to collect the $5,000. Rookie left-hander Al Downing was also out in the
Yankees bullpen hoping to catch the historic ball; 13 years later, he had an
even better view when Ruth lost his other cherished record to Henry Aaron's
historic 715th homer — he threw it.

Maris faced 24-year-old right-hander Tracy Stallard in the first inning
and flied harmlessly to left. In the fourth inning, Stallard's first two pitches
to Maris were balls and the crowd booed. Stallard then threw a fastball over
the plate, and Roger took that beautiful Yankee Stadium swing of his and
drove the ball into the lower right-field stands to break the record. Unfortunately for Ford's bank account, the ball landed just to the right of the
bullpen. Nineteen-year-old Sal Durante from Brooklyn jumped up on his
seat and made a nice barehanded catch of the $5,000 ball. Maris watched
the ball just for a second and then circled the bases in his usual head-down
home run trot. His teammates kept pushing him out of the dugout to
acknowledge the crowd, which was going nuts. Fittingly, Maris's homer was
the only run in a 1–0 Yankee victory. "Whether I beat Ruth's record or not
is for others to say," said Maris after the game. "But it gives me a wonder-
ful feeling to know that I'm the only man in history to hit 61 home runs.
Nobody can take that away from me."[11]

Roger won the American League RBI crown with 142 to go along with
his homer crown and tied Mantle for the AL lead in runs scored with 132.
For the second straight year, Maris narrowly edged Mantle in the MVP bal-

loting, 202–198. Ford finished fifth and Arroyo sixth.

Whitey's final record of 25–4 gave him a winning percentage of .862, which matched Wild Bill Donovan of the 1907 Detroit Tigers for the fourth-best mark in modern baseball history among pitchers with at least 20 wins, behind Grove, Preacher Roe (1951) and Smokey Joe Wood (1912). Furthermore, since the Yanks won nine of the 10 games he started in which he didn't get a decision, they were 34–5 in Whitey's 39 starts for a winning percentage of .872. (The Yankees played .610 baseball in

Ford showing off his 1961 Cy Young Award after finishing the season 25–4. There was only one award for both leagues at the time. (AP/Wide World Photos)

games started by all of their other pitchers.) He was the ultimate stopper: the Yanks were 17–1 in games he started after a Yankees loss. New York won all six of Whitey's starts against second-place Detroit, as compared to a 4–8 record behind their other pitchers. He led the league in innings pitched with 283, and his 209 strikeouts were second in the American League and established a new Yankee record for left-handers. Whitey also established a major league record for most consecutive innings without having a base stolen off him (243);[12] base runners stayed close because Whitey had one of the best pickoff moves in history. His ERA of 3.21 was only 10th-best in the AL and was the highest of his career up to that point, but it was still .81 better than the league ERA of 4.02.

While in general Whitey got excellent run support and excellent support from the bullpen, three of his losses were by scores of 1–0, 2–1 and 2–1 and the bullpen blew three saves in games he left with a lead, so with a little bit more luck he conceivably could have won 30 games. He was rewarded for his great season with the only Cy Young Award of his career, beating out Warren Spahn and Frank Lary at a time when there was just one award for both leagues.

Perhaps the most amazing statistic of Ford's 1961 season was his salary: $35,000, or $1,400 per win. In 2003, Pedro Martinez of the Red Sox was paid $15.5 million, which worked out to $534,483 for each of his 29 starts

Ford beating the Cincinnati Reds in the opening game of the 1961 World Series 2–0. He spun a two-hitter for his third consecutive shutout in Series play and his eighth career Series win, breaking the record he had shared with former Yankees Red Ruffing and Allie Reynolds. (AP/Wide World Photos)

and $1,107,143 for each of his 14 wins. Averaging about 100 pitches per game, Martinez earned approximately $5,345 *per pitch* in 2003. Every seven pitches, Martinez was paid more than Whitey had been paid for his entire 1961 Cy Young Award season.

The Yankees' final 1961 win total of 109 (aided by the eight extra games) had been exceeded only three times in major league history: by the 1906 Chicago Cubs (116), the 1927 Yanks (110) and the 1954 Cleveland Indians (111). Their 240 homers remained the major league record until the 1996 Baltimore Orioles broke the record after moving into their new homer haven. Besides the 115 homers that Maris and Mantle hit, four other Yanks hit more than 20 homers: Moose Skowron (28), Yogi Berra (22), Elston Howard (21) and Johnny Blanchard (21). On the mound, Ralph Terry finished second behind Ford in the AL in winning percentage with a 16–3 record (with Arroyo third), and rookies Bill Stafford (14–9) and Rollie Sheldon (11–5) picked up the slack when Art Ditmar and Bob Turley suddenly lost their effectiveness.

The World Series against the Cincinnati Reds opened on October 4 at Yankee Stadium in front of 62,397 fans. The Reds had a powerful lineup led by National League MVP Frank Robinson (.323, 37 HR, 124 RBI) and

Vada Pinson (.343), and they had three good pitchers: left-hander Jim O'Toole (19–9) and right-handers Joey Jay (21–10) and Bob Purkey (16–12). Although the Series ended up being a bit anticlimactic, it gave Whitey a chance to bask in the limelight a little after taking a back seat to the home run race during the season. He pitched a real masterpiece in the Series opener, yielding just two singles and a walk in hurling his third consecutive World Series shutout, tying the record held by Christy Mathewson of the New York Giants. The Yanks won 2–0, beating O'Toole on homers by Elston Howard and Moose Skowron. Whitey was in complete control; only one Cincinnati runner got as far as second base. He fanned six, including Robinson twice. Mantle sat out the game because of the golf ball-sized crater he still had in his hip and Maris went 0-for-4, so Ford had center stage for a day. The victory was his eighth in Series play, breaking the record he had shared with two former Yankees, Red Ruffing and Allie Reynolds.

After the game, baseball statisticians dug up the fact that Whitey was now very close to one of Babe Ruth's most cherished records. After Mathewson had thrown his three consecutive shutouts (all in the 1905 Series), he added only one more shutout inning in his next World Series start in 1911 before yielding a run. That gave him 28 consecutive scoreless innings in World Series play. That record was broken by none other than Babe Ruth, who recorded 29⅔ consecutive scoreless innings in 1916–1918 when he was with the Red Sox. The Babe won 23 games for the Sox in 1916, leading the league in ERA (1.75) and shutouts (nine, an AL record for left-handers). He gave up a homer in the first inning of his first World Series game in 1916 but then settled down and blanked the Brooklyn Dodgers for the next 13 innings as the Red Sox prevailed in 14 innings, 2–1. His next Series appearance was in 1918 against the Cubs, and he pitched a six-hit shutout to win the Series Opener, 1–0. He followed that up with seven shutout innings in Game 4 before yielding two runs in the eighth. That gave him 29 consecutive scoreless innings under today's rules that count only completed innings, but in 1961 the record was listed at 29⅔, counting a fractional inning. Ford now had 27 consecutive scoreless innings.

The two teams split Games 2 and 3. Joey Jay shut down the Yanks on four hits in Game 2 for a 6–2 win, but the Yanks regained the Series lead in Game 3 with a dramatic 3–2 win. Stymied through seven innings by Bob Purkey, the Yanks tied the score at 2 on an eighth-inning pinch-hit home run by Blanchard and won it on a ninth-inning blast by Maris.

Ford came back to pitch the pivotal Game 4 (again opposed by O'Toole) and retired the Reds in order in the first two innings. He gave up a harmless single to Darrell Johnson in the third, but when Elio Chacon grounded out to end the inning, Whitey had eclipsed Ruth with his 30th consecutive scoreless inning.

The record was now Ford's but the game was still scoreless when Mantle (who had insisted on playing) batted in the top of the fourth. He blasted a ball off the scoreboard in left center to help the Yanks score the first run of the game, but then had to leave the game for a pinch runner. The wound in his hip had opened, and blood had soaked through the thick bandages and was now soaking through his uniform. After watching the doctor treat the wound in the clubhouse, Tony Kubek said: "Most of the guys took one look and left. They couldn't take it.... It was awful. You could see the bone. I knew then what kind of guy Mantle was."[13] The sight of Mantle limping to first with the blood coming through his uniform after coming through with a key hit was one that none of his teammates would ever forget. There was no way they were going to lose the Series after that.

After retiring the Reds in the bottom of the fourth, Whitey walked in the top of the fifth and came around to score on singles by Richardson and Kubek to give the Yanks a 2–0 lead. A two-out single by Johnson in the bottom of the fifth gave the Reds a brief glimmer of hope, but Dick Gernert (batting for O'Toole) grounded to Boyer to end the inning.

Then Ford ran into trouble of the self-inflicted kind. Batting in the top of the sixth after Clete Boyer had already doubled home two runs, Whitey fouled a ball off the big toe on his right foot, badly bruising the knuckle. He then grounded into a double play and had to come right back out to pitch the bottom of the sixth. After giving up a lead-off single to Chacon, Whitey limped off with a 4–0 lead. "I wasn't going out to pitch in the sixth at all," he said after the game, "but we decided to give it a try. It was no go, though. Landing on that foot when I let the ball go hurt like blazes."[14] Jim Coates pitched the last four innings and the Yanks tacked on three more runs to win 7–0. The five shutout innings by Ford stretched his string of scoreless World Series innings to 32. "It's been a bad year for the Babe," quipped Ford after the game.[15]

That game broke Cincinnati's back, and the Yanks wrapped up the Series the following day with an easy 13–5 victory, sparked by Johnny Blanchard's second homer of the Series and a homer and triple by Hector Lopez. Ford was awarded the Babe Ruth Award as the outstanding player in the World Series and the Chevrolet Corvette awarded annually by *Sport Magazine* to the Series MVP. Other than Whitey's superb pitching, the Series was remarkable only for the ease with which the Yanks dispatched the Reds despite getting very little production from the M & M boys. Maris went two for 19, with his only meaningful contribution the game-winning home run in Game 3. Mantle had only six at-bats in the five games. The tremendous depth of the Yanks was never more apparent, as Skowron, Lopez and Blanchard picked up the slack.

Since the 1906 Cubs and the 1954 Indians had both lost the World Series in their great seasons, the 1961 Yanks could now stake a claim to being one of the two best teams in baseball history, along with the 1927 Murderers' Row Yankees of Ruth, Gehrig, Lazzeri, Meusel and Combs, who swept their World Series against Pittsburgh after posting a 110–44 regular-season record.

As for Ford, starting with the September 1960 stretch run he had now won 32 of his last 36 decisions, including four World Series wins. His career winning percentage of .715 (158–63) was the best in major league history among pitchers with at least 200 decisions and he had now won more World Series games than anybody else.

Ford's 1961 Season

	Date	Opponent	Score	Record	Reliever
L	04/11/61	Minnesota	0-6	0-1	Terry
W	04/17/61	Kansas City	3-0	1-1	CG
W	04/21/61	Baltimore (A)	4-2	2-1	CG
ND	04/26/61	Detroit (A)	13-11	2-1	Arroyo win
W	04/30/61	Washington (A)	4-3	3-1	Arroyo save
W	05/04/61	Minnesota (A)	5-2	4-1	Coates save
ND	05/09/61	Kansas City (A)	4-5	4-1	Arroyo BS
ND	05/14/61	Detroit	5-4	4-1	Clevenger BS
W	05/21/61	Baltimore	4-2	5-1	CG
W	05/25/61	Boston	6-4	6-1	Arroyo save
L	05/29/61	Boston (A)	1-2	6-2	Clevenger
W	06/02/61	Chicago (A)	6-2	7-2	CG
W	06/06/61	Minnesota	7-2	8-2	Arroyo save
W	06/10/61	Kansas City	5-3	9-2	CG
W	06/14/61	Cleveland (A)	11-5	10-2	Arroyo save
W	06/18/61	Detroit (A)	9-0	11-2	Arroyo save
W	06/22/61	Kansas City (A)	8-3	12-2	Arroyo save
W	06/26/61	Los Angeles (A)	8-6	13-2	Arroyo save
W	06/30/61	Washington	5-1	14-2	CG
W	07/04/61	Detroit	6-2	15-2	CG
W	07/08/61	Boston	8-5	16-2	Arroyo save
W	07/17/61	Baltimore (A)	5-0	17-2	CG
ND	07/21/61	Boston (A)	11-8	17-2	Arroyo win
W	07/25/61	Chicago	5-1	18-2	Arroyo save
W	07/29/61	Baltimore	5-4	19-2	CG
ND	08/02/61	Kansas City	6-5	19-2	Arroyo win
ND	08/06/61	Minnesota	7-6	19-2	Reniff win
W	08/10/61	Los Angeles	3-1	20-2	Arroyo save
L	08/15/61	Chicago	1-2	20-3	Arroyo
W	08/19/61	Cleveland (A)	3-2	21-3	Arroyo save
ND	08/23/61	Los Angeles (A)	8-6	21-3	Arroyo win
W	08/27/61	Kansas City (A)	8-7	22-3	Arroyo save
ND	09/01/61	Detroit	1-0	22-3	Arroyo win
W	09/06/61	Washington	8-0	23-3	CG
ND	09/10/61	Cleveland	7-6	23-3	Coates win
W	09/15/61	Detroit (A)	11-1	24-3	CG
L	09/19/61	Baltimore (A)	0-1	24-4	
W	09/23/61	Boston (A)	8-3	25-4	Arroyo save
ND	09/29/61	Boston	2-1	25-4	Arroyo BS

(A)   Away game
BS   Blown save
CG   Complete game
ND   No decision

ELEVEN

Another Near No-Hitter and Another Title

After the unbelievable seasons that Mantle, Maris, Ford and Arroyo had in 1961, it was not surprising that there was a drop-off in production from all four in 1962. For Mantle and Ford the problem was all too familiar — injuries. Both had physical problems on and off for much of the season, although they played up to their usual standards when healthy. Arroyo was a different story: he hurt his elbow early in the season and never fully recovered. After winning 15 games and saving 29 the previous season, he won only one game in 1962 and saved only seven, and his ERA ballooned from 2.19 to 4.81. He would pitch only six more innings the following season before retiring.

The drop in Maris's production was less easily explained. He had the exact same number of at-bats that he'd had in 1961 yet hit 28 fewer homers and knocked in 42 fewer runs. After two consecutive MVP years, Maris failed to garner even a single point in the 1962 MVP balloting. Although some of the drop-off could be attributed to some nagging physical problems, it was almost as if the physical and mental stress of 1961 had sapped his strength because he never approached that level of production again.

With their top four stars from 1961 all producing at a lower level, it became apparent early in the season that in order for the Yankees to win the pennant and World Series again in 1962, the rest of the players on the team would have to step up and pick up the slack. Fortunately for the Yankees, they did.

There was no hint of the problems to come at the start of the season. In fact, Opening Day seemed like a continuation of the previous season as the Yankees' three top sluggers all homered in a 7–6 win over the Orioles at the Stadium. Maris had a three-run shot and Mantle hit a game-tying eighth-inning homer, but Skowron hit one farther than either of them — 461 feet off the center-field wall on the fly for a two-run inside-the-park homer. Ralph Terry got the win in relief after blowing a lead handed over by Ford, and rookie Tom Tresh made his debut at shortstop in place of Tony Kubek, who was in the army and wouldn't return to the team until August. The *New York Times* actually pointed out that Maris was "ten games ahead of his 1961 pace," since he hadn't hit his first homer the previous season until the Yankees' 11th game.

Ford picked up his first win of the season on April 21 when the Yankees dealt the Indians their 19th straight loss at Yankee Stadium, 3–1. A three-run first-inning homer by Johnny Blanchard provided the offense and Whitey pitched eight solid innings before giving way to Arroyo in the ninth. He followed up that effort with his first complete game of the season on April 29, a 3–2 win over Washington in which he drove in the winning run with a sacrifice fly.

After losing a 1–0 heartbreaker to Chicago's Johnny Buzhardt in his next start despite allowing just four hits, Whitey held court in the clubhouse after the game, telling reporters that he planned to pitch "two to three more years before retiring." He also said he was seriously considering going into the business of breeding, training and driving harness horses, and was trying to buy 10 acres of farmland on Long Island for that purpose.[1]

When the Yanks returned home to Yankee Stadium, manager Ralph Houk gave right-hander Jim Bouton his first major league start in the second game of a double-header against Washington and the rookie responded with an 8–0 shutout of the Senators. Mantle hit homers from both sides of the plate for the ninth time in his career in that game, after slamming a home run about 460 feet into the last row of the distant right-center-field bleachers in the first game as the Yanks split the double-header.

Ford was next up in the rotation and he hooked up with Boston's Bill Monbouquette in a great pitching duel at the Stadium. Monbouquette was nearly perfect through six innings, facing just 18 batters as his only blemish (a walk to Berra) was quickly erased by a double play. Ford was nearly as good and the game remained scoreless into the seventh inning. Tresh broke up the no-hitter by bunting a little pop fly over Monbouquette's head that fell for a single, and then Maris reached on an error by center fielder Gary Geiger. After Berra walked again to load the bases, Elston Howard broke up the game with a three-run double over Carl Yastrzemski's head in left and came around to score on a single by Skowron. The only remaining suspense was whether Ford would get a shutout, and when Jim Pagliaroni lofted a pop fly to the infield with two out and nobody on in the ninth, it appeared he would. However, nobody took charge and the ball dropped in among Boyer, Tresh and Ford, and then Frank Malzone ruined the shutout with an RBI double before Whitey closed out the 4–1 win. The two pitchers were so efficient that the game took only an hour and 41 minutes.

Incredible as it may seem in light of today's Yankees attendance figures (an average of 50,499 for 81 home dates in 2005), only 6,058 fans witnessed this duel between two of the top pitchers in the league. The Yankees set attendance records just about everywhere they played that season, becoming the first major league team to draw more than 2 million fans on the road. They drew 70,918 for a game in Cleveland and even outdrew the Dodgers when they played the Los Angeles Angels in Chavez Ravine (Dodger Stadium). Yet for some reason they averaged only 18,670 fans for home games at Yankee Stadium, partly because they now had competition from the Mets, who were playing their inaugural season in the Polo Grounds while Shea Stadium was being built. Perhaps Yankees fans were getting a bit complacent from all the winning.

The Yankees' fortunes took a dip after that game as they dropped three out of four in Cleveland to fall half a game behind the Indians in the AL race. Things got worse on May 18 when the Twins beat Ford 4–3 on a two-run homer by Harmon Killebrew to move past the Yanks into second place. Worse still, Mantle tore the adductor muscle in his right thigh trying to beat out an infield grounder on the final play of the game and would be sidelined for a month. Three days later, Luis Arroyo was placed on the 30-day disabled list with a sore left elbow that had already kept him out of action for a month.

At this point in the season, Ford's record was only 3–3 and he had been unusually inconsistent. The Yanks needed a strong pitching performance out of him when they faced the surprising Los Angeles Angels at the Stadium on May 22. In only their second year of existence, the Angels were in fourth place, just two games behind the Yankees. Two rookie pitchers were leading the way: right-hander Dean Chance (who won 14 games that season) and flamboyant left-hander Bo Belinsky, who was 6–1 and had pitched a no-hitter on May 5 in just his fourth major league start. Chance got the nod against Ford in front of another sparse Yankee Stadium crowd of only 13,135.

The Angels got on the board in the first inning without the benefit of a hit. Little Albie Pearson (5'5") worked Ford for a walk and then had the temerity to steal second despite Whitey's well-known pick-off move. He advanced to third on an infield out and scored on a sacrifice fly by Steve Bilko. Ford stopped the Angels cold after the first inning but it took the Yanks six innings to get him even against Chance. They finally broke through in similar fashion to the Angels, on a walk to Tresh, a single by rookie Joe Pepitone and a sacrifice fly by Elston Howard.

Ford retired the Angels without a hit in the top of the seventh, and for the first time in his career he had a no-hitter after seven innings. Unfortunately, when he came into the dugout at the end of the inning he complained of pain in the back of his left shoulder. He said he had strained a muscle throwing an off-balance pitch back in the fourth inning. Since Whitey was never particularly concerned with personal achievements, he didn't object when Houk decided not to take any chances with his best pitcher's arm. Houk sent Phil Linz up to hit for Ford in the bottom of the seventh but the Yanks failed to score, leaving Whitey with just a no-decision to show for his efforts.

Jim Coates kept the no-hitter alive through the eighth but yielded a clean single to Bob Rodgers with one out in the ninth. The Angels failed to score, however, and the game moved into extra innings. Bud Daley and Bob Turley gave the Yanks three hitless innings and then Pepitone led off the bottom of the 12th with a triple to right. Los Angeles manager Bill Rigney ordered reliever Tom Morgan to walk Roger Maris and Hector Lopez intentionally to set up a play at any base, but Elston Howard foiled that strategy with his second sacrifice fly of the game to give the Yanks a 2–1 win and move them into first place by 13 percentage points over the Twins. The intentional walk to Maris was his fifth walk of the game, with four of them intentional — a major league record. He certainly missed having Mantle batting behind him.

Ford skipped two turns to rest his shoulder before testing it in a rematch with the Angels in front of 50,127 in Chavez Ravine on June 2. He was uncharacteristically wild and was reached for four runs in seven innings in a 6–1 loss, dropping his record to 3–4. It was the first time he had ever had a losing record as late as June. Matters didn't improve in his next start when he had to come out after just one inning because of pain in his left shoulder. Whitey said the pain was in a different part of the shoulder than the pain he had felt 17 days before, but it put him back on the shelf for another 13 days.

With Ford and Mantle both out of the lineup, the Yanks lost eight of their next 10 games and fell to fourth place, four games behind the first-place Indians and also trailing the Twins and Angels. Mantle made a dramatic pinch-hitting appearance during that stretch and hit a 450-foot three-run homer off Cleveland's Gary Bell to give the Yanks an eighth-inning lead, but they blew that game in the ninth inning and were swept in a four-game series by the Indians.

The Yankees started to turn their season around in Baltimore on June 21 when Ford returned to the mound and reassumed his role as stopper. He limited the Orioles to just three hits and was within one out of a shutout when he developed a blister on his left forefinger. He proceeded to walk Brooks Robinson and Jim Gentile, and Houk decided to go to the bullpen for the final out. With Arroyo still on the disabled list, Houk brought in left-hander Marshall Bridges, who retired Jackie Brandt on a pop-up to nail down the 3–0 win. The team was further buoyed when Mantle returned to the lineup the following day, playing right field in order to cut down the area he had to cover.

The momentum continued to build when the Yanks prevailed in an epic struggle against the Tigers in Detroit on June 24. The game lasted exactly seven hours, which broke the previous major league record by an hour and 41 minutes. The Yanks jumped all over long-time nemesis Frank Lary (previously 28–11 lifetime against New York) for six runs in the top of the first inning and chased him with another run in the second. However, Bob Turley, Jim Coates and Bill Stafford gave back seven runs by the sixth inning and the game eventually went into extra innings, tied at seven. It went through a second nine innings, still tied at seven. Finally, in the 22nd inning, Jack Reed (Mantle's frequent late-inning defensive replacement) hit his first major league home run with Maris on base to give the Yanks a 9–7 win. The game was four innings short of the major league record and two innings short of the American League record, and the two teams had played 40 innings in two days because they had split a double-header the day before. Jim Bouton pitched the last seven innings to pick up the win, but the real hero (besides Reed) was Yogi Berra, who at the age of 37 caught all 22 innings after not having caught a game in more than a year until a few days before.

The tired Tigers were overmatched against Ford the following day as Whitey shut them out on two hits for eight and a third innings before removing himself after experiencing a sharp twinge in his left shoulder. Once again, Bridges finished off the shutout as the Yanks won, 2–0. A double by Jake Wood and a single by Norm Cash were the only hits Whitey allowed, and he chipped in at the plate with a single that set up the first Yankees run. Ford's injury turned out not to be serious and he went the distance to beat the Angels with a four-hitter in his next start, 6–3. With this win, the Yanks crept to within half a game of the first-place Indians.

The Kansas City Athletics came into the Stadium on July 2 for a four-game series and the M & M boys went on a homer binge reminiscent of 1961. Both of them homered in the first game of the series, an 8–4 Yankee win, with Mantle's homer landing well up into the upper deck in right. The following night they upped the ante, hitting two each and driving in seven runs as the Yanks overcame a subpar effort by Ford and the bullpen to beat the A's again, 8–7. Maris's three-run shot in the eighth inning tied the game at seven and then Mantle followed with the game-winner. Neither connected in the first game of a July 4 double-header as the Yanks were pounded 11–1, but they resumed their barrage in the nightcap, with Mantle hitting two more and Maris one to drive in six runs in a 7–3 Yankees win. It was the third straight day that Mantle reached the right-field upper deck at the

Stadium, and the two homers moved him ahead of Duke Snider into seventh place on the all-time home run list with 389.

Mantle and Maris both slammed two more homers in the Yankees' next game on July 6 in Minnesota, driving in six runs in a 7–5 win over the Twins. That gave the M & M boys 13 homers and 21 RBIs in a five-game span. Moreover, Mickey's homers on his first two at-bats followed homers in his last two at-bats on July 4, so he tied a major league record with homers in four consecutive times at bat. He also had seven homers in his last 12 official at-bats and 17 homers on the season in only 141 at-bats, a homer rate of one every 8.29 at-bats. (At the time, the single-season record was a home run every 8.48 at-bats, set by Babe Ruth in 1920. Barry Bonds held the record as of the end of the 2005 season with a home run every 6.52 at-bats in 2001.) Mickey was also batting .326 and would have been contending for another Triple Crown if not for the month he had lost earlier in the season. Maris had 21 homers for the season, but in more than twice as many at-bats as Mantle.

The Yanks reached the halfway point of their season with a 46–35 record, which placed them three percentage points ahead of the Indians for the AL lead. The Angels were only half a game back, with the Twins three and a half games behind the Yankees. Ford reached the midway point with a very ordinary 7–5 record. The Yanks would certainly need a much better second half out of their ace if they were to hold off the three teams chasing them.

New York began the second half of the season with nine straight wins to put a little daylight between themselves and their pursuers. Ford contributed two of the wins, beating Kansas City 3–1 and Washington 3–2, with Mantle's two-run homer the big blow in the latter game. The Yankees' streak was stopped but Ford's personal streak continued. He beat Boston for his third straight win (striking out eight of the first 15 batters), although his shoulder stiffened again in the ninth inning, requiring help from Marshall Bridges to close out the 5–3 win.

After failing to complete nine innings in seven straight starts, Ford went 10 innings on August 1 to beat the Senators 5–2 when the Yanks pushed across three runs in the top of the 11th inning. Ralph Terry got the last three outs for Whitey, who had now won eight of his last nine decisions. The Senators claimed that Ford had been throwing a spitter, a claim that Whitey laughed off. "Ridiculous," he said. "Maybe they thought so because once, while pitching to Harry Bright, I crossed up Elston Howard. Instead of a slider, I threw a high fast ball which got away from my catcher."[2] Since his retirement, Ford has been very frank about which illegal pitches he did and didn't throw, and the spitter is one that he says he didn't throw, except on rare occasions such as the 1961 All-Star Game. However, he says he never made much of an effort to discourage such allegations because he felt that if the batters *thought* he was throwing a spitter, it gave him an edge.[3]

Tony Kubek rejoined the Yankees on August 4 after eight months in the army, which presented Houk with a dilemma. Kubek's erstwhile replacement, Tom Tresh, was in the process of running away with the AL Rookie of the Year Award and was one of the big reasons why the Yanks were in first place. He made it clear he should stay in the lineup by hitting five home runs in 10 days after Kubek rejoined the team. After initially experimenting with Kubek in left field, Houk gave Tony back his job at shortstop and moved Tresh to left field, where he had previously been platooning Lopez, Berra, Blanchard and Pepitone. (The extra outfielders came in handy because Mantle was hurt again, having wrenched his left knee in late July.) Kubek didn't have any trouble readjusting to American League pitching, homering in his first at-bat and hitting .314 in the 45 games that he played in. His return gave Houk three players at the top of the lineup who were outstanding leadoff men — Kubek, Richardson and Tresh — and they continually set the table for the big guns that came after them.

Ford beat Detroit 8–0 at Yankee Stadium on August 10, although once again he needed Marshall Bridges to close out the shutout, their third combined shutout of the season. The game was played in a cold drizzle but the weather didn't seem to bother Whitey as he struck out a season-high 10 batters and even added an RBI single. Ford frequently pitched well in cold weather, which certainly was to his advantage come World Series time.

Whitey finally went the distance on August 14 in Minnesota, beating the Twins 5–2 for his sixth straight win and his 10th in his last 11 decisions. His winning streak came to an end in his next start when he again went the distance but lost to Kansas City in the bottom of the ninth 5–4 despite homers by Mantle and Maris. Ford was now 13–6 on the season and with 10 scheduled starts left, he still had a chance to win 20 games.

At this point in the season, the Yanks were still being doggedly pursued by both Los Angeles and Minnesota, who were four and five games behind, respectively. After going 4–5 in the first nine games of a brutal 17-game road trip, the Yanks arrived in Los Angeles on August 21 for a three-game series against the upstart Angels. The first game matched Bill Stafford against Bo Belinsky, who had cooled off considerably after his remarkable start but was still pitching well. The Angels took a 3–1 fifth-inning lead but the Yanks fought back to tie the game on a two-run homer by Howard and the game eventually moved into extra innings, tied at four. The Yanks sent the crowd of 50,830 home unhappy by erupting for seven runs in the top of the 10th, with the last four scoring on a grand slammer by Maris.

In the second game, Ford fell behind 3–1 in the bottom of the first when Leon Wagner stroked his 30th homer of the season with two men on.

The Yanks closed to within a run on an RBI double by Dale Long in the fourth and then Berra won the game with a two-run homer in the eighth, with Rollie Sheldon getting the win in relief of Ford. The Angels salvaged the final game of the series in 13 innings, 5–4, but the Yanks still left town with a five-game lead.

New York finished off the road trip with five games in three days against Baltimore and proceeded to lose the first four. They hoped that Ford could stop the slide in the final game but he was beaten by future Hall of Famer Robin Roberts in a great pitching duel, 2–1. Roberts had resurrected his career with the Orioles after going 1–10 the previous year for the Phillies, for whom he had won 234 games. Ironically, the winning run was scored on a home run by Jim Gentile, who was normally a Ford patsy. Gentile had tied for third behind Maris and Mantle in the 1961 homer derby with 46, but he was a left-handed batter who swung from the heels and Ford normally made him look terrible. He previously had only one hit — a single — off Ford in three seasons with Baltimore, but he got hold of one on that day to send the Yankees to their first five-game sweep in three years and cut their lead to three games over both the Angels and the Twins.[4]

After going 6–11 on the road trip, the Yanks were glad to be back at the Stadium. However, they managed only a split of a four-game series with the Indians and now led the Twins by only two games, with the Angels one game further back. Ford pitched the opener of a key three-game series against Kansas City and won easily, 5–1, with the help of a 15-hit Yankees attack (including two by Ford) and the obligatory save by Bridges, who came on when Whitey tired in the eighth. The following day it was Ralph Terry's turn to shine, as he became the first 20-game winner in the AL with a 3–1 win over his former team, thanks to a two-run triple by Elston Howard. When New York won the final game of the series 2–1 on a ninth-inning double by Bobby Richardson, they had a lead of four games in the loss column over both Minnesota and Los Angeles, with the Angels coming to the Stadium for a four-game series.

After the teams split the first two games, Ford cruised into the seventh inning of the third game with a 4–0 lead. Then he suddenly lost his stuff, yielding three runs before departing in favor of Marshall Bridges with only one out. Unfortunately, the usually reliable Tony Kubek let a perfect double-play ball go right through his legs at shortstop and two more runs scored. Although a homer by Clete Boyer tied the game for the Yanks in the eighth, the Angels won it in the ninth to pull within three games of New York in the loss column. Faced with the unthinkable prospect of losing the pennant to a second-year expansion team, the Yanks came from behind against Dean Chance in the final game of the series to stave off the Angels, 6–5, on a two-run single by Tresh.

The Twins were now in second place, and Ford maintained New York's three-game lead with a 5–1 win over Boston, although he was forced to leave the game in the sixth inning after being plunked in the side by his opposing pitcher, Don Schwall. But when the Yanks dropped a double-header to the Red Sox the following day, the Twins were within two games in the loss column with three weeks left to play.

In perhaps the biggest game of the season, Ralph Terry took the mound against Detroit's Hank Aguirre, the league ERA leader. Aguirre had already beaten New York three times during the season without a loss and a first-inning homer by Al Kaline staked him to a 1–0 lead. But in the fifth inning, Mantle gave the Yanks a needed lift. Returning from yet another injury (an abdominal muscle strain that had sidelined him for six days), Mantle poled his 26th home run of the season over the center-field wall to bring the Yanks even. It was also the 400th homer of his career, making him only the seventh player in major league history to reach that plateau and the second-youngest (behind Jimmie Foxx).[5] Among active players, only Stan Musial (460) was ahead of him. Mickey came up again in the ninth inning with the lead run on second, but Detroit manager Bob Scheffing elected to put him on and pitch to Hector Lopez, who was hitless in his last 22 at-bats. The move backfired when Lopez singled home a run, and Mantle subsequently scored as well to nail down Terry's 21st win of the season 3–1.

Two days later, Ford followed up Terry's fine effort with a complete game of his own, beating Cleveland 5–2 with a six-hitter thanks to a long three-run homer by Mantle. The Yanks now led the Angels by five games and the Twins by five and a half with just 13 games left to play.

Ford's slim chance of winning 20 games evaporated in a 4–3 loss to Boston, with the bullpen allowing the winning run. The bullpen cost him a win in his next start, as Bud Daley, Marshall Bridges and Jim Coates blew a 6–1 ninth-inning lead for Whitey. Despite that debacle, the Yanks still had a four-and-a-half game lead over the Twins, and the Angels had finally fallen out of contention. Ford had the opportunity to clinch the Yankees' 27th American League pennant on September 25 against the Senators and he came through with a complete-game 8–3 win. Despite winning 13 fewer games than the 1961 juggernaut, the Yanks finished five games ahead of the second-place Twins. The pennant was the team's 12th in 14 years, and Whitey's ninth.

Ford finished the season with a 17–8 record; his winning percentage of .680 was second in the league, just behind Chicago's Ray Herbert. His ERA of 2.90 was third in the AL behind Aguirre (2.21) and Roberts (2.78). It was a strange year for Whitey in that he was constantly battling arm problems but missed only a few starts. The injuries were reflected more in his complete game total: he completed only seven out of 37 starts (well below his usual percentage) and he didn't have a single complete-game shutout. Nevertheless, his 257.7 innings tied Minnesota's Camilo Pascual for the fourth-highest total in the league, and because his ERA was 1.07 runs below the league ERA of 3.97, Whitey was second in the league to Aguirre in pitching runs with 31.[6] After his 3–4 start, Ford had been 14–4 over the remainder of the season to salvage not only his season but also the team's. The Yankees were 9–3 in Ford's no-decisions with several blown saves, so with a little luck Whitey could have won 20 again despite missing nearly a month of the season.

Mantle won his third MVP Award, joining Jimmie Foxx, Joe DiMaggio, Stan Musial, Roy Campanella and Yogi Berra as three-time MVPs. Though injuries limited him to only 123 games, Mantle batted .321 (second to Pete Runnels) and had 30 homers, 89 RBIs, and 96 runs scored in only 377 at bats. Opposing pitchers walked him so many times (122) that he had a league-leading .488 on-base percentage.

Maris slipped to "only" 33 homers and 100 RBIs from his record-setting 1961 season, while batting just .256. (He would never hit as many as 30 homers in a season again.) The Yankees' depth was evident in the fact that despite getting 52 fewer homers from Maris and Mantle than in the previous year, they still hit 199 home runs, second in the league behind Minnesota's 209 homers. Moose Skowron's 23 home runs were no surprise, but the other members of the Yankees infield performed well beyond expectations. Bobby Richardson hit .302, led the league in hits (209) and defensive double plays (116) and finished second in the MVP balloting. Certainly no one expected Rookie of the Year Tom Tresh to bat .286 with 20 homers and 93 RBIs. Even slick-fielding Clete Boyer stepped up his offensive production, batting .272 with 18 homers. Elston Howard was solid as a rock behind the plate and hit 21 homers with 91 RBIs.

Several pitchers stepped up as well. The decrease in Ford's win total was almost entirely made up by Ralph Terry, who led the league in wins with 23, seven more than he had the previous season. Bill Stafford (14–9) was an able number three starter, and Marshall Bridges was 8–4 with 18 saves after replacing Arroyo in June as the Yankees' primary reliever.

In some respects, the 1962 baseball season bore an eerie resemblance to 1951. At the end of the final day of the regular season, the same three teams were still alive. The National League pennant race had been a season-long dogfight between the Giants and the Dodgers. The Dodgers' pitching duo of Sandy Koufax and Don Drysdale was nearly unbeatable that year, with Koufax headed for a possible 30-win season until a circulatory problem in his pitching hand ended his season in mid-July. Drysdale picked up the slack and won the Cy Young Award with a 25–9 mark, but they both took a back seat to teammate Maury Wills, who broke Ty Cobb's 47-year-old record of 96 stolen bases by swiping 104 in only 117 attempts. Wills also had 208 hits and scored 130 runs to beat out Willie Mays of the Giants for the MVP Award. Tommy Davis of the Dodgers finished third in the balloting after leading the NL in batting (.346), hits (230) and RBIs (153).

The Giants were equally good. Led by Mays (.304, 49 HR, 141 RBI), Orlando Cepeda (.306, 35 HR, 114 RBI), Felipe Alou (.316, 25 HR, 98 RBI) and Willie McCovey (20 homers in only 229 at-bats), they finished first in the National League in batting and home runs. On the mound, right-hander Jack Sanford went 24–7 (including 16 straight wins) to finish second to Drysdale in the Cy Young balloting, while left-hander Billy O'Dell was 19–14 and Juan Marichal was 18–11. However, one of the keys to the Giants' season was the off-season acquisition of left-hander Billy Pierce from the Chicago White Sox. The Giants badly needed another left-hander to pitch at Candlestick Park and Pierce filled the bill perfectly, going 12–0 at Candlestick (16–6 overall).

The Dodgers were in first place when Koufax got hurt, but the Giants made a run and got to within half a game of the Dodgers on September 12. Then they lost six straight games and trailed Los Angeles by four games with seven to play. No team in baseball history had ever come back from such a deficit in the final week of the season. But the Dodgers somehow lost five of their next six while the Giants were winning four of six, so the Giants trailed by only one game on the final day of the regular season. Mays hit an eighth-inning homer to beat Houston, 2–1, while the Dodgers were losing a 1–0 heartbreaker down in Los Angeles. As they had in 1951, the two teams would play a three-game playoff for the right to play the Yankees.

Two more home runs by Mays led the Giants to a win in Game 1 as Pierce pitched a three-hit shutout at Candlestick, but the Dodgers came back to win the second game and force a third and deciding game on October 3, 11 years to the day after the Miracle of Coogan's Bluff.

Following the 1951 script almost to the letter, the Dodgers took a 4–2 lead into the ninth inning of Game 3, but a single and two walks loaded the bases for Mays with one out. Mays lined a ball off pitcher Ed Roebuck's leg for a single that scored one run, and then Cepeda tied the score with a sacrifice fly. The Dodgers had won all season long with pitching and defense, but a wild pitch and two walks by Stan Williams forced in the go-ahead run and a Dodgers error made it 6–4. Billy Pierce came on in the last of the ninth to pitch a 1–2–3 inning and the Giants were headed for a rematch with the Yankees, to whom they had lost in 1951.

The World Series started at Candlestick Park with Ford opposing O'Dell. The latter was no stranger to the Yankees, having pitched for the Orioles for five seasons before being traded to the Giants. Maris gave the Yanks a 2–0 lead with a two-run double after Richardson and Tresh set the table with a couple of singles. Roger's ball was actually over the fence, but right fielder Felipe Alou made a desperate leap for the ball and managed to knock it back onto the field.

Ford retired the Giants in order in the first, but his World Series consecutive scoreless innings streak came to an end in the second inning. Not surprisingly, the Giants' rally was started by Willie Mays, whose career batting average against Whitey in All-Star competition was a robust .857 (six for seven). Willie led off the second with a single and advanced to third on a single by Jim Davenport. Ford nearly escaped, but Jose Pagan surprised the Yanks with a beautiful two-out bunt down the third-base line and beat it out to score Mays. Willie continued his tormenting of Ford in the third inning, singling home Chuck Hiller from third to tie the game at two.

The two southpaws cruised through the middle three innings without trouble but Clete Boyer hit his first World Series homer leading off the seventh. The Yanks chased O'Dell with two runs in the eighth and added another run off Don Larsen and Stu Miller in the ninth. Meanwhile, Ford scattered four harmless singles (including another one by Mays) over the final six innings to complete the 6–2 win, his fifth straight in Series play. He became the first pitcher to win 10 World Series games, and his Series record of 33 consecutive scoreless innings still stands, although New York's Mariano Rivera threw 33 1/3 consecutive scoreless postseason innings in 1998–2000, only nine of which were in World Series play. (Ford's record was originally recorded as 33⅔ innings since there were two out when the streak-ending run was scored, and that's how the record is listed on his Hall of Fame plaque. However, major league baseball rule makers decided years later that only completed innings should count, so Ford's record was reduced to 33 innings.)

Ford had all four of his pitches (fastball, curve, sinker and slider) working in this game and said the cool weather helped him. He summed up his effort by saying: "Good pitching is mainly a matter of getting the batter to hit the pitch you want him to hit, not the one he wants to hit."[7] This approach obviously hadn't worked with Mays (3-for-4), of whom Whitey said: "Willie hit a different pitch each time. I finally got him with a fastball that he probably didn't expect. I was beginning to think he owned me — or at least was a major stockholder."[8] Added Houk: "We thought we had a good book on Willie, but I guess we're just not any smarter than the other guys in his league who haven't been able to stop him either."[9]

Ralph Terry and Jack Sanford squared off in Game 2 for the first of three times in the Series. Sanford shut out the Yanks 2–0 on three hits, escaping a ninth-inning jam when Roger Maris was robbed of a base hit with Mantle on second and two out. The second Giant run scored on a long home run off Terry by Willie McCovey, who would hit 521 homers in his

Hall-of-Fame career, an NL record for left-handed batters until Barry Bonds broke it in 2001. Terry had a tendency to throw the long ball (he'd given up 40 homers during the regular season), and McCovey was just the type of left-handed slugger that gave him trouble. "Stretch" was 6'4" with long arms and he had a vicious uppercut swing. Pitchers so feared him that he was intentionally walked a record 45 times one year. He still holds the NL career record for grand slams with 18.

The Yanks came back to win Game 3 at Yankee Stadium 3–2 behind the four-hit pitching of Bill Stafford, who lost his shutout on a two-run homer by Ed Bailey with two out in the ninth. Billy Pierce had matched Stafford for six innings but was undone by consecutive seventh-inning singles by Tresh, Mantle and Maris plus an error in right field by McCovey that led to the eventual winning run.

Ford got the ball for Game 4, opposed by Juan Marichal, who was making his first World Series start. The following year, the "Dominican Dandy" would supplant Sanford as the ace of the San Francisco staff, going 25–8 en route to 243 career wins and the Hall of Fame. But in 1962, despite winning 18 games, Marichal was the number four starter on the Giants' staff. He struck out Mantle with a man on to end the first inning, and then San Francisco catcher Tom Haller hit a slider from Ford into the lower right-field stands with a man on in the second inning to give his pitcher a 2–0 lead. "I made the perfect pitch," said Ford after the game, giving Haller credit. "If I had to do it all over again, I'd make the same pitch."[10]

Whitey settled down after Haller's homer but Marichal wasn't giving the runs back, stranding Skowron after a two-out triple in the second and then cruising through the third and fourth innings, as did Ford. In the fifth inning, however, Marichal injured the index finger on his pitching hand trying unsuccessfully to bunt a run home from third with two strikes and had to leave the game. The Giants left the bases loaded when Whitey fanned Chuck Hiller to end the inning.

Reliever Bob Bolin escaped a bases-loaded jam in the Yankees' fifth by inducing Richardson to hit into a double play, but he wasn't as lucky in the sixth. He walked Mantle and Maris with one out and then gave up consecutive two-out RBI singles to Skowron and Boyer that tied the game, 2–2. With Ford due up, Houk made a decision that may have cost the Yankees the game. Whitey had just retired the heart of the San Francisco order (Mays, Alou and Cepeda) in order in the top of the sixth and still appeared to have plenty of gas left in the tank, but Houk sent Berra up to pinch-hit for him in an attempt to grab the lead. Yogi walked, but then Kubek grounded out to end the inning and Houk had to go to his bullpen. Marshall Bridges hadn't pitched yet in the Series, but Houk opted to try to get an inning out of Jim Coates despite his 4.44 ERA during the season.

Coates promptly got into a jam in the top of the seventh. He walked Davenport and allowed a double by pinch hitter Matty Alou. With men on second and third and one out, Houk brought in Bridges to pitch to left-handed pinch hitter Ed Bailey. Giants manager Alvin Dark recalled Bailey and sent up Bob Nieman, a dangerous .295 lifetime hitter who was in the final days of his 12-year career. Houk ordered an intentional pass to Nieman, loading the bases. When Bridges retired former AL batting champ Harvey Kuenn on a pop-up to Boyer, he needed only to retire light-hitting second baseman Chuck Hiller to get out of the inning. Hiller was a left-handed batter who had hit only three homers in 602 at-bats during the regular season and was hitting .154 in the Series, but he proceeded to take Bridges deep for the first grand slam home run hit by a National Leaguer in the World Series. (Seven American Leaguers had done it — six of them Yankees.) The Giants hung on for a 7–3 win that tied the Series at two games apiece. Ironically, Don Larsen (in relief) was the winning pitcher for San Francisco, on the sixth anniversary of his perfect game.

Typically, Ford refused to second-guess Houk after the game. "Ralph asked me how I felt after we had tied the score and had two on and two out in the sixth," said Whitey. "I told the skipper that I wasn't tired, but that my breaking stuff was not as good as I thought it should be.... If I were the manager, I would have called for a pinch hitter in that situation, too."[11]

It was Terry against Sanford again in Game 5, and Tresh broke a 2–2 tie in the eighth inning with a three-run homer to give Terry his first Series win after four losses. The Giants threatened in the ninth when McCovey tagged Terry for a double and subsequently scored, but Terry completed the 5–3 win to put the Yanks within one game of their second straight Series win.

At this point the Series was put on hold as the San Francisco area was deluged with rain, causing Game 6 to be cancelled three times. When the rain finally stopped, the Giants brought in helicopters to hover over the soggy outfield in an attempt to dry it enough to be playable. The game was finally played on October 15, and the four off days allowed Houk to bring Ford back to try to close out the Series. He was opposed by Billy Pierce, with his 12–0 record at Candlestick Park. The two of them had hooked up in many great pitching duels when Pierce was with the White Sox, with Ford coming out on top more often than not. But Pierce was unbeatable at Candlestick Park that season and he sent the Yankees down in order over the first four innings.

Ford brought about his own downfall in the bottom of the fourth. With one out, Felipe Alou reached on an infield hit off Boyer's glove and advanced to second on a walk to Mays. Ford then attempted to pick Alou off second, but his throw was way off the mark and ended up in the soggy outfield. "I had the pickoff play on with Kubek," Ford explained after the game, "but when I whirled around to throw to second, I saw I had no chance to get Alou. I tried to check my throw, but the ball sailed out of my hand and that was that."[12] By the time the ball was retrieved, Alou had scored and Mays was perched on third. The usually imperturbable Ford seemed shaken by this turn of events and allowed two more runs to cross the plate on a double by Cepeda and a single by Davenport, putting the Yankees in a 3–0 hole.

Roger Maris broke up Pierce's perfect game in the top of the fifth with a one-out homer, and then an error and a walk put the tying runs on base with two out and Ford due up. Faced with the same decision as in Game 4, Houk decided to let Ford bat for himself this time. "We still had four more turns at bat and Whitey's my best pitcher," said Houk later.[13] Whitey popped up to end the inning and that was essentially the game, as the Giants chased Ford with two more runs in the bottom half of the inning and coasted to a 5–2 win behind Pierce's three-hitter. The loss was Whitey's first in Series play since 1958 and was the fifth of his career, tying the record shared by three Hall of Famers: Christy Mathewson, Eddie Plank and Rube Marquard.

Because of the three-day rain delay after Game 5, the managers were able to bring back Terry and Sanford to pitch the climactic seventh game. For Terry, it was a chance for redemption for surrendering the famous ninth-inning homer to Bill Mazeroski that won the 1960 World Series for the Pittsburgh Pirates.

Sometimes one mistake defines a player's entire career. Fred "Bonehead" Merkle had a solid 14-year major league career but is remembered only for his "boner" in a crucial 1908 game between the Giants and the Cubs, who were battling for the pennant in the final week of the season. The Giants had a runner on third and Merkle on first in the bottom half of the ninth inning, and when the batter drilled a single to center field and the crowd began to swarm onto the field, Merkle ran for the clubhouse without ever touching second base. Johnny Evers of the Cubs grabbed a ball and tagged second base. Merkle was eventually ruled out, the game was replayed, and the Cubs won the game and the pennant.

Mickey Owen was a fine catcher for the Brooklyn Dodgers, but is remembered only for letting what should have been a game-ending third strike from Hugh Casey to Tommy Henrich get by him in Game 4 of the 1941 World Series, allowing Henrich to reach first base. The Yankees rallied to win the game and the Series.

Among Red Sox fans, Johnny Pesky is remembered more for one moment of hesitation than he is for his .307 lifetime batting average and his six consecutive seasons with more than 100 runs scored. In Game 7 of the 1946 World Series, he stood in short left field holding on to a relay throw from center field just long enough for Enos Slaughter of the Cardinals to go tearing around third base and score the Series-winning run all the way from first base on what looked like an ordinary single. But Pesky's burden pales in comparison to that of Boston's Bill Buckner, whose 2,715 career hits and 1980 NL batting title are completely overshadowed by his imitation of a croquet wicket in the 10th inning of Game 6 of the 1986 World Series against the Mets, after the Red Sox had been one strike away from the world championship.

Lastly, Brooklyn pitcher Ralph Branca (who averaged nearly 14 wins per season for the Dodgers between 1947 and 1951) became forever Ralph "Gopher Ball" Branca when he surrendered "the shot heard round the world" to Bobby Thomson in the ninth inning of the third and deciding NL playoff game in 1951, thus giving the pennant to the Giants. Now, two years after surrendering the second-most famous home run in history, Ralph "Gopher Ball" Terry had a chance to either redeem himself or go down in history as the pitcher who blew two seventh games for the Yankees.

The Yanks scored first when Tony Kubek hit into a double play in the fourth inning with the bases loaded and nobody out. Terry pitched brilliantly, retiring the first 17 batters before Sanford broke up the perfect game with a single. In the bottom of the seventh, Tom Tresh made one of the key plays of the Series, racing deep into the left-field corner to make a back-handed stab of a line drive hit by Willie Mays. McCovey (who by now must have felt like he owned Terry) followed with a triple, but was stranded.

Terry carried a two-hit shutout into the bottom of the ninth. Pinch hitter Matty Alou led off with a bunt single, but Terry fanned the next two batters. Mays then followed with a double to right, and only a fine play by Roger Maris kept Alou from scoring. Up came McCovey, with the tying run on third and the winning run on second. Every Yankees fan watching the game assumed Terry would walk McCovey, since his run was meaning-less and he'd been killing Terry. It also would have set up a play at any base. But the dangerous Orlando Cepeda was on deck, and Houk decided to take his chances with McCovey.

Seconds later it looked like a bad decision when McCovey hit a tow-ering drive into the right-field stands, but the Candlestick Park wind pushed it foul. Houk still refused to walk McCovey, and Willie absolutely crushed the next pitch on a line toward right field. The ball was hit so hard that the cameraman couldn't follow it fast enough, and by the time the camera swung around toward right, the ball was already in Bobby Richardson's glove and the Yankees had their 20th world championship. A foot or two in either direction and Terry would have been the goat again. Instead, he won the Babe Ruth Award and *Sport Magazine* Corvette as Series MVP, and wiped the slate clean with Yankees fans for the gopher ball to Mazeroski.

Although the 1962 season had been an up-and-down year for Ford due to his arm problems, he had finished strong and appeared to be fine. Despite his early season comments to the contrary, it certainly appeared that Ford (who turned 34 shortly after the World Series) was still in his prime and could pitch for another five years. His career record was 175–71; his winning percentage of .711 was unparalleled among pitchers with at least 110 wins. With 26-year-old Ralph Terry coming off a big year and two hard-throwing young pitchers (Jim Bouton and Al Downing) about to come into their own, Yankees pitching appeared set for years to come. (They also had a young right-hander named Mel Stottlemyre who had burned up the Carolina League that season.) New York's infield of Boyer, Kubek, Richardson and Skowron was the best in the league and Elston Howard was about to establish himself as the best catcher in the league. Most importantly, the Yankees had Mantle, Maris and Tresh in the outfield. Certainly no one thought it would be 15 years before the Yanks would win another World Series.

TWELVE

Ford vs. Koufax

After slugging their way to two straight world championships, the Yanks had to find another way to reach the World Series in 1963. Mantle missed most of the season due to injuries and Maris missed 71 games as well. The Yanks got a total of only 88 RBIs from the M & M boys, and Berra drove in only 28 runs in limited action in his final season. Moose Skowron was traded to the Dodgers before the season started in return for right-hander Stan Williams, so the heart of the lineup from the great 1961 team was either injured or gone. The Yankees were forced to rely primarily on their pitching and their depth to carry them through the season, and the results were so good that they ran away and hid from the rest of the league, winning the pennant by 10½ games over the White Sox and 13 games over the Twins.

Manager Ralph Houk was able to field his regular lineup in only 10 games all season due to a steady stream of injuries, but the bench players performed admirably and the pitching staff was superb. Ford had the second-most productive season of his career and the Yankees also got excellent pitching from Jim Bouton (21–7), Ralph Terry (17–15) and Al Downing (13–5). Stan Williams (9–8) was a bit of a disappointment on the mound, but Skowron's replacement at first base (Joe Pepitone) stepped up and hit 27 homers with 89 RBIs. Elston Howard won the American League MVP Award, batting .287 with 28 homers and 85 RBIs while leading the team from behind the plate. Tom Tresh played center field in Mantle's stead for much of the season and hit 25 homers, and the two reserve outfielders who filled in for the injured Maris and the relocated Tresh (Johnny Blanchard and Hector Lopez) combined for 30 homers and 97 RBIs.

The injury that was the toughest for Houk to work around was Mantle's. Despite missing most of April with a muscle tear along his rib cage, Mickey had 11 homers by June 4 and appeared headed toward a big year. Included among those homers was a blast at Yankee Stadium on May 22 that was one of the most memorable home runs of his career. The Yankees blew a 7–0 lead against Kansas City that night and the game went into extra innings. Batting left-handed against Bill Fischer in the bottom of the 11th inning with the score 7–7, Mantle came as close as he would ever come to realizing his ambition of becoming the first man to hit a fair ball out of Yankee Stadium. He would always refer to this one as "the hardest ball I ever hit," and it may have been the hardest ball *anyone* ever hit. The ball struck the facade on top of the three-tiered right-field grandstand, a few feet from the top. Had it been hit a little to the left, it would have been out. The facade was 374 feet from home plate and 108 feet high, and a physicist calculated that if the ball was at its peak when it hit the facade, it would have gone 620 feet if unimpeded. Most observers reported that the ball was still rising when it hit the facade.[1] Of the three times that Mickey hit this facade in his career, this one was the most impressive.

Unfortunately for the Yanks, Mantle knew only one way to play the game, and on June 5 he ran full speed into a chain-link fence in Baltimore trying to catch a drive by Brooks Robinson. He caught his spikes in the fence, breaking a bone in his left foot and doing cartilage and ligament damage to his left knee (his "good" one). He missed the rest of June and all of July, and batted only eight times in August, all as a pinch hitter.

Ford had some injury problems of his own. A sore arm during spring training set his preparation back and he started the season slowly, losing his first two starts. Houk rested him for 11 days before testing him again on April 28 at the Stadium and Whitey returned to form with an impressive outing. Not only did he shut out the Indians for seven innings on only two hits, but he also hit the third home run of his career. After hitting his homer in the fourth inning off Mudcat Grant, Ford came back to the dugout and got the silent treatment for a while before his teammates crowded around congratulating him. Hal Reniff finished off the shutout as the Yanks beat the Indians, 5–0. Ford followed up that effort four days later with a four-hit shutout in Los Angeles, striking out 10 and yielding but four singles and a walk in beating Dean Chance and the Angels, 7–0.

Earlier that day, Ford had gone to see Dodgers team physician Robert Woods, who told Whitey that the circulation in the tip of his left index finger was impaired by about 10 to 15 percent. Dr. Woods prescribed medication and said he did not consider the ailment to be serious, but in retrospect this was a precursor of the circulatory ailments that would eventually end Whitey's career.[2]

Ford stretched his winning streak to four with wins over Detroit and Minnesota before getting roughed up by the Angels at the Stadium on May 19, dropping his record to 4–3. It would be more than two months before Whitey would lose another game.

He started his streak with a complete-game win over Washington and then pitched a three-hit shutout against Cleveland on May 31. A pair of two-

Ford beating Chicago 9–1 on July 4, 1963, for his ninth straight win. Whitey struck out 12 in raising his season record to 13–3 on his way to a 24–7 season. (AP/Wide World Photos)

run homers by Tresh and Howard powered the Yanks to a 4–0 win as Ford limited the Tribe to three measly singles and struck out eight.

Whitey carried the team during June. The Yanks entered the month trailing the Orioles by a game in the standings but moved into first place as Ford went 6–0 in June to raise his record to 12–3. (New York was only 13–13 for the month in games in which Whitey was not involved in the decision.) When Ford beat the White Sox 9–1 on July 4 (striking out a season-high 12), his winning streak was at nine. His 13 wins at the halfway point of the season were the most in the league.

Ford stretched his winning streak to 10 games with a 3–2 win over the Angels in his first start after the All-Star break. A two-run homer by Hector Lopez offset two unearned runs off Ford and then Elston Howard won the game with a 10th-inning RBI single. After a no-decision against Kansas City, Whitey beat Cleveland and Los Angeles to draw within two wins of the Yankees' record of 14 consecutive wins that he shared with Jack Chesbro. He was now 16–3, and there was still a week left in July. The Yanks were moving inexorably away from the rest of the American League, lead-ing the second-place Twins by eight and a half games and the White Sox and Orioles by nine games each.

The streak ended with a thud when Ford yielded all five Minnesota runs in a 5–1 loss to the Twins on July 28, and he lost his next two starts as well. The last of these three losses was one of the worst outings of Ford's career: eight earned runs on 10 hits in six innings of work against Washington. The Senators reached him for four homers, including two by light-hitting Chuck Cottier, who hit only three other homers all season. But after this brief slump, Whitey finished the season with 12 consecutive high-quality starts.

After beating Dean Chance and the Angels 2–1 to finally record his 17th win, Ford went the distance against the Indians but came out on the short end of a 2–1 score. He then pitched a typical Whitey Ford game against Chicago on August 24, requiring only 98 pitches to shut out the White Sox 3–0 on six hits (all singles) to drop the second-place White Sox 12 games behind the Yanks. He walked none and struck out eight and didn't allow a runner as far as second until the ninth inning. The Yankees' outfielders recorded only one putout as one Chicago batter after another either grounded out or struck out. He followed that up with a 4–1 win over Boston, yielding just five hits but losing a shutout on a home run by Dick Stuart. For the second consecutive game, Whitey didn't walk a single batter as he finished August with a 19–7 record.

Mantle returned from his injury in August, appearing as a pinch hit-ter in a game the Yankees were losing, 10–9. The Yankee Stadium crowd gave Mickey a huge standing ovation and he responded with a game-tying homer, one of his most dramatic. The Yanks went on to win the game. Mantle hit another dramatic pinch-hit homer on September 1 at Memor-ial Stadium in Baltimore to propel the Yanks to another late-inning come-back win, 5–4 over the Orioles. This homer became part of the Mantle legend, because by all accounts he was considerably under the weather when he hit it. Figuring he wouldn't be playing in this game, Mantle had partied long and hard the night before with Ford and some friends of Mickey's who lived on a farm outside of Baltimore. He was half asleep in the dugout the following day when Houk roused him to pinch-hit with a man on in the eighth inning and the Yanks trailing 4–1. After finding his cap (Ford had been sitting on it), Mantle trudged to the plate, armed with Whitey's advice to "swing at the first fastball." Oriole coach and former teammate Hank Bauer had seen Mantle when he arrived at the ballpark and told the Balti-more manager to go ahead and pitch to Mickey because he was in no con-dition to hit. Left-hander Mike McCormick tried to blow a high fastball by Mantle on the first pitch and Mickey hit it out of the park, setting up a game-winning two-run homer by Tresh later in the inning.[3]

Ford reached the 20-win plateau for the second time in his career by beating the Tigers 5–4 in Detroit on September 2, yielding just one earned run in seven innings but having to sweat out the last two innings as the Yankees' bullpen nearly blew the game. Whitey struck out seven, bringing his career total to 1,532 and breaking Red Ruffing's Yankees record of 1,530. What made the win even sweeter was that it came at the expense of Tigers pitcher Frank Lary, who had tormented the Yankees for so many years. Whitey then beat Detroit's Hank Aguirre 2–1 for win No. 21 when the two teams met again at the Stadium four days later.

After beating Kansas City for his 22nd win in his next start, Ford recorded New York's 100th win of the season on September 15 with a neat two-hitter against the Twins in Minnesota, out pitching right-hander Lee Stange 2–1. Third baseman Clete Boyer knocked in both Yankees runs with a second-inning single and Ford made the two runs stand up, yielding one clean single and one scratch single off his glove. The bullpen blew a 4–1 lead in Ford's next outing, but Whitey picked up his 24th win on September 24 with seven shutout innings against the Angels, striking out nine. That game marked the first time since June 1 that Houk had been able to field his regular lineup.

Ford finished the season with a 24–7 record, leading the AL in wins, winning percentage (.774) and innings pitched (269) while recording an ERA of 2.74 (seventh in the AL). His 189 strikeouts ranked fourth in the league and he tied for sixth in complete games with 13. He walked only 1.87 batters per nine innings, well below his previous best. In May, June, July and September, Whitey's record was 20–2. After his bad outing on August 6, Whitey was 8–1 with an ERA of 0.98 in his last 12 starts and allowed more than one earned run only once (in the August 2–1 loss to the Indians).

Although Ford was named the American League Pitcher of the Year by *The Sporting News* and finished third in the American League MVP balloting (behind Elston Howard and Al Kaline), he didn't receive a single vote in the Cy Young Award balloting. At the time there was still only one Cy Young Award for both leagues and Sandy Koufax captured all 20 votes after having his first great season and one of the best pitching seasons of all time. Koufax was 25–5 and led the NL in wins, ERA (1.88) and strikeouts (306) to win the Triple Crown of pitching. His 11 shutouts were the most since 1916 and broke Carl Hubbell's record for shutouts by a left-hander, establishing a mark that still stands. For good measure, on May 11 he tossed a no-hitter against the defending National League champion Giants of Mays, McCovey and Cepeda, retiring the first 22 batters before a walk spoiled his perfect game. These accomplishments earned Sandy the National League MVP Award, one of the few times a pitcher has won it. Since the Dodgers had won the National League pennant by six games over the Cardinals, Ford and Koufax would be facing each other in the World Series.

There were many similarities between these two great left-handers. Both grew up playing baseball on the sandlots of New York City — Ford in Queens and Koufax in Brooklyn. Both battled arm problems that curtailed several seasons and shortened their careers. They finished their careers with nearly identical earned run averages (Ford 2.75, Koufax 2.76) and both were elected to the Hall of Fame. However, Koufax took much longer to reach stardom.

Sandy's primary sport at Lafayette High School was basketball and he was good enough to make the University of Cincinnati freshman basketball team in 1953 as a walk-on. Playing for Ed Jucker (who would coach the Bearcats to consecutive national championships in 1961 and 1962), Koufax showed promise as a 6'2" forward, averaging nearly 10 points a game. In the spring he also played baseball, and after his freshman year he attracted some notice from scouts during the summer while playing sandlot ball. He could throw a ball through a brick wall, though he walked nearly as many as he struck out.

Signed by the Dodgers at age 19 for $20,000 ($14,000 of which was a bonus), Sandy could not be farmed out to the minors because of the then-existing rule requiring that "bonus babies" (any player receiving a bonus in excess of $4,000) be kept by the parent club for two years. The rule was intended to discourage large bonuses so that the poorer teams would not be at a disadvantage in signing new talent. Unfortunately, all the rule did was delay the development of some very talented players such as Koufax and Johnny Antonelli. Instead of learning his craft pitching in the minor leagues as Ford had, Koufax wasted two years sitting on the Dodger bench, winning a total of only four games. After six seasons he had a sub-.500 career record (36–40). He had a tremendous fastball and a vicious curveball, but he hadn't yet learned to control them. He was averaging 5.3 walks per nine innings.

There were periodic stretches of brilliance. He tied Bob Feller's major league record (and broke Dizzy Dean's NL record) by striking out 18 Giants (including 15 of the last 17 batters) to win a crucial game on August 31, 1959; the Dodgers went on to catch the Giants and win the pennant and the World Series. Combined with 13 strikeouts in his previous game and 10 strikeouts in his next game, Sandy also set major league records of 31 strikeouts in two consecutive games and 41 strikeouts in three consecutive games, eclipsing Feller and Walter Johnson. But then he went 8–13 in 1960 and nearly quit baseball.

After working with catcher Norm Sherry during spring training the following year, Sandy finally learned to control his pitches. Sherry convinced him to ease up a little and just concentrate on getting the ball over instead of trying to throw every pitch 100 mph. Sherry's message sunk in during a spring training game against the Minnesota Twins. Sandy walked the first three batters, trying to throw each pitch harder than the last. Sherry came out to the mound and pleaded with Sandy to ease up and just let the batters hit the ball. Koufax relaxed his delivery noticeably and proceeded to strike out the side. After pitching seven no-hit innings, Sandy was sold on a whole new approach to pitching.[4] He led the NL in strikeouts in 1961 with 269 (breaking Christy Mathewson's NL record) and walked only 96 batters in 255 innings while going 18–13.

In 1962 he was the best pitcher in baseball during the first half of the season, winning 14 games by mid-July and striking out 216 batters in only 184 innings. He struck out 18 Cubs on April 24, becoming the first pitcher to twice strike out 18 batters in a game. In May he began to experience numbness in his left index finger, but at first it didn't affect his pitching so Sandy didn't worry about it. Pitching with a completely numb index finger, he threw a no-hitter against the Mets on June 30.

In his second start after the no-hitter, he allowed only two hits against the Giants but had to leave the game in the ninth inning because his hand went numb. Sandy finally went to a vascular specialist, who discovered a giant arterial blood clot in his palm between the thumb and index finger that was almost completely cutting off circulation to the finger. Had Sandy waited a few more days, gangrene would have set in and the finger would have had to be amputated. The injury ended his season, which not only cost him his first 20-win season but also cost the Dodgers the pennant (they lost to the Giants in a playoff). Nevertheless, he won his first ERA title with a mark of 2.54.

When Koufax returned in 1963, he totally dominated National League batters. The Dodgers were 34–6 in games Sandy started, and 22 times he allowed one run or less. Baseball fans were anxious to see how he would do against the Yankees, who were favored to win their third straight Series. He had pitched well in his only previous World Series start, losing 1–0 to the White Sox in 1959. Ford was 10–5 with a 2.31 ERA in nine previous World Series.

Game 1 of the Series was played at Yankee Stadium in front of a capacity crowd of 69,000. Koufax tied a World Series record by fanning the first five Yankees he faced: Kubek, Richardson, Tresh, Mantle and Maris. Ford struck out two in the top half of the first inning but ran into trouble in the second when Frank Howard (the Dodgers' 6'7" outfielder) hit a line drive to straightaway center field that was "the hardest ball that was ever hit off me," according to Ford.[5] It was never high enough to go out but was hit so hard that it struck the center-field wall on the fly (461 feet from the plate) and rebounded 75 feet straight back to Mantle, who nearly threw Howard out at second. Old friend Moose Skowron followed with a run-scoring single to give the Dodgers the lead. Dick Tracewski followed with a single, and then catcher Johnny Roseboro unloaded a three-run homer to give his batterymate an unaccustomed 4–0 lead. Another RBI single by Skowron in the third plated a fifth Dodgers run.

Skowron looked out of place in a Dodgers uniform. He had come up through the Yankee farm system and had helped the Yanks win seven pennants and four World Series championships in his nine seasons with them. "I felt bad playing against guys I played with all my life," he said later.[6]

Koufax didn't allow a base runner until two were out in the fifth. Elston Howard singled to break up the perfect game, and when Joe Pepitone and Bobby Richardson followed with singles to load the bases, the Yanks had a chance to get back in the game. But Hector Lopez (batting for Ford) went down swinging for Koufax's 11th strikeout. The Yanks averted a shutout when Tom Tresh homered with two out in the eighth, but Koufax ended the game with his 15th strikeout, a new World Series record, 10 years to the day after Carl Erskine struck out 14 Yankees. The last victim, pinch-hitter Harry Bright, said after the game: "I waited all my life to get into a World Series, and when I did everybody was rooting for me to strike out." Yogi Berra said: "I can see how he won twenty-five games. What I don't understand is how he lost five."[7]

The Yankees lost Game 2 to an old nemesis, Johnny Podres, who had beaten them twice (including the seventh game) back in the 1955 Series. A fourth-inning homer by Skowron off New York left-hander Al Downing helped the Dodgers to a 4–1 victory that put the Yanks in a deep hole as the Series moved to Los Angeles.

Game 3 matched Don Drysdale against Jim Bouton. This was Bouton's first World Series game, and he was so nervous before the game that teammate Ralph Terry tried to calm him down by telling him: "Jim, just remember that whether you win or lose, there are six hundred million Chinese out there who don't give a shit what happens one way or the other."[8] The 55,912 fans at Dodger Stadium who presumably did care saw a great pitching duel. The Dodgers manufactured a run in the first inning on a walk, a wild pitch and a bad-hop single by Tommy Davis. That was all the scoring in the game, as Drysdale's three-hitter bested Bouton's four-hitter. Joe Pepitone's bid for a game-tying homer with two out in the ninth was caught against the right-field fence.

Therefore, when Koufax and Ford squared off again in Game 4, the Yankees were trying to avoid being swept in four games for the first time in 28 World Series. (In 1922 they had been swept by the Giants, but there had been a tie game.) This time Ford had his good stuff and the two pitchers matched zeroes for the first four innings, with the only hits being a broken-bat single off Ford and a dropped pop fly "double" off Koufax. But in

Ford (left) poses with Sandy Koufax of the Los Angeles Dodgers before the two southpaws squared off in Game 4 of the 1963 World Series. Koufax prevailed for the second time in the Series, winning 2–1 to complete a Los Angeles sweep even though the Dodgers managed just two hits off Ford. (AP/Wide World Photos)

the bottom of the fifth, Frank Howard hit a monstrous 450-foot homer into the upper deck in left to give the Dodgers a 1–0 lead. The way Koufax was pitching it looked like it would be enough, but with one out in the Yankee seventh, Mickey Mantle blasted a fastball from Koufax into the pavilion in left-center, tying the score at 1–1. It was Mantle's 15th World Series home run, tying Babe Ruth's record.

Jim Gilliam opened the Dodgers' half of the seventh with a high chopper to third baseman Clete Boyer. First baseman Joe Pepitone was a little late getting over to the bag and lost sight of Boyer's throw against the background of white shirts in the box seats behind third. The ball hit him on the wrist and bounced away, and by the time Joe chased the ball down, Gilliam had gone all the way to third on the error. "Boyer's throw was perfect," Pepitone said after the game. "I just lost it in the crowd."[9] Willie Davis followed with a deep fly ball to Mantle in center field, whose strong throw to the plate was too late to get the speedy Gilliam. Once again, the Yanks were in a hole against the best pitcher in baseball, with only six more outs.

The Yanks put the tying run on base in each of the last two innings, but Koufax fanned Tresh and Mantle in the ninth and got Hector Lopez to ground to short to end the game and the Series. Koufax had recorded another eight strikeouts and yielded just six hits, but Ford had out pitched him with a two-hitter in defeat. This was one of four World Series games in his career in which Ford pitched brilliantly but was denied victory either because of poor fielding or because a reliever failed to hold a lead. His record total of 10 World Series wins could easily have been 14.

Koufax was voted Most Valuable Player of the Series. When he returned to New York to pick up the award and the new Corvette that went with it, he got a $15 parking ticket outside the restaurant where the ceremony was held, prompting Ford to quip: "Koufax has only two apparent weaknesses. He can't park and he can't hit."[10] (His lifetime batting average was only .097.)

Koufax pitched for three more seasons after the 1963 World Series. In 1964 he was 19–5 with an ERA of 1.74 and 7 shutouts before an elbow injury (incurred diving back into second on a pick-off play) ended his season in mid-August. He also threw his third no-hitter on June 4 against the Phillies, missing a perfect game because of a walk to Richie Allen on a very close 3-and-2 pitch. When his season ended on August 16, Sandy was leading the league in all three Triple Crown categories. Had he not missed his last 12 starts, this might have been his best season.

It was after this injury that it was discovered that Koufax had traumatic arthritis in his left elbow. He had taken his next two turns after the initial injury, but the morning after the second start (a 13-strikeout shutout of the eventual world champion Cardinals), he couldn't straighten his arm. His elbow was swollen to twice its normal size. Tests confirmed the diagnosis, and since there was no cure for traumatic arthritis and since arthroscopic surgery and elbow reconstructions ("Tommy John surgery") did not yet exist, it was clear that Sandy had no long-term future as a pitcher and that even his short-term future was in doubt.

When Koufax returned for the 1965 season, he began the routine that he would follow for the rest of his career. Before each game he would rub his arm with Atomic Balm and take anti-inflammatory drugs, and after the game he would soak his throbbing left arm in an ice bath for 30 minutes, wearing a rubber sleeve to prevent frostbite. He got periodic cortisone shots in the joint. Despite this routine, the elbow would swell after every game and sometimes turn colors. Nevertheless, Koufax refused to alter his every-fourth-day pitching schedule or skip a start, and he pitched more innings that season than any pitcher in either league. At one point he won 11 straight games. He threw eight shutouts, and on September 9 he pitched a perfect game against the Cubs (striking out 14) to become the first pitcher in major league history to pitch four no-hitters. The Dodgers were in the midst of a four-team pennant race at the time, and Sandy struck out the last six batters to nail down both the perfect game and an important 1–0 win. The Dodgers still trailed the Giants by half a game, but three more shutouts by Koufax put the Dodgers in first place and then Sandy came back on two days' rest to clinch the pennant with a 3–1 win over the Braves on the final weekend of the season.

Koufax won his second Triple Crown and led the major leagues in all of the following categories: wins (26), winning percentage (.765), ERA (2.04), strikeouts (382), innings (335.7), and complete games (27). His 382 strikeouts smashed Bob Feller's modern-day record of 348 and Rube Waddell's all-time record of 349 set in 1904, and have been surpassed since only by Nolan Ryan in 1973 (383).

The World Series against the Minnesota Twins started four days later, but the opening game fell on Yom Kippur, the Jewish Day of Atonement. Koufax solidified his status as a Jewish icon by refusing to pitch, and Drysdale got hammered that day in his stead. When Koufax lost Game 2 despite giving up only one earned run, the Dodgers fell behind, two games to none. But Drysdale and Claude Osteen beat the Twins in Games 3 and 4 to even the Series, and then Koufax shut out Minnesota on four hits in Game 5 and came back on two days' rest to pitch a three-hit shutout in Game 7 to give the Dodgers their second world championship in three years. Koufax was again voted World Series MVP and he nearly won the National League MVP Award again as well, finishing second to Willie Mays, who hit 52 home runs that year. The Cy Young Award balloting was no contest, as Koufax again received every vote.

It was after this season that Koufax and Drysdale (who had won 23 games) tried to negotiate their salaries with Dodger owner Walter O'Malley as a pair, represented by a lawyer. This was pre–players' union, pre–Marvin Miller and pre–free agency. Owners refused to deal with agents. Because the reserve clause (which bound players to their teams) had not yet been struck down, the players had little leverage; consequently, salaries were miniscule compared to today's outrageous salaries. Only a few superstars such as Mantle and Mays were making $100,000 per year. Koufax and Drysdale made considerably less and demanded big raises. They figured the Dodgers couldn't do without them, but O'Malley knew they didn't really want to be Hollywood actors (as they threatened to become) and he simply waited them out. They were finally forced to negotiate for themselves, separately, and they both settled for less than they had demanded. Still, they got big increases: Koufax signed for $125,000 and Drysdale for $110,000.[11]

To put these salaries into perspective, Koufax's final season at that new salary brought his total career earnings to $430,500 for his 12 years with the Dodgers.[12] During the 2004 season, Pedro Martinez of the Red Sox was paid $17.5 million, which worked out to $530,303 for each of his 33 starts. Imagine getting the entire career of Sandy Koufax for $100,000 less than the price of one Pedro Martinez start.

While Koufax and Drysdale were only partially successful in their joint salary negotiation, it had far-reaching ramifications for the economics of baseball. This was the first real challenge to the baseball establishment, and its partial success opened the eyes of the players and helped pave the way for the hiring of Marvin Miller as executive director of the Players Association, the 1969 challenge of the reserve clause by Curt Flood, and the 1975 arbitration decision that liberated Andy Messersmith and Dave McNally and led to the advent of free agency. In 1976, the owners insisted on language in the Players Association contract that would preclude joint negotiation by players, repeatedly citing the Koufax-Drysdale negotiations as an example of why the clause was necessary. Miller agreed, on the condition that reciprocal language be added that would preclude the owners from acting in concert as well. This latter clause backfired on the owners in 1985 when they were forced to pay $280 million to settle a collusion case. "We have Koufax and Drysdale to thank," said Miller.[13]

In his final season of 1966, Koufax again led the major leagues in wins (27), complete games (27), strikeouts (317), innings (323) and ERA (1.73). He was the first pitcher in major league history to win five consecutive ERA titles. Only two other pitchers in baseball history have won three Triple Crowns — Grover Cleveland Alexander and Walter Johnson. Once again the Dodgers were embroiled in a three-way pennant race (with the Giants and Pirates), and once again they needed a superhuman effort from Koufax down the stretch to get them into the World Series. He won six games in September, clinching the pennant on the final day of the season by beating the Phillies on only two days' rest. Sandy won his third unanimous Cy Young Award in four years and narrowly lost the MVP Award to Roberto Clemente despite receiving more first-place votes. It was after this season that Major League Baseball decided that a separate Cy Young Award was needed for each league.

The Dodgers were swept by the Baltimore Orioles in the World Series, with Koufax losing Game 2 to Jim Palmer despite allowing only one earned run in his final game. The Dodgers made six errors behind him in six innings that day, leading to three unearned runs. But with Koufax, as with Ford, there were never any histrionics on the mound, no glaring at teammates who had committed errors. He simply called for the ball and got ready for his next pitch.

Although Ford holds most World Series pitching records because of the number of Series he pitched in (11), Koufax's record in his eight World Series starts was also remarkable: an ERA of 0.95, with 61 strikeouts and only 36 hits allowed in 57 innings pitched. With a little support, his 4–3 record could easily have been 8–0.

Shortly after the Series, Koufax retired at the age of 30, fearing that if he continued to pitch he might lose the use of his left arm for the rest of his life. At his retirement press conference, he said: "I've got a lot of years to live after baseball, and I would like to live them with complete use of my body. I don't regret one minute of the last twelve years, but I think I would regret one year that was too many."[14] In 1972 at the age of 36, Sandy became the youngest player ever inducted into the Hall of Fame.

Koufax's final record was 165–87; his winning percentage of .655 was the sixth best in the 20th century among pitchers with at least 200 decisions. After his rocky start, his winning percentage during his last six years was an incredible .733. Among his contemporaries, Sandy's career ERA of 2.76 was bested only by Ford (2.75), with Juan Marichal (2.89), Bob Gibson (2.91) and Warren Spahn (3.09) trailing behind. His career average of 9.28 strikeouts per nine innings was the major league record until Nolan Ryan (9.55) broke it, and his average of 6.79 hits allowed per nine innings is second only to Ryan (6.56).[15]

While Koufax's arm problems prevented him from achieving career totals anywhere near those of Warren Spahn, the last five years of Koufax's career may have been the best five consecutive seasons recorded by any pitcher in major league history, although on a purely statistical basis, Walter Johnson and Lefty Grove both had better five-year runs. (See chart on page 174 for a comparison of great five-year pitching runs.) He was 111–34 with an ERA of 1.95 during this period, and he accumulated 100 complete games, 33 shutouts, four no-hitters and 1,444 strikeouts. His five-year haul of five ERA titles, three Triple Crowns, three unanimous Cy Young Awards, two World Series MVP Awards and one NL MVP Award will be hard to equal. What makes his record all the more remarkable is that during the last four of those years, the Dodgers scored fewer runs than any team in the National League except for the two new expansion teams (New York and Houston), yet L.A. was 114–36 (.760) in the 150 games that Koufax started, mostly because Sandy allowed just one run or less in nearly half of those games. The most telling measure of how much Koufax meant to the Dodgers is that the season after he retired, they dropped all the way to eighth place.

Despite Koufax's brilliance over his last five seasons, Ford's career numbers were better. He had more wins, a better winning percentage and a slightly better ERA. He also had more "good" seasons: 10 seasons in which he won at least 16 games (versus five for Koufax), 12 seasons with at least six more wins than losses (versus five for Koufax), and 16 consecutive seasons in which his ERA was at least three-quarters of a run better than the league average (versus five for Koufax). At his peak, Koufax was the more spectacular of the two, but Ford was "Steady Eddie" for 16 seasons and one of the best "money" pitchers of all time. During the 1963 season, both were money in the bank. Koufax got the better of Ford in the World Series, but if not for the error by Pepitone, it might have been a standoff.

Best Five Consecutive Seasons

Pitcher	Team	Years	W	L	Win %	Net Team Win %	Pitcher Wins	ERA	League ERA	Pitching Runs
Walter Johnson	Wash. Senators	1911-'15	149	63	.703	.472	49.0	1.54	3.05	294
Lefty Grove	Phil. Athletics	1928-'32	128	33	.795	.626	27.2	2.56	4.36	282
Sandy Koufax	L.A. Dodgers	1962-'66	111	34	.766	.542	32.5	1.95	3.58	246
Pedro Martinez	Boston Red Sox	1999-'03	82	21	.796	.520	28.4	2.10	4.65	266
Randy Johnson	Seattle/Hous./Ariz.	1998-'02	100	38	.725	.535	26.2	2.63	4.43	255
Grover Alexander	Phil. Phillies	1913-'17	143	58	.711	.512	40.0	1.91	2.81	178
Christy Mathewson	New York Giants	1908-'12	138	51	.730	.599	24.8	1.71	2.95	217
Greg Maddux	Atlanta Braves	1993-'97	89	33	.730	.595	16.5	2.13	4.17	262
Hal Newhouser	Detroit Tigers	1944-'48	118	56	.678	.526	26.4	2.35	3.66	212
Mordecai Brown	Chicago Cubs	1906-'10	127	44	.743	.678	11.1	1.42	2.61	196

Net Team Win percentage: The winning percentage of a pitcher's team in games in which he is not involved in the decision.

Pitcher Wins: The difference between a pitcher's winning percentage and his team's net team win percentage, multiplied by the pitcher's total number of decisions. This statistic measures the number of extra wins that a pitcher earned for his team beyond the number that the other members of the team's pitching staff would have won (on average) in the same number of decisions.

Pitching Runs: The difference between a pitcher's ERA and the league's ERA, multiplied by his total innings divided by nine. This statistic measures the number of runs that the pitcher saved his team over the course of the season, as compared to the average pitcher in the league over the same number of innings.

THIRTEEN

Chasing Ruth Again

After breaking Babe Ruth's consecutive scoreless innings record in Game 4 of the 1961 World Series, Ford had joked that "maybe I'll get together with Wally Moses (the Yankees' batting coach) next spring and work on my hitting so I can go after some of the Babe's batting records, too."[1] In 1964, Whitey did make a run at another one of the Babe's most cherished records—his American League record for shutouts in a season by a left-hander. Ruth's record of nine shutouts (established in 1916) had stood for 48 years, although it had been threatened by Ford in 1958, when he had seven by early August before a sore elbow derailed him. Of course, Ford didn't start the 1964 season with this record in mind and he probably barely gave it a thought even as he approached it, but Whitey did some of the very best pitching of his career that season before injuries once again ruined what might otherwise have been his finest season.

Ford had some extra duties to worry about that spring. Yogi Berra had retired at the end of the previous season after 18 seasons in pinstripes and had been named the Yankees' manager when Ralph Houk was moved up to the front office as general manager. Berra had asked Ford to double as pitching coach and Whitey had accepted the responsibilities, hoping to do whatever he could to help his long-time friend and batterymate succeed as manager.

The Yankees opened the season at home against Boston with Ford going for career win number 200 in Berra's managerial debut. The field was so soggy due to two days of steady rain that two second-inning pop flies hit by the Red Sox stuck in the mud upon landing with a run scoring on each. However, the Yanks battled back to tie the game at 3–3 and send the game into extra innings, with Ford still on the hill. Because of the sodden outfield turf, Mantle couldn't quite reach a fly ball to deep center in the top of the 11th that he normally would have caught and the ball fell for a one-out triple. Whitey then threw a sinker to Dick Williams that bounced off the plate and got by Howard, scoring what held up as the winning run.

The Yanks stumbled through the first week of the season and were actually in last place with a 1–4 record when Ford faced the White Sox in

Ford warms up during spring training in preparation for the 1964 season.
(National Baseball Hall of Fame Library, Cooperstown, N.Y.)

his second start of the season, opposed by Chicago ace (and 1963 ERA
leader) Gary Peters. Clete Boyer broke up a scoreless duel with a fifth-
inning home run and Whitey blanked the White Sox on six hits, 3–0, for
his 200th major league win. Although 59 previous pitchers had reached
that milestone (many of them before the turn of the century), none had done
so with as few losses.[2] After reaching the century mark with only 36 losses,
Ford had won his next 100 games with 43 losses, giving him a record of

Ford talks to reporters on May 1, 1964, after two-hitting the Washington Senators 1–0 for his second of eight shutouts that season, nine days after reaching the
200-win mark with the fewest losses of any 200-game winner in major league
history. (AP/Wide World Photos)

200–79 for a winning percentage of .717, which was significantly higher
than Lefty Grove's modern baseball record for pitchers with at least 200
decisions. (Former Yankee pitcher Spud Chandler had a winning percentage of .717 during his abbreviated career, in which he went 109–43.) The
only pitcher before or since to come close to matching Ford's record at the
200-win mark was Grove, who reached 200 wins with 83 losses, a winning
percentage of .707. Grove went on to win exactly 100 more games but lost
another 58 to finish his career with a record of 300–141, a winning percentage of .680.

The shutout against Chicago was the start of perhaps the best two
months of Ford's career. He had won 13 straight games within a two-month

period in 1961 and 12 straight within two months in 1963, but he pitched
better between April 22 and June 20 in 1964. He pitched a masterful two-
hit 1–0 shutout against the Washington Senators on May 1, striking out
eight. After yielding ground ball hits to Ken Hunt in the second inning and
Don Zimmer in the third, Whitey pitched no-hit ball the rest of the way.
He nearly duplicated the effort in his next start against the Tigers (carrying a two-hit shutout and a 2–0 lead into the eighth inning), but got
knocked out in the ninth inning and settled for a no-decision when the
Yankees won the game in the 10th, 4–3.

Ford picked up his third win of the season in a 6–2 win over the Indians but encountered the first sign of an injury that would become more serious as the season progressed. Leading 5–1 after six innings, Whitey removed
himself from the game as a precautionary measure because his right hip had
stiffened up. The hip was okay in his next outing four days later against the
Tigers and he retired the first 12 batters in a game played in 48-degree weather.
However, an infield hit and a misjudged fly ball put him in a jam in the fifth
inning and he wild-pitched in the tying run. The game ended in a 1–1 tie when
it was halted after six innings due to rain. Ford threw only six wild pitches
all season, but this was the second one that had cost him a win.

Ford got back on the winning track with a four-hit shutout on May
17, beating Kansas City 8–0 at the Stadium behind Joe Pepitone's two home
runs. But then Whitey strained his right hip again against the Los Angeles
Angels and took himself out after three innings in a game the Yanks won,
4–3. The hip hurt when he planted his right leg at the end of every pitch.

Ford took his regular turn four days later against Cleveland at Yankee
Stadium in a game enlivened by a controversy concerning Whitey's wedding ring. As he admitted years later in his autobiography *Slick,* it wasn't
his actual wedding ring but rather a substitute that had been made for him
by a jeweler friend of one of Whitey's closest friends. With all the physical
problems that he was beginning to have as he neared the end of the line at
the age of 35, Ford was looking for any advantage that would help him
maintain his edge against the hitters. He had found that the slightest nick
or cut on the surface of the ball would give the pitch a little extra move-
ment, usually downward. The "wedding ring" (worn on his glove hand) had
a rasp on one of the edges that Whitey used to scratch the ball while he was
"rubbing it up." Most of his own teammates didn't even know what was
going on; in fact, Pepitone had innocently tossed a cut ball to the first-base
umpire in an earlier game and got some rather pointed advice from Whitey
in the dugout at the end of the inning.[3]

Ford had thus far avoided detection but ran into trouble against the
Indians when opposing pitcher Mudcat Grant noticed a nick in the ball
when he came out to start an inning. Cleveland manager Alvin Dark began

to save foul balls hit into the dugout, and when he had several cut balls he went out to talk to plate umpire John Rice and the two of them converged on the mound to confront Ford with the evidence. They definitely noticed the ring: the next day's *New York Times* reported that "Whitey Ford was accused by the Indians of defacing new baseballs with his wedding ring."[4] However, they didn't notice the rasp (which was concealed by tape) and Whitey convinced them that the ring was just his wedding ring. I suspect that both Dark and Rice knew better, but Ford was such a respected and popular player that neither wanted to make a big deal out of the incident. Dark had made his point and Whitey knew the jig was up. He gave the ring to trainer Joe Soares, who got rid of the evidence.[5]

Ford not only lost his cutting tool in this game but also was deprived of a win when the Indians tied the game 2–2 in the seventh inning when Grant was called safe at first on what appeared to be an inning-ending double play. Ford gave way to reliever Pete Mikkelsen with one out in the top of the ninth after striking out 10, and Mikkelsen picked up the win when the Yanks won the game in the bottom half of the inning.

Ford was not above trying to get a slight advantage against the hitters but he certainly didn't need to cut the ball to win. Pitching totally on the up-and-up (except for an occasional mud ball), he won his next six starts, allowing a total of four earned runs in 50 innings and lowering his earned run average all the way down to 1.39. First he beat Kansas City 9–1 with a five-hitter, losing a shutout when an error by Clete Boyer on an easy grounder gave the Athletics their run. He followed that up with his fourth shutout of the season (beating Minnesota 3–0 with a four-hitter on June 3), and then beat the Angels 9–3 for his seventh straight win.

The shutouts kept on coming. The White Sox came to town in first place, five games ahead of the third-place Yankees, who were only six games over .500 after 48 games. Ford threw a four-hit shutout in the second game of a Friday night double-header and the Yanks swept the five-game weekend series to draw even with Chicago, one game behind Baltimore. After allowing one earned run in a 7–5 win over Boston, Whitey pitched a gem in Chicago on June 20, shutting out the White Sox 1–0 in 11 innings for his 10th straight win. Ford out dueled Gary Peters as he spaced out six hits and fanned nine for his sixth shutout of the year and the 40th of his career, tying the Yankee record held by Red Ruffing. Among active pitchers, only Warren Spahn (with 63) had more career shutouts than Whitey. It was the fourth straight time (including one at the end of the previous season) that Ford had shut out the White Sox, the team that would battle the Yankees down to the final weekend of the season. They hadn't scored off him in 43 innings.

Ford had now started 15 games since his Opening Day loss and the Yankees had won 14 and tied one. They were 21–22 in games not started by their pitching coach. With the season barely one-third over (104 games remained on the schedule), Ford was 10–1 with a 1.39 ERA and six shutouts, and it seemed certain that he would eclipse his 1961 and 1963 seasons. The Cy Young Award race appeared to be between Ford and Sandy Koufax (who was 9–4 with four shutouts and an ERA of 1.84), with Whitey having the clear edge. Kansas City manager Eddie Lopat (Ford's former teammate and mentor) declared: "Whitey is a better pitcher now than he's ever been in his life."[6]

As it turned out, this was the statistical apex of Ford's career. His career record stood at 209–79, for an unheard-of winning percentage of .726. No one would have believed that from that point on, Ford would have a record of 27–27 for the remainder of his career.

The day after Ford's masterpiece, the Yanks continued their total domination of the White Sox (9–0 on the season) by sweeping a double-header to move into first place for the first time all season. A homer by Mantle helped Jim Bouton win the first game 2–0 and then Al Downing and Bill Stafford combined to win the nightcap 2–1 in 17 innings. Ford's pitching staff was starting to come around and Mantle was getting hot. After undergoing off-season surgery on his left knee, Mickey had been in and out of the lineup all season with one pulled muscle after another in addition to his bad knee. The homer against Chicago was his fifth in 11 days since coming back from his latest injury and his 13th of the season.

Ford's great season began to unravel on June 24 in Baltimore. He was clearly not himself and was pounded for four runs on seven hits in just two innings of work, although the Yanks eventually tied the game and got him off the hook, preserving his winning streak. But he fared little better in his next start, yielding four more runs in just three innings against the Tigers at the Stadium. Once again he escaped with a no-decision as the Yanks came back to win the game 5–4, aided by Mantle's 15th homer of the season.

Ford got off to another rocky start on July 1 against the A's, yielding two first-inning runs. But Mantle hit number 16 with a man on in the bottom half of the inning to give his buddy a 3–2 lead and Ford settled down and held that lead through seven innings, after which he came out of the game due to the heat. Unfortunately the bullpen couldn't hold the lead and the Yanks lost when Ralph Terry served up a gopher ball in the 11th inning.

Mantle continued his hot hitting, celebrating July 4 at the Stadium by hitting a ball into the third deck in right field with two on and two out in the bottom of the eighth inning to beat Minnesota, 7–5. Ford, however, continued to struggle. His 10-game winning streak came to an end on July 5 against the Twins, who rocked him for eight hits and four runs in four innings. This time his teammates were unable to bail him out. The Yanks broke for the All-Star Game in third place, three games behind Baltimore

and percentage points in back of Chicago. Mantle, Howard and Richardson all started for the American League in the All-Star Game (played at
Shea Stadium), but Ford, though selected for the team, opted to rest his
tired arm.

Ford rallied briefly after the All-Star break. He beat Washington 4–1
on July 10 but needed relief help from Bill Stafford after aggravating the
pulled muscle in his right hip again in the sixth inning. The hip seemed
fine in his next start five days later, a first-place showdown against the Orioles at Yankee Stadium. He needed just 98 pitches to temporarily move the
Yanks past the Birds as he threw a three-hitter to best southpaw Dave
McNally, 2–0. He walked none and retired 19 men in a row at one point as
he moved past Ruffing on the Yankee shutout list with his 41st. With almost
exactly half the season left (80 games), Ford was 12–2 with an ERA of 1.92.
Mantle scored the winning run after a single and a stolen base and was hitting an unbelievable .515 for the season right-handed and .334 overall.

It would be 41 days before Ford won another game, and the Yanks went
20–21 during this period to stumble along in third place behind the Orioles
and the White Sox. His slump started with a game against Cleveland that
looked like a mismatch: Ford against the eighth-place Indians and a rookie
hurler just called up from the Pacific Coast League and making his major
league debut. The two teams were playing a double-header at the Stadium
that day and pitching coach Ford gave Rollie Sheldon the task of facing "Sudden Sam" McDowell while Whitey got the rookie. After Sheldon beat
McDowell 6–2 in the opener, things didn't work out as planned for coach
Ford as rookie Luis Tiant pitched a four-hit 3–0 shutout for the first of his
229 major league wins. Whitey was out of sync again and removed himself
after the fifth inning. His troubles worsened in his next start when his hip
strain flared up again and he had to come out after only two innings in a
Yankees win over Detroit.

Whitey took himself out of the rotation and rested the hip for 11 days
before testing it against the A's in Kansas City. Mantle's 22nd homer of the
season gave Ford a 1–0 lead in the sixth inning but two walks and two Yankees errors led to three runs off Ford and another loss, his fourth of the season. He said after the game that his hip had hurt from the fourth inning
on and that he would likely miss his start in the upcoming series against
Baltimore, with whom they were neck-and-neck.[7]

To no one's surprise, Ford gave it a go against the Orioles after the
Yanks lost the first game of the series. This time Whitey felt a sharp pain
in his hip right from the start and he removed himself after pitching two
scoreless innings. The Yanks lost the game in 10 innings and fell to third
place, behind the White Sox. Worse still, it was obvious that Ford would
need to be removed from the rotation again for several weeks and the Yanks

faced 13 games against Baltimore and Chicago in the next 12 days. In addition to Ford's problems, Bill Stafford was injured and Stan Williams had been ineffective (1–5). The Yankee brass decided to bring right-hander Mel Stottlemyre up from their Richmond farm club, where he was burning up the International League with a 13–3 record and 1.45 ERA.[8]

After splitting a double-header with Baltimore, the Yanks dropped both ends of a double-header against Chicago. In desperation, Berra started Stottlemyre on August 12 against the White Sox at the Stadium, and the rookie responded with a 7–3 complete-game win in his major league debut. He was not the big story, however, as Mantle switch-hit homers in the same game for the 10th and final time in his career, a major league record until Eddie Murray broke it in 1994. The left-handed shot (off Ray Herbert) traveled straight over the 461-foot sign in dead-center field and landed 15 rows deep in the bleachers, 502 feet from home plate.[9] The only other ball ever hit into those bleachers in the long history of Yankee Stadium had also been hit there by Mantle, but the other one (back on June 21, 1955) had been hit *right-handed.*

Three days later, Mantle hurt his left knee, causing him to miss a week. It was the seventh time that season that he had been sidelined with an injury. Maris was also having increasing physical problems and was having a very poor year, particularly against left-handers, against whom Berra occasionally sat him down. Just three years after his 61-homer, 142-RBI season, Roger was struggling through a season in which he had only 15 homers and 40 RBIs in early August.

On August 17 the Yanks went into Chicago for an important four-game series. With Mantle unable to play, the Yanks dropped all four games to fall four and one half games behind the White Sox and four games behind the Orioles. Ford pitched three innings in the final game of the series, and though he said the hip felt better, he was clearly rusty after not pitching for 12 days and was hit hard. His record fell to 12–5, after being 10–1 on June 20.

It was on the bus to the Chicago airport after the fourth loss that the famous Phil Linz harmonica incident occurred. Linz had just bought a harmonica and he started to play "Mary Had a Little Lamb" in the back of the bus. Berra (sitting in front) turned around and told him to shove the harmonica up his ass, but Linz didn't hear what he said and asked Mantle to repeat it. Mickey told him: "He says if you're going to play that harmonica, play it louder," which Linz proceeded to do. An enraged Berra stormed to the back of the bus and knocked the harmonica out of Linz's hand. It was the first time he showed that he had made a complete transition from teammate and buddy to manager, and it proved to be a turning point in the Yankees' season. (Plus Linz got a $5,000 endorsement contract from a harmonica company out of the incident, which far outweighed the $200 fine that Berra levied on him.)

Things got a little worse before they got better. The Yanks lost the first two games of a four-game series against the Red Sox at Fenway Park, extending their losing streak to six and dropping them six games off the pace with only 41 games remaining. But Mantle had returned to the lineup (hobbling and playing left field instead of center) and he and Maris each homered and drove in three runs to help Stottlemyre end the skid with an 8–0 shutout. Mickey added a two-run homer the following day to jump-start a 4–3 Yankees win in the series finale.

The momentum gained by New York in the last two games in Boston got a significant boost when Ford returned to form two days later against the Senators at Yankee Stadium. His hip problem had been diagnosed as a calcium deposit but X-ray treatments and rest had improved his condition enough so that he could finally land on his right foot without a stabbing pain in his hip. He pitched eight solid innings, yielding but five hits and striking out seven, but trailed 1–0 until the Yanks erupted for four runs in the bottom of the eighth to give Ford his first win in six weeks. He followed up that effort with seven shutout innings as the Yanks swept a doubleheader from the Red Sox on August 29, with Pepitone hitting three homers in the twin bill. Mantle hit his 28th homer of the season in the first game but later achieved the dubious distinction of tying Babe Ruth's career record of 1,330 strikeouts, reaching that total in 650 fewer games than the Babe. New York still trailed Baltimore by four games and Chicago by two and a half.

After the Yanks lost two out of three in Los Angeles, Ford opened a three-game series in Kansas City on September 4 and turned a 5–3 lead over to the bullpen in the seventh inning. Unfortunately Pete Mikkelsen yielded a game-tying homer to Ken "Hawk" Harrelson with two out in the ninth and the Yanks needed to work overtime to win the game, thus depriving Ford of his 15th win. The win by New York was the first of five straight wins that propelled them to within a game of the first-place Orioles, but then Detroit southpaw Mickey Lolich pitched his third consecutive shutout to beat the Yanks 4–0, with the Tigers scoring all of their runs in the seventh inning to break up a scoreless duel between Lolich and Ford.

In early September, the Yanks fortified their bullpen by trading for Pedro Ramos, who was nearing the end of his career. Pedro was glad to finally be on the same team as Mantle, who had hit 12 homers off him in his career. Ramos paid his first dividend when he had to take over for Ford in the fifth inning of a game against Minnesota on September 13 after Whitey bruised his right heel beating out a hit. The Yanks were leading 4–1 at the time, but rather than try to pitch one more inning in order to be eligible for the win, Whitey removed himself. "He's good, he tells you," said Berra appreciatively. "Another guy might stay in and try to pick up the win. But he tells you right away when he's not right."[10] Ramos pitched the last five innings and picked up his first win as a Yankee.

The Yankees' charge toward the top was momentarily stalled on September 15 when Dean Chance of the Angels two-hit them, 7–0. Chance was having a second half that was even better than Ford's first half and he had dominated the Yanks that season like no pitcher before or since. He had beaten New York four times, including three shutouts, and in a fifth game had pitched 14 scoreless innings without getting a decision. In that game, a seventh-inning single by Roger Maris was the only hit Chance allowed through 11 innings, and in all he allowed only three hits and struck out 12 before leaving for a pinch hitter and watching the Angels lose the game in the 15th. In 50 innings he had allowed the Yanks just 14 hits and one solitary run (a homer by Mantle) for an ERA of 0.18. Though Chance would finish the season with just 20 wins pitching for the fifth-place Angels, he recorded 11 shutouts (five of them by a 1–0 score), matching Ed Walsh (1908) and Walter Johnson (1913) for the second-best mark in American League history behind Jack Coombs' 1910 record of 13. His ERA of 1.65 was nearly two runs below the league average of 3.63 and was the lowest in either league since Walter Johnson in 1919, with the exception of Spud Chandler's 1.64 ERA in the watered-down World War II 1943 season. With the two mid-season Cy Young Award front-runners (Ford and Koufax) both derailed by injuries, Chance would walk away with the award.

The Yanks resumed their charge the following day and surged into first place on September 17 with a 6–2 win over the Angels at the Stadium. Mantle led the way with a double, a single (his 2,000th hit) and a two-run homer (his 450th). He was the fifth Yankee to reach 2,000 hits (Ruth, Gehrig, DiMaggio and Berra were the others) and the third Yankee to hit 450 homers, trailing only Ruth and Gehrig.

Recovered from his bruised heel, Ford kept the momentum going the following night by throwing his eighth shutout of the season, an efficient 6–0 win over the A's in which only one Kansas City runner got as far as third base. The eight shutouts tied the Yankees' record set by Russ Ford in 1910 and were only one less than Ruth's AL record for left-handers. Were it not for the shutout he had lost due to an error back on May 30, Whitey would have been tied with the Babe.

After Jim Bouton kept the winning streak going two days later with a two-hit shutout over Kansas City, Ford beat Cleveland 8–1 for his 16th win of the season behind four Yankees home runs, including Mantle's 33rd of the season. When Stottlemyre pitched a two-hit shutout (while going 5-for-5 at the plate) to beat Washington 7–0 on September 26, the Yanks had won 11 straight games (and 19 out of 22) to take a four-game lead over both Baltimore and Chicago in the AL standings with just eight games to play.

The Washington Senators finally ended New York's winning streak on September 27 despite the best efforts of Ford and Mantle. Whitey allowed just one run on four hits in seven innings and Mantle hit his 34th homer and an RBI double, but the Yankees' bullpen let this one slip away in 11 innings, 3–2. That cut the Yanks' lead over both of their pursuers to three games. They left the door open by splitting their next four games and then sent their money pitcher to the mound in the opener of a three-game series against Cleveland on the final weekend of the regular season, needing to win two of the three games to win the pennant. Ford fell behind 1–0 in the first inning and then an unearned run in the second inning doubled the deficit. However, the Yanks erupted for five runs in the third inning and Whitey was nearly perfect over the final seven innings, allowing just one walk and retiring the last 16 batters he faced without a ball leaving the infield. The 5–2 win clinched at least a tie for the pennant. When they beat Cleveland again on Saturday, they had their 29th AL flag, completing a remarkable comeback. The White Sox finished one game behind, with the Orioles another game back.

In his last nine starts coming down the stretch, Whitey was 5–1 with an ERA of 1.55, allowing more than one run only twice. He finished with a 17–6 record and an ERA of 2.13, third in the league behind Chance and Chicago's Joel Horlen. His winning percentage of .739 and his eight shutouts were both second-best in the AL. Although this was an excellent season for Whitey, one couldn't help but wonder (as in 1958) what he might have accomplished if not for his injury problems.

Mantle finished with 35 homers, third in the AL behind Harmon Killebrew and Boog Powell. He was also third in RBIs with 111 (trailing Brooks Robinson by seven), and fourth in batting at .303 (20 points behind Tony Oliva). Had he not missed 21 games completely and appeared only as a pinch-hitter in many others, a Triple Crown was not out of the question. His on base percentage of .426 was the best in the majors. For the third time in his career, Mickey finished second in the MVP balloting, behind Oriole third baseman Brooks Robinson. Elston Howard finished third in the balloting.

Mantle and Ford were not the only late-season heroes. Maris hit 11 homers and knocked in 31 runs from early August on. Stottlemyre went 9–3 with an ERA of 2.06 after being called up in mid-August and Pedro Ramos won or saved nine games in September with an ERA of 1.25. Unfortunately, Ramos had been acquired by the Yankees after the September 1 deadline and would not be eligible for the World Series. Neither would shortstop Tony Kubek be available for the Series: he had injured his wrist in a fit of anger during a late September slump.

Over in the National League, one of the most amazing pennant races in years took place. The Dodgers were the defending champions, but injuries and a drop-off in performance from some key players gradually dropped them out of the race. They eventually finished tied for sixth. The race was between the Cardinals, Phillies, Reds, Giants and Braves, and it went right down to the final day with three teams still in contention.

The Cardinals started slowly and in mid-June were in seventh place with a sub-.500 record. Then St. Louis general manager Bing Devine made a trade that eventually turned the team around, although ironically it was initially ridiculed by Cardinals fans. Looking to inject more speed into his lineup, Devine sent pitcher Ernie Broglio (18–8 the previous season) to the Cubs in exchange for Lou Brock, a .258 hitter with only 37 RBIs the previous year. As it turned out, it was one of the most-lopsided deals ever — in the Cardinals' favor. Broglio won only seven more games in the majors, losing 19. Meanwhile, Cardinals manager Johnny Keane turned Brock loose on the base paths and he went on to become one of the greatest base stealers of all time, leading the NL eight times and setting stolen base records for a season (118) and career (938). He also hit .293 lifetime and was subsequently inducted into the Hall of Fame. All he did for the Cardinals during the remainder of the 1964 season was hit .348, steal 33 bases and score 81 runs. Still, the Cards continued to play .500 ball and in late August were still mired in fifth place, eleven games behind the first-place Phillies.

In addition to having a powerful lineup that included Johnny Callison, Richie Allen and Frank Thomas (acquired in August from the Mets), the Phillies had the deepest pitching staff in the league, featuring Jim Bunning (who had pitched a perfect game against the Mets on Father's Day), Chris Short, Ray Culp, Art Mahaffey and Dennis Bennett. Culp and Bennett came down with sore arms in September but Philadelphia hung tough, and when Bunning won his 18th game against the Dodgers on September 20, the Phillies still had a six-and-a-half-game lead over the Reds and a seven-game lead over the Cardinals, with only 12 games left to play. But then the Phillies pulled one of the biggest chokes of all time, losing 10 straight games. In the final two weeks of the season, manager Gene Mauch six times pitched either Bunning or Short on only two days' rest instead of sticking to his normal rotation, and the Phillies lost all six games.

On the final day of the season, the Reds and Cards were tied and the Phillies were one game back, and the potential existed for the first three-way tie in history if the Phillies beat the Reds and the Mets beat the Cards. Bunning finally pitched with his normal rest and shut out the Reds 10–0 for his 19th victory. The Reds and Phils finished in a tie at 92–70. The Cards were 92–69 when they started their game with the Mets. They fell behind 3–2 in the fifth inning, but Bob Gibson came on in relief and shut down the Mets while his teammates exploded for nine runs to win the game, 11–5, and the pennant.

After the frantic finishes to both pennant races, the two survivors had only a few days to regroup for the World Series. In Game 1 at Busch Stadium, Whitey Ford pitched his eighth World Series opener. He was opposed by Ray Sadecki (20–11), since Gibson had pitched twice in the previous five days to help the Cards get into the Series. Despite Whitey's great pitching down the stretch, he had not been as dominating as he had been in the first half of the season and he was not 100 percent healthy. In the latter part of August, he had begun experiencing numbness in the fingers of his left hand, making it difficult to grip the ball properly. It was the first sign of the circulatory problems that would eventually end his career.[11]

The Cards nicked Ford for a run in the first inning on a sacrifice fly by Ken Boyer, but the Yanks came back with three in the second on a two-run homer by Tom Tresh and an RBI single by Ford. A throwing error by Mantle in right helped the Cards narrow the gap to 3–2, but the Yanks added a run in the fifth on singles by Mantle and Howard and a double by Tresh, and Ford held the 4–2 lead into the last of the sixth inning. Then the roof fell in on him.

After Boyer led off with a single, Ford made Bill White his 94th and final World Series strikeout victim, a record that still stands. But then he hung a slider to Mike Shannon, who hit a tremendous home run off the Budweiser sign atop the scoreboard at the back of the left-field bleachers, tying the game. Whitey was losing the feeling in his arm, but he pitched to one more batter, allowing a double to Tim McCarver. When he got the ball back, suddenly he didn't have the strength to grab it out of his glove. According to Ford: "Suddenly my left hand went numb; it just went dead. No blood was getting down from the shoulder: the artery was blocked. The blood was just coming down through the little capillaries, and I didn't have a pulse for a year."[12] He was replaced by Al Downing and walked off the mound for the last time in a World Series game. Carl Warwick pinch-hit for Sadecki and singled in Boyer, and then Curt Flood was credited with a triple on a routine fly ball to left field that Tresh lost in the sun, making the score 6–4.

There was concern for Ford in the clubhouse because numbness in the left arm is a classic sign of a heart attack. Although the problem was determined not to be a heart attack, it was obviously a serious circulatory problem that would need to get checked out. The Yankees held out some hope that Whitey would make a miraculous recovery and be able to pitch again in the Series, but it didn't happen.

After Ford's departure, the Yanks tried to come back. In the seventh, Mantle hit a ball off the screen in right, but was limping so badly that he only got a single out of it and the Yanks couldn't bring him around. They cut the lead to 6–5 the following inning on a pinch double by Johnny Blanchard and a single by Bobby Richardson, but before they could get their final shot in the ninth, the Cards tagged the weak New York bullpen for three more runs in the bottom of the eighth, aided by two walks and an error. (The Yanks missed Pedro Ramos in this game, and throughout the Series.) The final score was 9–5, and since Ford had put the go-ahead run on base before leaving, he was saddled with his fourth straight Series loss.

Bob Gibson and Mel Stottlemyre faced each other in Game 2, the first of three times they would do so in the Series. The fact that Berra picked Stottlemyre over Bouton (who was 18–13 during the regular season) showed the confidence the Yankees had in their rookie hurler. Stottlemyre's nine wins (including several crucial ones) after being brought up with eight weeks left in the season had been reminiscent of Ford's 9–1 record after being called up midway through the 1950 season. Just as the Yanks wouldn't have won the pennant in 1950 without Ford, they never could have held off the White Sox and Orioles in 1964 without Stottlemyre.

This was the first of Gibson's nine career World Series starts (of which he won seven), and he was sharp in the first two innings, fanning Richardson, Maris, Mantle, Howard and Tresh. Stottlemyre was sharp as well, retiring the first six Cardinals in order.

The game turned on a controversial play in the top of the sixth inning with the score tied 1–1. With Mantle on first and one out, umpire Bill McKinley ruled that Joe Pepitone had been hit on the thigh by a pitch. Gibson and McCarver argued that the ball had hit Pepitone's bat, but to no avail. (Joe dropped his pants for a crowd of reporters after the game to show off the telltale red mark on his thigh.) Mantle scored from second on a single to center by Tresh to give the Yanks the lead.

The lead grew to 4–1 in the seventh when Richardson singled in Linz and then scored himself on a ground out by Mantle, and the Yanks pounded three relievers for four runs in the ninth, keyed by a Linz home run and an RBI double by Mantle. Stottlemyre finished off a seven-hitter to win, 8–3.

Game 3 at Yankee Stadium was a classic that is remembered by anyone who saw it. It was a pitcher's duel between Jim Bouton and Curt Simmons, with one of the most dramatic endings of any World Series game. The Yankees scored first on a double by Clete Boyer but the Cards tied it in the fifth when McCarver singled to right, went to second when Mantle misplayed the ball, and scored on a single by Simmons that deflected off Boyer's glove into left field. Bouton allowed no more runs and the game went into the bottom of the ninth with the score tied 1–1.

The Cards had pinch-hit for Simmons in the top half of the inning, so Barney Schultz came in to pitch the bottom of the ninth. The 38-year-old

Schultz was their best reliever, having saved 14 games during the last two months of the season after being recalled from the minors. He had pitched in half of the Cardinals' final 60 games during their stretch run to the pennant, with a minuscule ERA of 1.64. His best pitch was a knuckleball.

Mickey Mantle was the first batter for the Yanks, and he was determined to atone for his error in the fifth inning that had contributed to the Cardinals' run. He walked up close to the plate while Schultz warmed up, taking a few vicious practice swings. Then he walked over to Elston Howard in the on-deck circle and said: "You might as well go on in. I'm gonna hit the first pitch I see out of the park."[13] Schultz's first pitch was a knuckleball that didn't knuckle enough, and Mantle belted it high up into the third deck in right field, almost hitting the facade again. It was one of the most memorable home runs of his career, not only because it won the game in dramatic fashion but also because it was his 16th World Series homer, breaking Babe Ruth's record that he had tied the previous October with his blast off Koufax. Years later, Mickey said that this home run was one of his biggest thrills in baseball.

With Ford not available for the rest of the Series, Berra started Al Downing in Game 4 against Ray Sadecki, the winning pitcher in Game 1. This time, Sadecki didn't even get out of the first inning as the first four Yankees hit safely. Linz led off with a double and scored on a double by Richardson. Maris singled Bobby to third, and when Mantle followed with a single to right, Richardson scored to make it 2–0. However, Mantle tried to take second when right fielder Mike Shannon momentarily bobbled the ball, and Shannon nailed him with a great throw. Sadecki got the hook after a brief workday of 10 pitches, and Roger Craig replaced him, the same Roger Craig who had beaten the Yanks as a Dodgers rookie in the crucial fifth game of the 1955 Series and who had lost 46 games for the Mets in their first two years of existence before being rescued by the Cards in 1964. Elston Howard greeted Craig with a single to right — the Yankees' fifth straight hit — to score Maris with the Yanks' third run of the inning, but Craig escaped without further damage. Mantle's failed gamble had short-circuited a potential big inning and would loom large later in the game.

Craig pitched through the fifth inning, allowing only one more hit and striking out eight. Trailing 3–0, the Cards mounted a rally in the top of the sixth. Carl Warwick (batting for Craig) singled and went to second on a single by Curt Flood. With one out, Groat hit what should have been an inning-ending double-play grounder to Richardson, who had trouble getting the ball out of his glove and ended up getting nobody. Ken Boyer then hit a high change-up into the left-field stands, fair by five feet, and all of a sudden it was 4–3, Cards. He gave his brother Clete a "Can you top that one?" look as he passed him rounding third. It was the ninth grand slam homer in Series history, and only the third by a non-Yankee.

Keane brought in Ron Taylor to pitch in the bottom of the sixth and he pitched no-hit ball over the final four innings, allowing one measly walk. After the first five Yankees batters in the game had hit safely, who would have believed that the Yanks would be shut out on one hit the rest of the way? They had squandered a chance to take a 3–1 Series lead; instead the two teams were even at 2–2.

Game 5 was a rematch of Game 2: Stottlemyre versus Gibson. Both pitchers allowed but one hit and no runs through four innings. With one out in the fifth, Gibson blooped a single to left. Flood then hit a double-play ball to Richardson at second, but the ball bounced off his glove and chest and the Cards had two runners on with only one out. After a single by Brock scored Gibson with the first run of the game, White grounded to Richardson, giving the Yanks another chance to turn a double play and get out of the inning. Richardson fielded this one cleanly and got Brock at second, but Linz short-hopped his relay throw to Pepitone, making the play just close enough for the first-base umpire to blow the call, allowing Flood to score the second run. All of the controversial calls seemed to be going against the Yankees.

It was ironic that for the second consecutive game, Bobby Richardson had made a costly fielding error. He was having another great Series at the plate (he would set a new record with 13 hits to go along with his Series RBI record from 1960), but he was hurting the Yanks in the field. Usually the reverse was true: he was a .266 lifetime hitter with no power, but usually sure-handed in the field.

Stottlemyre, who had pitched well enough to win but had been victimized by poor fielding, left for a pinch hitter in the bottom of the seventh. Pete Mikkelsen held the Cards in the eighth and ninth, and the Yanks came up for their last shot at Gibson, who had yielded just four hits.

Mantle led off and reached first on an error by Groat. After Howard struck out, Pepitone lined a shot right back at Gibson, who was finishing his follow-through. The ball hit Gibson in the butt and bounced off him toward the third-base line. The third baseman was playing deep and had no chance to get Pepitone, but Gibson sprang off the mound and pounced on the ball. As his momentum carried him across the third-base line, he whirled and fired a sidearm fastball to White at first. Pepitone and the ball appeared to arrive at first base at the exact same instant (even in slow-motion replay), but again the call went the Cardinals' way, and the Yanks had only a runner on second with one out instead of two on and no out.

Gibson's incredible play and the umpire's call were both key, since Tresh hit Gibson's next pitch into the right-center-field bleachers to tie the score at 2–2. The Series was dead even again, but only for about 10 minutes. White drew a walk from Mikkelsen leading off the 10th and Boyer beat out a bunt. Elston Howard then picked White off second on a missed bunt attempt by Groat, but the Yankees botched the rundown and White made it to third safely. Groat forced Boyer at second (with White holding third), bringing up the red-hot Tim McCarver, who hit .478 in the Series. McCarver was a left-handed batter and Berra had Steve Hamilton, his ace left-handed reliever (7–2 on the year and particularly tough on lefties), ready in the bullpen. He opted to stay with Mikkelsen, and McCarver ripped a three-run homer over the right-field fence to give the Cards a 5–2 lead. Gibson retired the Yanks in the bottom of the 10th (notching his 13th strikeout of the game in the process), sending the Series back to St. Louis with the Yanks needing to win two straight games.

Game 6 was a rematch of Game 3, Bouton versus Simmons. Again it was a tight pitcher's duel through five innings (1–1), but the Yanks broke through in the sixth when Maris and Mantle hit back-to-back homers. Maris's homer was a shot onto the right-field roof, just fair. Then Mickey hit one *over* the roof in right center for his 17th Series homer and a 3–1 Yankees lead.

The Yanks put the game away in the eighth when Howard singled home a run off Schultz and Pepitone unloaded the 10th grand slammer (and seventh by a Yankee) in Series history onto the right-field roof off left-hander Gordon Richardson. Bouton went eight and one third innings before giving way to Steve Hamilton, who closed out the Cards 8–3. This game was the last bright spot in Bouton's career; he would slip to 4–15 the following year after hurting his arm and then drift around the majors until his retirement in 1970, never again winning more than four games in a season. He is best remembered for his best-selling baseball expose *Ball Four*, which made Bouton an outcast among all major league players because it violated the locker room code, "What you hear here, stays here." His uncomplimentary stories about Mantle particularly angered the Yankees players as well as players throughout the league, because Mickey was the most revered player in the game.

Gibson and Stottlemyre both came back with only two days of rest to face each other for the third time in Game 7. The Yanks loaded the bases with two out in the second, but Gibson fanned Stottlemyre. The game was scoreless through three innings, but the Yankees self-destructed in the Cardinals' half of the fourth.

After Boyer led off with a single, Stottlemyre walked Groat on four pitches. Then there was deja vu all over again: a tailor-made double-play grounder to Pepitone. They got Groat at second, but Linz threw wildly to first and Boyer scored, with Stottlemyre jamming his pitching shoulder diving for Linz's throw. Mike Shannon singled McCarver to third. Next, the

Cards attempted a double steal, and after a bad throw to second and a worse throw home, both runners were safe and the score was 2–0. Dal Maxvill singled to right, scoring Shannon to make it 3–0.

After the Yanks pinch-hit for Stottlemyre in the top of the fifth (without scoring), Al Downing was brought in to try to hold the Cardinals. After a 400-foot homer by Lou Brock, a single by White and a double by Boyer, Rollie Sheldon replaced Downing. Sheldon retired the Cards, but not before both White and Boyer scored to make it 6–0.

The Yanks finally got on the board in the sixth. Richardson and Maris singled, and Mantle hit an opposite-field homer into the left-center-field bleachers to cut the lead in half. It was his 18th and final World Series homer.

Richardson singled to center with two out in the Yankees' seventh for his record 13th hit of the Series, but Gibson retired Maris. When Ken Boyer homered to left off Steve Hamilton in the bottom half of the inning, the Cardinals had a four-run lead. Mantle made a bid for another homer leading off the eighth, but his towering drive to center didn't quite have the distance.

Gibson fanned Tresh to open the Yankees' ninth. Then Clete Boyer homered into the left-field bleachers to bring the Yanks within three; this was the first time in Series history that two brothers homered in the same game. Gibson struck out pinch hitter Johnny Blanchard — his ninth strikeout of the game and 31st of the Series, establishing a new World Series record. (This record would last only until the 1968 Series, when Gibson whiffed 35 Tigers, including a record 17 in one game.) Then Phil Linz hit a ball into the left-field bleachers, and the Yanks were within two with Richardson, Maris and Mantle coming up. But Gibson got Richardson to pop up to Maxvill at second and the last gasp went out of the Yankees dynasty.

It was one of Mantle's best World Series. He batted .333, and with his six walks he reached base 14 times in 30 trips to the plate. His eight RBIs gave him a career Series total of 40, a record that still stands (as does his homer record). However, the Babe Ruth Award (World Series MVP) went to Gibson, the hero of the last two Cardinals wins.

The next few days saw some of the strangest managerial maneuvering ever seen after a World Series. Before the Series even started, the owners of both teams had already decided to replace their managers afterward. When it had looked like the Cardinals were out of the NL race, Gussie Busch had decided to fire Keane at the end of the season, and allegedly had offered the job to Leo Durocher. When the Cards came back to win the pennant and the World Series, Busch realized that he would look like an idiot if he fired Keane, so he hurriedly called a press conference to announce that Keane had been rehired. However, Keane had heard about Busch's discussions with Durocher and handed him a letter of resignation before the press conference started.

At about the same time, Berra was being fired as manager of the Yanks. General Manager Ralph Houk felt that Berra had lost control of the team during the second half of the season and he wanted more of a disciplinarian as manager. Nothing that had happened in the Series had changed his mind; in fact, Yogi's failure to bring in Hamilton to face McCarver in the tenth inning of Game 5 had angered Houk. After Berra was fired, Keane was offered and accepted the Yankees job. It turned out to be a mistake, both for the Yanks and for Keane. Berra would later manage the Mets to the 1973 NL pennant, becoming the first manager since Joe McCarthy to win pennants in both leagues.

After the Series, Ford went to see Dr. Denton Cooley (the famous Houston heart surgeon), who found a blockage in his left arm. Dr. Cooley thought that the injury had been caused over time by wear and tear, possibly by a little injury in the artery that kept healing from the inside, forming scar tissue that gradually narrowed the artery. During the sixth inning of the Series opener, some scar tissue had apparently broken loose and blocked the artery. The problem called for bypass surgery, but Dr. Cooley was afraid that type of surgery might end Ford's career and he performed a procedure called a sympathectomy instead. He deflated one of Whitey's lungs, went in under his left armpit and put a little silver clip on a particular area of his spine to keep the little capillaries open all the time instead of having them open and close. Although the operation helped a little, there still wasn't a big enough supply of blood to Whitey's arm, and he would eventually need the bypass operation in order to regain complete feeling in his arm.[14]

FOURTEEN

End of an Era

The decline of the Yanks was both sudden and precipitous. Very few people saw it coming. The 1965 Yanks were almost the exact same team that had won 99 games the previous year and reached the seventh game of the World Series, except that now they would have Mel Stottlemyre for the entire season. Yet they fell all the way to sixth place, finishing eight games below .500 and 25 games behind the first-place Minnesota Twins. It was their worst finish in 40 years.

The most obvious reason was injuries. The accumulation of 14 years of injuries caught up with Mickey Mantle in 1965 and he suffered through the worst year of his career, batting .255 with just 19 homers and 46 RBIs, a huge drop-off from his near-MVP 1964 season. He missed 40 games with the usual assortment of leg and shoulder injuries and appeared only as a pinch hitter in 14 others. His legs and his right shoulder hurt so badly that he grimaced with pain on every left-handed swing. He had always been a better hitter right-handed (his career batting average right-handed was .350), but the disparity was becoming greater as his right knee and right shoulder deteriorated. For the rest of his career, there would be occasional periods when he would be healthy for a few weeks and would shine as brightly as ever. But those periods gradually became shorter and less frequent.

Roger Maris had an even tougher year. After an extended early season stay on the disabled list with a pulled hamstring, Roger dislodged a bone chip in his right wrist in late June and missed 49 games. In all, he missed 116 games and contributed just eight homers and 27 RBIs. His wrist never fully healed enough for him to be a home-run hitter again.

Equally damaging was the loss of Elston Howard, who injured his right elbow on Opening Day and missed most of the first half of the season. After catching 150 games the previous season and driving in 84 runs, Howard caught only 95 games in 1965 and knocked in only 45 runs. His batting average dropped 80 points.

The litany went on and on. Tony Kubek hurt his left shoulder and missed 53 games. Joe Pepitone and Clete Boyer missed a total of 33 games

Ford shows off his form during one of his final spring trainings. (National Baseball Hall of Fame Library, Cooperstown, N.Y.)

with injuries. Jim Bouton's arm was shot and he fell to 4–15; although he hung on for another five years, he would never win more than four games in a season again. Bill Stafford also had arm problems and went 3–8; he never won another major league game.

No team could have coped with so many injuries to so many of its regulars, but the problem was exacerbated by the fact that the famous Yankees depth was gone. They no longer had capable back-ups at every position ready to step in and pick up the slack. They also no longer had a steady stream of prospects coming out of their farm system to continue the dynasty. As their aging stars broke down physically and retired one by one, they had nobody to whom to pass the torch. The Yankees were now paying dearly for their earlier shortsightedness in not signing black players. They had been one of the last major league teams to sign a black player — Elston Howard in 1955 — eight years after the Dodgers signed Robinson. In an era dominated by black players such as Willie Mays, Hank Aaron, Roberto Clemente, Ernie Banks, Frank Robinson, Willie McCovey, Billy Williams, Willie Stargell, Richie Allen, Maury Wills, Juan Marichal and Bob Gibson, black stars were conspicuously absent from the Yankees' lineup as the team floundered in the middle and late 1960s.

Ironically, the player whose physical status was most uncertain entering the season (Ford) held up his end fairly well. After his physical breakdown in the previous year's World Series and his off-season operation, Ford was definitely a question mark entering the 1965 season. He had to battle his circulatory problem all season long, but the drop-off in his productivity was much less than that of most of his teammates.

Statistically, Ford's 1965 season was the worst of his career up to that point. He finished with a 16–13 record and a 3.24 ERA, the highest of his career. The losses were also a career high and his winning percentage of .552 was a career low. Yet considering the fact that the Yanks won just 77 games that season, his season wasn't that bad. Only four pitchers in the league (including Mel Stottlemyre) won more games than Whitey, and he finished in the top 10 in complete games and strikeouts. His ratio of 1.84 walks per nine innings was the best of his career and the fourth-best in the league, and despite significant physical obstacles, he pitched more innings (244.3) than all but five AL pitchers. There were at least six games in which he pitched well enough to win but didn't due to lack of run support, sloppy fielding or blown saves. He could easily have won 20 games, and almost certainly would have if the 1965 version of the Yankees had been anywhere near as good as the previous year's team. In his 14th season in the majors, Whitey finally found out what it was like to pitch for an also-ran.

The fact that Ford pitched as many innings as he did was a testimonial to his resourcefulness and determination. The operation performed by Dr. Cooley after the 1964 World Series was only partially successful and Whitey still didn't get enough blood flow to his left forearm and hand. Afraid that the permanent solution to Ford's arterial blockage problem — a bypass operation using a vein graft — might end Whitey's career considering his age and other arm problems, Dr. Cooley had opted for the less intrusive sympathectomy procedure that left the capillaries in Whitey's left shoulder continuously open instead of alternating open and closed. Unfortunately, the resulting blood flow was still considerably less than that of a normal arm with a healthy artery. His arm was always cold and he didn't sweat on his left side where the sweat glands had been cut through during the operation, giving rise to all sorts of clubhouse jokes about how he was the only person who could get 10 days out of a five-day deodorant pad.

This condition resulted in the most bizarre season of Ford's career, one in which the meteorologist became almost as important as the manager in determining when Whitey would pitch. Cold weather exacerbated Ford's circulation problems to the point where he would lose feeling in his left hand and be unable to grip the ball properly. The tips of his fingers would shrivel up as if they had been under water for a long time and his fingers would cramp. After a few rough early season outings in cool weather, it became clear that the temperature needed to be within a certain range in order for Ford to pitch well. He pitched best when the temperature was around 70 degrees; if it fell much below that, the Yankees would scratch Ford and start someone else. That meant they always had to have a starter in reserve on days when Whitey was scheduled to pitch. If the weather was warm Ford was fine, unless the temperature got too hot, in which case Whitey's inability to sweat on the left side sometimes caused him to overheat. Seventy-degree weather therefore became known as "Whitey Ford weather."

The correlation of the weather to Ford's performance was startling. He was 13–4 with a 2.52 ERA in day games when it was usually warm, but only 3–9 with a 4.48 ERA in night games. During the cooler months (April, May, September and October) he was 7–10 with a 3.82 ERA, versus 9–3 with an ERA of 2.77 during the hotter months of June, July and August. Occasionally he got by in cold weather: he picked up his first win of the season on a raw April afternoon at the Stadium (beating the California Angels 3–2), but had to come out of the game in the seventh inning because of the 51-degree cold. "My fingers were numb," he said. "I couldn't feel the seams on the ball. I threw mostly fastballs."[1] He picked up another win on a mild afternoon at the Stadium in his next outing, striking out nine in a complete-game 9–4 win over Baltimore. The Orioles complained that New York third baseman Phil Linz was rubbing up the ball for Whitey, the implication being that the two of them were somehow loading up or doctoring the ball. While unlikely, it could have been true, given Whitey's frank confessions 20 years after he retired.

In his 1987 autobiography *Slick: My Years in and Around Baseball,* Ford said he began doctoring the ball late in his career when he needed an edge to make up for the erosion of his natural stuff. He said he never threw a spitter, both because he couldn't control it and because sometimes it did nothing, making it a fat pitch to hit. His weapons of choice were the mud ball and the cut ball.

Ford began experimenting with the mud ball in 1963. He learned it from Lew Burdette, the master of illegal pitches. Whitey said he would put a dab of saliva on the ball, pretend to rub it in, and then bend over to get the rosin bag with the ball in his hand and touch the ball to the dirt. He threw the pitch like a fastball, with the dirt on the top of the ball. The action was similar to that of a screwball, moving down and away from a right-handed batter. "The weight of the mud and the resistance it gives the air will finally force the ball to drop like a screwball," according to Ford. "It's the same as if you cut the ball, keep the cut on top, and fire it like the fastball. It'll drop like hell." On the other hand, he said that if the pitch were thrown with the dirt on the bottom of the ball, it would tail in on a right-handed batter. But unlike a spitter, the mud ball rotated, so it did not appear to be an illegal pitch and it was hard to detect after the fact because the dirt would fly off when the ball was caught or hit. As Whitey pointed out, all baseballs are rubbed up with mud before a game anyway — he would just add a little extra.[2]

Ironically, the originator of the cut ball (originally called the emery ball) was another Yankee pitcher named Ford — Russ Ford, whose Yankees record of eight shutouts in 1910 had been tied by Whitey in 1964. As the story goes, Ford was warming up one day when a pitch got away from him and sailed over the catcher's head, slamming into a concrete wall. When his next pitch suddenly broke sideways just as it reached the catcher, Ford examined the ball and found a scuffed spot as big as a dime where the ball had hit the concrete. He kept throwing the scuffed ball, experimenting with the location of the scuffed spot in his grip. He found that the ball broke differently depending on how it was held. From then on, the emery ball became his "out" pitch, but very few of his teammates knew about it.

One teammate who did know what was going on was shortstop Roger Peckinpaugh, a teammate of Ford's in 1913. "The emery ball broke even sharper than a curve," said Peckinpaugh in a 1953 interview. "Ford was smart. He had a piece of sandpaper on a ring. When he went to the mound he'd slip it over a finger of his glove and at the inning's end, he'd whisk the sandpaper into his pocket. No one saw him use it. What's more, he never scuffed the ball bigger than a dime."[3]

Whitey was cutting balls as early as 1964, as evidenced by the May 1964 game in which the Indians caught him cutting balls with a phony wedding ring. Many players thought that Elston Howard was cutting the ball for Whitey by nicking it with one of the little metal rivets on his shin guards, and Ford confirmed this in his 1977 autobiography.[4] Whitey is fond of saying that they didn't call him "Slick" for nothing, but he emphatically denies cheating during his prime, including his 1961 Cy Young Award season.[5] Be that as it may, by 1965 both the mud ball and the cut ball were part of his regular repertoire.

Unfortunately the Yankees hadn't quite figured out the weather correlation yet and three of Ford's next four starts after his win over the Orioles were in night games played on cool May evenings. For the first time in his career, Whitey lost four straight games. On one cold and windy night at Fenway Park, Whitey couldn't get a good grip on the ball and walked the bases full before a triple scored the eventual winning runs. His record now stood at an unsightly 2–5, with an even more unsightly ERA of 6.33. There was widespread speculation in the New York press that perhaps the "Chairman of the Board" had reached the end of the line.

Ford insisted that he was fine and that there was nothing physically wrong with him that some warm weather wouldn't cure. Nevertheless, manager Johnny Keane banished him to the bullpen to work on his control and try to straighten himself out. After three days of throwing in the bullpen without being called upon, Whitey took his regular turn against the Senators on a nice balmy afternoon at the Stadium. He produced a vintage Ford performance — a three-hit 6–0 shutout in which he struck out eight and was in total control the entire game. It was his 43rd career shutout (extending his Yankees record) and it gave Yankees fans hope that the team, which was mired in eighth place with a record of 15–20, could still make a run with a healthy Ford. Reality returned five days later when Keane started him in a night game in Detroit with the temperature in the low 50s. He couldn't feel the ball properly and left after one inning, getting tagged with the loss after allowing the first Detroit run in a 4–1 Tigers win.

It was now crystal clear how Ford would need to be used for the remainder of the season. On the final day of May, Whitey took advantage of a warm afternoon at the Stadium to beat Denny McLain and the Tigers, 3–1. After the first three Tigers batters singled to give Detroit a 1–0 lead, Ford settled down and allowed only three singles thereafter, requiring only 88 pitches to get through eight innings before turning the game over to Pedro Ramos in the ninth. The win started him on what would prove to be his final winning streak of any considerable length in his career.

At the age of 36 and in his 14th season in the majors, there weren't many "firsts" left for Ford in baseball. However, one occurred on June 4 when he made the first appearance of his career as a pinch hitter. In the bottom of the 15th inning against the White Sox after the Yanks had fallen behind 2–0 in the top half of the inning, Keane had run out of position players and sent Whitey (who led the pitching staff in hits that year with 15) up to bat for Pete Mikkelsen. Facing the league's premier relief pitcher, right-hander Eddie Fisher (15–7 with a 2.40 ERA in 82 appearances that season), Ford worked the count full before flying out to center field. Afterward he joked that Fisher must have thrown him a spitter. There wasn't much else to joke about as the 2–0 loss dropped the Yankees eight games below .500 at 19–27 and left them mired in ninth place.

A warm, sunny afternoon at Yankee Stadium was just what the doctor ordered for Ford two days later as he beat Tommy John and the second-place White Sox, 6–1, in the first game of a Sunday double-header. The 33,029 fans on hand enjoyed the second game as well, as Tom Tresh hit three consecutive homers to back a three-hit shutout by Al Downing. Tresh hit one homer right-handed and two left-handed; this was the third time he had switch-hit homers in a game, second in major league history behind Mantle's 10 times.

Ford was now 5–6 on the season, with all five wins coming in afternoon games at Yankee Stadium and all six losses suffered in chilly night games on the road. He finally won a game on the road in sunny Los Angeles on June 13, beating the Angels in an afternoon game, 3–0. He had a three-hitter going with two out in the ninth, but needed Pedro Ramos to come in and strike out Vic Power after two singles brought the tying run to the plate. This was the first time all season that Ford had his regular catcher behind the plate, since Howard had been out almost the entire season with his elbow injury.

Back at the Stadium for an afternoon game against Minnesota in mild temperatures, Ford out pitched Mudcat Grant (the league's leading winner that season), 5–3, for his fourth win in a row. His streak reached five with an 8–3 win over Kansas City at home, although he needed relief help from Steve Hamilton since the temperature was about 20 degrees above "Whitey Ford weather." With the thermometer at a near-perfect 74 degrees for an afternoon game at the Stadium on June 27, the Angels had little chance against Ford and he beat them 7–2 for his sixth straight win. His ERA during this streak was 1.81 and he was now a perfect 8–0 at Yankee Stadium for the season.

The streak ended in a night game in Baltimore, with the two deciding runs scoring as a result of two consecutive fly balls that right fielder Hector Lopez lost in the lights. Ford then split his next two decisions before pitching one of his best games of the season on a warm afternoon at Yankee Stadium on July 22. He struck out 10 and went the distance to beat Chicago 3–1, yielding a first-inning RBI single to old friend Moose Skowron and then blanking the White Sox thereafter. When he beat Detroit 4–3 in his next start (his 10th straight win at Yankee Stadium) to raise his record to 12–8, he took over the league lead in wins. He got to 13–8 with his 44th career shutout, a masterful five-hitter against the White Sox in Chicago. Strangely, Keane used him in relief two nights later, bringing him in with the bases loaded and two out in the bottom of the ninth with the Yanks ahead, 6–5. Whitey retired Jerry Lumpe on a grounder to Richardson to save the win for Stottlemyre.

With 12 scheduled starts remaining, Ford was on pace to win 20 again. (Mel Stottlemyre also had 13 wins at the time and went on to win 20.) Instead, wins suddenly became very hard to come by for Whitey. On this date his career record stood at 229–92 for an unprecedented winning percentage of .713, but his record over the remainder of his career would be 7–14. He didn't pitch badly; in fact, his ERA from that point until he retired (41 appearances later) was only 2.38, which was well below his lifetime ERA of 2.75. Yet lack of support consistently kept him out of the win column. It was almost as if he was paying dues for having pitched for the best team in baseball for so many years.

Ford won only three of those last 12 starts in 1965 (against five losses), despite pitching well enough to win most of those games. He allowed four hits and one earned run in seven innings against Minnesota, but an error and a terrible relief job cost him a win. Two more solid efforts were wasted due to lack of run support, and then Steve Hamilton blew a save for him with two out in the ninth.

The next game was a crusher. Whitey allowed just two hits (an infield hit and a bunt) through the first eight innings of a night game in Kansas City, but the game remained scoreless as the Yanks managed just four hits themselves. The Athletics pushed across a run in the bottom of the ninth on a bunt single and two legitimate singles and Ford had his ninth loss of the season.

After five quality starts in a row without a win, Ford finally picked up his 14th win of the season, beating the Angels for the ninth straight time with a complete-game four-hitter on a warm afternoon in Los Angeles. Mantle drove in four runs with a homer and single as the Yanks romped 8–1. Then it was back to purgatory for Ford on September 6 as he lost a 2–1 decision to Baltimore on a homer off the left-field foul pole, with the Yanks collecting only three hits on his behalf. It was his first loss of the season at Yankee Stadium, and there would be three more in the final three weeks of the season.

Ford reached an important milestone on September 11, tying Red Ruffing for most wins by a Yankees pitcher by beating Chicago 3–1 for his 231st win in pinstripes. (Ruffing lost 124 games for the Yanks while amassing his win total, as compared to only 94 for Ford.) The amazing part was that the game was played on a raw 50-degree night in Chicago, yet Whitey had a shutout until an unearned run spoiled it in the ninth. He said later that he had a hot-water bottle on the bench that he rested his left arm on between innings.

In his first attempt to break Ruffing's record, Ford hooked up with Detroit's Mickey Lolich in a southpaw pitching duel at the Stadium and held the Tigers to two runs in nine innings before losing on a 10th-inning home run by Norm Cash. He took a one-hit shutout into the seventh inning of his next start against Cleveland but surrendered a three-run homer to Fred Whitfield and lost 4–3 on a run walked home by Steve Hamilton. In his third unsuccessful attempt (all at the Stadium), he had a two-hit shutout and a 3–0 lead in the seventh before allowing a game-tying homer to Pete Ward. Moose Skowron beat him with a two-out eighth-inning single after an infield hit prolonged the inning. Whitey finally passed Ruffing with a win over the Red Sox at Fenway Park in the final game of the season, though it was his least impressive outing of the final two months (four earned runs in seven innings). Mercifully, the season was finally over.

In retrospect, Ford should have had the bypass operation he needed during the ensuing off-season. However, he had pitched reasonably well and felt that he could continue to pick his spots based on the weather, with the help of a hot-water bottle between innings. He had also been so encouraged by his successful outing in cold weather on September 11 that he had convinced himself that he would be fine in 1966. "I haven't seen my surgeon [Dr. Cooley] since last April," he told Joseph Durso of the *New York Times* in a January interview at his home in Lake Success on Long Island. "But as far as we're concerned, the operation was a success.... Five years ago, my shoulder hurt and I didn't think I could last. But now I would like to pitch four more years—I mean four good years."[6]

Whitey went on to express the hope of all Yankee fans—that the 1965 season had been just an aberration (similar to 1959) and that all of his teammates would somehow be healthy again and return to their form of championship years past. "We could come all the way back," he said. He concluded the interview by saying how much he admired Joe DiMaggio, Stan Musial and Ted Williams for retiring when they did. "Some guys hang around too long," he said, "but they went out good. Mickey will be that way, and I want to be that way, too."[7] Unfortunately it wouldn't work out that way for either of them. Ford's last two partial years with losing records would drag his lifetime winning percentage down to .690 after it had been comfortably above .700 his entire career, and Mantle always said one of his biggest regrets was that he hung on so long that his lifetime batting average dropped down below .300 to .298. Both players loved the game so much that they found it hard to walk away.

The week after this interview, Whitey signed a contract for the 1966 season at a salary of $55,000, the same salary he had received in 1965. The Yankees said they needed to "stay within President Johnson's anti-inflation guidelines."[8]

During the off-season, Mantle had a four-hour operation at the Mayo Clinic to remove bone chips and calcium deposits from his right shoulder. Because the Yankees badly needed Mantle as a drawing card no matter what his physical condition, General Manager Ralph Houk convinced him to return for the 1966 season. (The impact of Mantle on attendance, both at Yankee Stadium and on the road, had been demonstrated in 1963, when Mickey missed 97 games with his broken foot. Despite winning the pennant by 10½ games that year, the Yankees' home attendance was the lowest it had been since 1945, and American League overall attendance sank to its lowest level in five years.) Remarkably, though he could do little more than lob the ball from the outfield, Mickey was in the Yankees lineup on Opening Day.

Ford appeared to be reasonably healthy for the opener, although he had been removed from a spring training game several weeks before after developing soreness in his shoulder. The weatherman didn't cooperate when Ford took the mound against the Tigers at Yankee Stadium: it was a chilly 35 degrees, a full 35 degrees below "Ford weather."

Right off the bat, Ford became embroiled in a controversy. In an effort to keep his fingers warm, Whitey stashed a little bottle of hot water in his back pocket to grab between pitches. Detroit manager Charlie Dressen noticed this immediately and asked plate umpire Jim Honochick to make him get rid of it. Honochick reluctantly enforced the rule against a player having a "foreign substance" in his pocket, and Whitey had a few words for Dressen as the latter walked off. Dressen died suddenly of a heart attack four months later, and Whitey always felt bad that the last words he had exchanged with Dressen had been somewhat heated.

After the controversy died down, Ford and Detroit's Mickey Lolich engaged in a great pitching duel. Whitey allowed but three hits through the first eight innings, although two of them had led to a Detroit run in the sixth that offset a fifth-inning home run by Joe Pepitone. Ford weakened in the top of the ninth, allowing a two-out RBI single to Norm Cash. When the Yanks left the tying run on third in the bottom of the ninth, Whitey absorbed another hard-luck loss.

Ford also tried out another little aid in this game in addition to the hot-water bottle. He put a mixture of Johnson's baby oil, turpentine and resin into a Ban roll-on deodorant bottle with a rolling ball dispenser, and he applied the mixture to his fingers between innings to help him get a better grip on the ball in the cold weather. According to both Ford and Mantle, Berra routinely mooched deodorant from their lockers, and Mickey took the bottle out of Whitey's warm-up jacket pocket after the game and put it on the top shelf of Ford's locker as bait. Yogi took the bait and applied the "deodorant." Within minutes, Berra's upper arms were stuck to his body and he was creating a scene. Mantle hustled him off to the trainer's room before the writers caught on and the trainer had to use alcohol and scissors to release Yogi's arms.[9]

Ford's luck didn't improve any in his next start, as he turned a 4–3 lead over to the bullpen (despite two unearned runs) and then watched Pedro Ramos blow the save and the game. It was "déjà vu all over again" his next time out against Boston when he turned a 4–2 lead over to Ramos with nobody out and a man on first in the ninth. Ramos again blew the save, although the Yankees eventually won this one with three runs in the bottom of the ninth. Then Whitey lost a 1–0 heartbreaker to ex-teammate Rollie Sheldon and the Athletics despite yielding just five hits in eight innings. By now Ford must have thought it had been he who had been traded to Kansas City instead of Sheldon.

The Yanks reached a new low on May 6 when two New York errors and shoddy relief work hung yet another hard-luck loss on Ford and dropped the team's record to 4–16. They were in last place, and it was painfully clear that there would be no miracle rebound that would return them to the top of the heap. Something had to give, and the Yanks fired manager Johnny Keane. Both Ford and Mantle spoke out in Keane's defense, saying that the team's demise was not his fault. While this was obviously true, a fall guy was needed, so Keane was axed and Ralph Houk returned to the bench.

Five starts into the season, Ford was now 0–3 with a 2.19 ERA. He could easily have been 5–0. Unfortunately things were about to go from bad to worse for Whitey. After pitching two scoreless innings against Kansas City on May 13, Ford had to leave the game because of soreness in his left elbow that made it difficult for him to throw a curveball. The problem was diagnosed as a strained (and inflamed) ligament on the inside of the elbow and Whitey skipped a turn. There was no improvement when he pitched an inning against the Angels on May 24, so the Yankees placed him on the disabled list.

After waiting a full month for the inflammation in his elbow to subside, Ford pitched two innings in relief on June 25 and then threw three perfect innings against the Mets in the Mayor's Trophy exhibition game. Encouraged by these efforts, he made his first start in nearly six weeks on July 2 but was shelled for 15 hits (including four homers) in six innings by the ninth-place Washington Senators. As always, even at what had to be one of the lowest moments of his career, Whitey stuck around after the game and talked openly with the press. He offered no excuses, saying his arm felt fine. The season was nearly half over and the greatest pitcher in Yankee history was 0–4.

After one final start against Boston in which he pitched fairly well but had to come out after five innings, Ford asked Ralph Houk to take him out of the starting rotation and use him out of the bullpen. "For three or four innings he can pitch with good stuff," said Houk. "Then his arm just seems to lose its life."[10] Yankee team physician Sidney Gaynor attributed the problem to Whitey's lack of circulation in the arm, saying that the muscles in his forearm became numb from lack of blood flow. Houk said Ford would be used in short relief, just a couple of innings at a time. Whitey said all the right things about doing whatever was best for the team and giving the younger pitchers a chance to start, but by now he could see that the end of his career was near and that there wouldn't be four more years. "It was nice while it lasted," he had told Arthur Daley of the *New York Times* a few weeks earlier.[11]

Ford did a respectable job as a relief pitcher, logging a 2–1 record and 2.25 ERA in 12 appearances. However, pitching in a mop-up role for a team fighting to get out of the cellar was not how he wanted to end his career. His circulation problem was getting worse instead of better, so he decided to gamble on the permanent solution that might rejuvenate his arm and give him another few years. On August 22 he went onto the disabled list for the rest of the season and flew to Houston to have the bypass operation.

Dr. Cooley took a six-inch vein out of Whitey's left leg and transplanted it into his left shoulder to bypass the circulatory blockage. He woke Ford up in intensive care after the operation and said, "Feel it. You've got a pulse again." Whitey immediately set his sights on the 1967 season, planning to go to the Yankees' Florida complex in October to begin the rehabilitation process.

While his buddy was struggling, Mantle was having injury problems of his own. He played in only 108 games in 1966 and had only 333 at bats. But when he played, he played very well, batting .288 and hitting 23 homers. His average would have tied Al Kaline for third in the AL if he'd had enough at-bats to qualify. He also had one of the most remarkable eleven-day stretches of his career.

On June 28, Mantle hit two homers against the Red Sox at Fenway Park, the first a blast well into the right-center-field bleachers and the second an opposite-field shot into the screen atop the Green Monster. The next day he hit two more homers (giving him homers on three consecutive at-bats), knocking in four runs to help the Yanks beat the Red Sox, 6–5. In the final game of the series on June 30, the Sox walked him three times.

On July 1, Mickey went 3-for-3 with a home run against Washington at D.C. Stadium, keying a Yankees win. The following day he hit two home runs right-handed against Mike McCormick in his last two at-bats, the first one hitting the facing of the mezzanine in dead-center field, 450 feet from the plate. In the third game of the series, he lined a homer to right his first time up, batting right-handed. For the second time in a week, Mantle had hit home runs on three consecutive at-bats; the first time, all lefty, and the second time, all righty. He now had eight homers in six games.

Mantle went homerless July 4–6 but resumed his barrage on July 7 at Yankee Stadium. With two out and two on in the bottom of the ninth inning of a 2–2 ballgame, Mantle homered into the right-field seats batting left-handed against Don McMahon. On the 11th and final day of his streak (July 8), Mickey went five for eight in a double-header against the Senators, including two long home runs. The second homer, hit lefty off Jim Han-

nan, landed in the center-field bleachers above the 461-foot sign. It was the
third time he had hit a ball into this section of the bleachers in his career.
He now had 11 homers in 11 days, giving him 18 for the season, only two
behind eventual Triple Crown winner Frank Robinson for the league lead.

Inevitably, the injury jinx struck again. Mantle's fifth hit of the July 8
double-header was a shot into the left-field corner that would have been a
triple had Mickey not pulled his left hamstring rounding first. He had probably precipitated the pull by beating out a bunt in his previous at-bat. It
seemed as if nearly every time he pulled his hamstring, it was while he was
putting it in his top gear trying to beat out a bunt, or soon thereafter. He
had learned to make many concessions to his chronic injuries, but he never
stopped trying to beat out bunts. This time he missed two weeks.

As soon as he got back in the lineup, he picked up where he had left
off, hitting three homers in a week (including his ninth career grand slam)
to pass Lou Gehrig for sixth place on the all-time home run list with 494.
It seemed certain that he would reach the 500-homer mark by the end of
the season, but after hitting No. 495 on August 14, he pulled a leg muscle
and missed 11 days. In his first at-bat after that injury, Mantle pinch-hit at
the Stadium with a man on and the Yanks trailing Detroit 5–4 in the bottom of the ninth. Batting right-handed against Hank Aguirre after receiving a huge standing ovation, Mantle delivered a game-winning home run
that most scriptwriters would have considered too improbable. In his 126
at-bats since he had started his rampage on June 28, Mickey had hit 16
homers, an average of one every 7.9 at-bats. Unfortunately that home run
(No. 496) would be his final one of the season because every time he tried
to return to the lineup, he injured something else.

Without a healthy Ford and with Mantle only a part-time player, the
Yanks stumbled home in last place. They lost 89 games, the most by a Yankees team since 1913. Poor Mel Stottlemyre lost 20 games after winning 20
the previous year, and his 12 wins tied rookie Fritz Peterson for the most
on the team. Other than Mantle, no regular hit higher than .256, and only
Joe Pepitone (31 HR, 83 RBI) and Tom Tresh (27 HR, 68 RBI) supplied any
punch at all at the plate.

Ford asked for his unconditional release after the season and went to
camp without a contract as a nonroster invitee. After three strong spring
training outings of gradually increasing length (three, four and five innings),
he looked and felt good and signed a contract reported to be somewhere
between $55,000 and $65,000.

The first sign of trouble came in his very next spring start, after which
Ford reported soreness in his elbow after pitching six innings against the
Cincinnati Reds. After a few X-ray treatments and a few more tune-ups,
he pronounced himself ready for the season.

Since the Yanks had made no major changes during the off-season, there wasn't much chance of a major turnaround in 1967. Houk shifted Mantle to first base in an effort to keep him in the lineup but he pulled a hamstring on Opening Day anyway. Ford pitched the home opener on April 14 and pitched well, holding the Red Sox to one run until two were out

Mantle (left) and Ford pose after being elected to the Baseball Hall of Fame on January 17, 1974. (AP/Wide World Photos)

in the eighth, when Joe Foy reached him for a two-run homer. Those two runs were irrelevant anyway, since the Yanks didn't even have a hit yet off 21-year-old left-hander Billy Rohr, who was making his first major league appearance. Rohr came within one strike of a no-hitter before surrendering a clean single to Elston Howard on a 3-and-2 pitch, much to the dismay of most of the fans at Yankee Stadium who wanted to see the kid get a no-hitter. Ford must have thought: "Here we go again."

Despite that shocking loss to a pitcher who would win a total of only three major league games, the Yanks actually started the season fairly well, with Mel Stottlemyre pitching shutouts in his first two starts and Ford and Al Downing both pitching well. Ford threw the 45th shutout of his career (the most by any active pitcher) in his second start, beating Chicago 3–0 with a seven-hitter at Comiskey Park. His sinker and slider produced 17 ground balls (including eight in a row), and only two White Sox runners reached second base. It was Whitey's first complete game since September 2, 1965, and he reported no problems despite frigid 46-degree weather. In fact, he joked that he had thought about pretending to have a hand-warmer in his back pocket in the first inning in order to bait White Sox manager Eddie Stanky into protesting and looking foolish, and then using a hand-warmer in subsequent innings. "But I didn't," he said, laughing. "I should have. That would've been a lot of fun."[12]

Ford followed up that effort with another complete game, beating Chicago again six days later at the Stadium with an eight-hitter, 11–2. He needed just 93 pitches to polish off the White Sox and chipped in with two hits of his own. Whitey hadn't looked this good in nearly two years and his circulatory problems were a thing of the past. After three consecutive solid outings, no one could have guessed that this would be the final win of his career.

Whitey made it four straight solid outings on April 30, yielding only one unearned run against the Angels at the Stadium. Unfortunately, he was gone by the time Mantle hit a three-run homer into the right-field upper deck in the bottom of the 10th inning to win the game, 4–1. The homer was Mickey's 2,214th career hit, tying him with Joe DiMaggio for third place on the all-time Yankees list behind Ruth (2,873) and Gehrig (2,721). He passed DiMaggio with a pinch-hit double in the next game.

A fifth straight solid outing by Ford (six hits and no walks in seven innings) was wasted when shoddy Yankee fielding led to three unearned runs and another tainted run as the punchless Yanks lost to Kansas City, 4–1. Whitey was now 2–2 on the season despite an ERA of 1.35. He was also just four innings from the end of his illustrious career.

In his next start, Ford pitched just three innings against Baltimore before leaving because of pain in his left elbow, saying afterward that he "couldn't get loose." He left trailing 1–0 on an RBI single by Frank Robinson and was saddled with another loss when the Yankees bullpen opened the floodgates while the inept Yankees were being shut out by Jim Palmer, 14–0. For the second time in Ford's six starts, the Yanks were held to a single hit — a seventh-inning single by Horace Clarke. By this time the Yankees were used to being embarrassed and were more worried about Ford's status.

The diagnosis this time was a bone spur in his left elbow, and Ford rested the elbow for eight days before testing it against the Tigers in Detroit on May 21. The pain was worse than ever and Whitey walked off the mound for the last time after just one inning. Fittingly, Mantle homered in this game, as he had done in so many of Ford's games over the years. Mickey was in the midst of another one of his home run streaks (eight homers in 13 games) that had started with his 500th home run on May 14, but on this day he lost his sidekick. To add insult to injury, Ford had yielded a run before leaving and was charged with his third straight loss when the Yanks were blown out again, 9–4.

Ford left the team and flew home to be examined by Dr. Gaynor, who told him that another operation would be needed to repair the bone spur. Whitey declined, saying: "I won't have another operation. If I were 33 or 34 years old, I definitely would, and try again. But not now."[13] Instead, he

From left, Mickey Mantle, Yogi Berra, Whitey Ford, Joe DiMaggio and Casey Stengel on Old Timers' Day, August 3, 1974. Mantle and Ford were inducted into the Baseball Hall of Fame nine days later. (AP/Wide World Photos)

retired on May 30, 1967, at Yankee Stadium, receiving a standing ovation from the crowd of 41,136 that was on hand for the day's game. "This is a much tougher job than I ever thought it would be," he told the assembled media, "but I have no complaints. I came in wearing a $50 suit, and I'm going out wearing a $200 suit, so that's pretty good."[14]

The following day, Arthur Daley of the *New York Times* summarized Ford's career nicely in his column titled "The Chairman Retires." After fondly recalling the "delightfully impudent, brash and irreverent young man" who had joined the Yanks at midseason back in 1950 and helped the team win a world championship, Daley reflected on how much Whitey's warmth, friendliness and joie de vivre had meant to the team and to everyone associated with it over the previous 17 years. Then he captured the essence of Whitey Ford perfectly when he said: "Through all of his lively ways, though, fun ended for the slick little lefty when he stepped on the mound. Then he was all business and a truly marvelous pitcher, a clutch performer who was at his best when the stakes were highest."[15]

Despite yielding just eight earned runs in his seven starts and posting an ERA of 1.64, Ford's record in his final abbreviated season was 2–4. Excluding his two wins over Chicago, the Yanks allowed more unearned runs (three) than they scored runs (two) for Whitey in his five other starts. He could have gone on the disabled list for the rest of the season and been paid his full salary (as today's players do), but he didn't want to get paid if he wasn't pitching. Instead, he agreed to scout National League teams (at a significantly reduced salary) when they came to Shea Stadium, which was near his home on Long Island. There was very little need to scout National League teams, though, since the Yanks moved up only to ninth place that season.

Ford had several coaching stints with the team, serving as Ralph Houk's first-base coach in 1968 and as Bill Virdon's pitching coach in 1974 and 1975. He quit in May of 1975 after suffering chest and arm pain and passing out after pitching batting practice. The Yankees retired his number 16 in 1974 on Old Timers' Day.

Ford was not voted into the Hall of Fame in his first year of eligibility (1973), receiving only 255 votes of the 284 necessary to be elected. (Players had to be named on 75 percent of the ballots cast.) This was not unexpected, since there was an unwritten custom among the voting sportswriters back then to make players wait at least a year before voting them in. So Whitey was forced to wait a year, just as Joe DiMaggio and Yogi Berra had been forced to wait before him. Ironically, the only player to be voted into the Hall in 1973 was Warren Spahn, Whitey's former rival. The following year, Ford was voted in. Fittingly, he went in along with his best friend and sidekick—Mickey Mantle. Reflecting back on his career after this crowning achievement, Whitey said: "It has been a great life, especially because I was able to do the thing I loved to do best—play baseball—and do it for a living. You can't be luckier than that."[16]

FIFTEEN

Where Ford Ranks

When Major League Baseball nominated 26 pitchers in 1999 for the All-Century Team pitching staff, Ford was one of those nominated. However, when the nine-man staff was selected, Whitey didn't make the cut. In general, when baseball fans talk about the greatest pitchers in history, Ford is regarded as one of the all-time greats but not as one of the truly elite.

Predictably, the fan voting for the All-Century Team favored the more recent pitchers, as Nolan Ryan edged Koufax for the most votes, with Clemens fourth and Bob Gibson fifth. The voters did include two old-timers on the team — Cy Young (third) and Walter Johnson (sixth) — but they left it to the Major League Baseball selection committee (set up to compensate for oversights in the fan voting) to add three all-time greats: Lefty Grove, Christy Mathewson and Warren Spahn. Since Ford had the best winning percentage of the 26 pitchers and since his ERA as a percentage of the league's ERA was the fourth-lowest in the group (behind Ed Walsh, Johnson and Grove), there are many who believe Whitey belonged on the All-Century Team. There are three main reasons why he wasn't selected.

The first rap against Ford is that he won only 236 games, well below the 300-win benchmark for baseball immortality. There are several reasons why he fell short. First, he lost two full seasons to military service. Since he won nine games in his half season before going into the army and averaged nearly 18 wins in the four years after he returned, it is reasonable to assume that he would have won 36 games during those two lost seasons, which would have given him 272 career wins.

The second reason why Ford fell short of 300 wins was that Casey Stengel pitched him every fifth, sixth or even seventh day and frequently held him back to open a series against a contending team. Whitey averaged only 29.7 starts during his eight full seasons under Stengel, not counting the 1957 season when he was injured and started just 17 games. Since he averaged 37 starts per season during the five seasons immediately following Stengel's departure, he lost an estimated 49 starts as a result of the way Casey used him. Since he won 52 percent of his 438 career starts (losing 23

211

percent and not getting a decision in the other 25 percent), it is reasonable to assume that he would have won another 25 games had Stengel pitched him every fourth day.[1] Some might question whether he would have been as effective had he pitched with less rest, but his winning percentage was actually higher during the five seasons in which he averaged 37 starts than it was during his first eight and a half seasons.[2] An additional 25 wins would have raised his career total to 297.

The third factor that kept him from winning 300 games was injuries. He lost anywhere from 13 to 20 starts in 1957 due to injuries, and he lost most of the 1966 season to injuries before retiring in May of 1967 due to his arm problems. Since he was still pitching effectively during those last two seasons when able to pitch (as evidenced by a combined ERA of 2.15), he probably would have won at least another 30 to 35 games had he been healthy during these three seasons (1957, 1966 and 1967). These wins would have put him well above the 300 mark for his career.

The second main reason why Ford wasn't selected is that he was not an overpowering pitcher and never threw a no-hitter. As a result, he is overshadowed in the minds of many by contemporaries Sandy Koufax and Bob Gibson, even though he had a better winning percentage and a lower ERA than either of the others. Neither Koufax nor Gibson won 300 games, but Koufax put together what many baseball historians consider to be the greatest five-year pitching performance in history from 1962 through 1966, and that's what people remember. He did little of note prior to those years and was forced to retire at the age of 30 due to traumatic arthritis in his left elbow, but during his last five years he outshone Ford, Gibson and everyone else, throwing four no-hitters and winning three Cy Young Awards and an MVP trophy. Gibson then became the dominant pitcher in baseball, and though his career statistics are inferior to Ford's, his unbelievable 1968 MVP season (1.12 ERA with 13 shutouts) secured his place in the upper echelon of pitchers. It always rankled Gibson that Koufax was considered better; in his 1994 autobiography, *Stranger to the Game*, he said: "It bothers me somewhat ... to hear and read so often that Koufax was the leading pitcher of our generation. A generation lasts more than five years."[3] Ford never expressed any such feelings, but he had the best career of the three and yet takes a back seat to the other two in the minds of many baseball fans.

Nolan Ryan's inclusion on the All-Century Team (as the leading vote-getter, no less) is an even bigger injustice to Ford. Some of Ryan's accomplishments defy belief, such as his 5,714 strikeouts and seven no-hitters, the last one at age 44, 18 years after his first one. However, while he may have been one of the most amazing pitchers of all time (as well as one of the most popular), statistically he was not one of the nine best pitchers of all time. He lasted long enough to amass 324 wins, but he also lost 292 games and his career ERA was 3.19. Neither his winning percentage nor his ERA merit comparison with Ford's, and all other pitching statistics are pure window dressing. Strikeouts are a popular statistic, but a pitcher's job is simply to get batters out, and an out is an out regardless of how gotten. Ryan was 21–16 for the California Angels in 1973 when he struck out 383 batters (the major league record), while Bobby Shantz fanned only 152 batters while going 24–7 for the 1952 Philadelphia Athletics, who won the same number of games (79) as the 1973 Angels. Ryan heads the all-time career list in such statistics as hits allowed per nine innings (6.56) and opponents' batting average (.204), but his career winning percentage was only .526.

The third main reason why Ford was overlooked for inclusion on the All-Century Team is that his achievements are somewhat discounted by some because he pitched for the Yankees, the best team in baseball during that era. Yet the differential between his winning percentage and that of his team when he wasn't involved in the decision is better than that of three of the nine pitchers who were selected ahead of him and very close to the marks of Koufax and Mathewson:

Pitcher	Winning %	Net Team Winning %[4]	Differential
Roger Clemens[5]	.665	.515	.150
Walter Johnson	.599	.460	.139
Cy Young	.618	.495	.123
Lefty Grove	.680	.561	.119
Sandy Koufax	.655	.544	.111
Christy Mathewson	.665	.560	.105
Whitey Ford	.690	.587	.103
Bob Gibson	.591	.516	.075
Warren Spahn	.597	.526	.071
Nolan Ryan	.526	.491	.035

This statistic recognizes the fact that it was harder for Steve Carlton to win 27 games for the 1972 Philadelphia Phillies (who won only 59 games) than it was for Sandy Koufax to win 27 games for the pennant-winning 1966 Los Angeles Dodgers, who won 95 games. Not surprisingly, Ford's team had a higher net winning percentage than that of any of the other pitchers' teams. But while Whitey's career winning percentage undoubtedly would have been lower had he not pitched for the Yankees, the above statistics indicate that he would have stood out no matter whom he pitched for. Some people have pointed out that Yankee Stadium was a good ballpark for a left-hander to pitch in because of its "Death Valley" in left-center field, but Ford won 120 games at home and 116 on the road, so he was just as effective in the other American League ballparks as he was at Yankee Stadium.

It also doesn't help Ford's case that he won just one Cy Young Award (as compared to seven for Clemens, three for Koufax and two for Gibson), but he probably would have won at least three had there been one awarded in each league during his entire career. He was the best pitcher in the AL in 1955 but the award wasn't initiated until the following year. In 1956 he might have won the award in the AL, but there was only one awarded for both leagues (until 1967) and Brooklyn's Don Newcombe had a monster year. Similarly, Ford would have been a shoo-in for the award in the AL in 1963 but Koufax had one of the best individual pitching seasons of all time and captured every vote. If a Cy Young Award had been awarded for the 12-year period 1953–1964, Ford quite likely would have won it.[6] Unfortunately, spectacular single seasons and accomplishments are often remembered more than consistent excellence over a long period of time.

Comparing pitchers across eras has always required a fair amount of subjectivity in addition to statistical analysis. Baseball has changed tremendously over the years and the resulting impact on pitching statistics has been significant. For example, the league average ERA in the American League has fluctuated significantly from year to year since the league's inception in 1901 but overall has risen nearly two full runs since the early years, for a variety of reasons. Since 1901, the baseball itself has evolved from the dead ball to the lively ball to the even livelier ball. Ballparks in general have gotten smaller; for example, the center-field wall at Yankee Stadium is now only 408 feet from home plate instead of 461 feet as it was before the Stadium was remodeled in the mid-1970s. Hitting 50 home runs used to be the gold standard for power hitters—it was done only 18 times during the years 1901–1994. During the next eight years, it was done another 18 times.

Other factors have contributed to the steady rise of earned run averages over the years. Either the fielding was poorer in the early part of the 20th century (possibly due to the very small gloves) or the scorekeeping was much stricter. When Cy Young posted an ERA of 1.62 in 1901, he gave up 112 runs in 371.3 innings but only 67 of the runs were scored as earned. On the other hand, when Koufax recorded an ERA of 1.88 in 1963, he yielded 68 runs and 65 of them were scored as earned. Therefore some of the miniscule earned run averages of the first 20 years of the century are somewhat suspect.

The biggest change of all occurred in 1947 when Jackie Robinson of the Brooklyn Dodgers broke the color barrier. Until then, the great pitchers faced a restricted talent pool of white Americans. Since 1947, the tremendous growth in the number of African-American and foreign players has greatly expanded the talent pool. This has been somewhat counterbalanced by the expansion in the number of major league teams from 16 to 30 (requiring today's teams to go deeper into the talent pool), but one can only wonder how many more games Warren Spahn would have won if he had never had to pitch to Hank Aaron, Willie Mays, Frank Robinson, Ernie Banks, Roberto Clemente, Roy Campanella, Jackie Robinson or any of the other great African-American players of his era. This needs to be factored in when evaluating pitching performances prior to 1947.

Subsequent changes to the game include the introduction of the designated hitter in the American League in 1973; the gradual shrinking of the strike zone so that letter-high pitches are no longer strikes; the introduction of the five-man pitching rotation, thereby making it easier on the pitcher but reducing his opportunities for wins; and the advent of the specialized relief pitcher (middle reliever, set-up man and closer).

It is impossible to quantify the impact on pitching performance of any one of these factors, but it is safe to say that the difference in talent between the great players and the average players was greater during the first half of the 20th century than in the second, resulting in inflated season statistics that have rarely been approached in the last 60 years. The following chart demonstrates this point, showing the number of times the 30-win milestone was achieved in each of the four eras of modern baseball:

Era	30 Wins
1901–1925	18
1926–1945	2
1946–1970	1
1971–2005	0

It was clearly easier for pitchers to put up impressive numbers during the first era. The way the game is played today, it is inconceivable that any pitcher could pitch 464 innings and win 40 games with an ERA of 1.42, as Ed Walsh did for the White Sox in 1908.

Given the trends of fewer wins and higher earned run averages over the past 100 years, the most reliable statistics for comparing pitchers are winning percentage and ERA as a percentage of the league's ERA. Appendix C shows the top 25 winning percentages since 1900 for pitchers with a minimum of 200 decisions, as of the end of the 2005 season. Ford's winning percentage of .690 was at the top of the list from the time he retired until 2002, when Pedro Martinez reached the 200-decision mark with a higher percentage. Martinez's career winning percentage at the end of the 2005 season was .701, but it is highly likely that his percentage will drop as his career winds down (as Ford's did), restoring Whitey to the top of the list.

With respect to earned run average, Appendix D shows that Ford's career mark of 2.75 is the lowest of any starting pitcher who has retired since 1930. (Hoyt Wilhelm had a better career ERA pitching primarily in relief, and Pedro Martinez's career ERA was 2.72 at the end of the 2005 season but will almost certainly rise above Ford's before Martinez retires.) There are numerous career earned run averages lower than Ford's among pitchers who retired prior to 1930, but since earned run averages in general were so much lower in the early years of the 20th century than they were in subsequent years, a simple comparison of earned run averages for pre-1930 pitchers versus post-1930 pitchers would be meaningless. However, comparing a pitcher's ERA to the average ERA in the league for that year is a statistic that can be consistently applied across the entire century.

Appendix E shows that Ford's career ERA was 71.6 percent of the league ERA during his career, which trails only Ed Walsh (65.9 percent), Walter Johnson (67.0 percent) and Lefty Grove (69.2 percent) among retired pitchers. Among pitchers still active as of the end of the 2005 season, Pedro Martinez (61.1 percent) was on track to surpass all of the above and Roger Clemens (71.4 percent) was also ahead of Ford. Appendix E also shows that Ford is one of only seven pitchers in major league history with a career ERA more than a full run better than the league average. Interestingly, four of the seven (Martinez, Roger Clemens, Randy Johnson and Greg Maddux) were still active as of the end of the 2005 season.

One question that generates a lively debate among baseball fans is where Ford ranks among the greatest left-handers of all time. Appendix F shows a comparison of the seven left-handers nominated by Major League Baseball for the All-Century Team, plus Randy Johnson, who clearly would have been in that group had it been selected several years later. Of those eight southpaws, one could make a legitimate case for five: Lefty Grove, Warren Spahn, Sandy Koufax, Randy Johnson and Ford. The answer really depends on the time frame selected. If the time frame is total career, the two most viable candidates are Warren Spahn and Lefty Grove. Spahn has the sheer weight of the numbers on his side because he pitched for so long, and his 363 career wins are tops among left-handers. However, Grove won 300 games and his career numbers are simply better than Spahn's: a winning percentage of .680, a winning percentage differential of .119, and an ERA differential versus the league average of 1.36 runs. Furthermore, when his ERA differential is converted into Pitching Runs (which incorporates innings pitched in order to calculate how many runs a pitcher saved his team over the course of the season), Grove's total of 595 is by far the best of any of the eight southpaws.[7] In fact, only Cy Young (753) and Walter Johnson (706) exceed Grove's total among all pitchers.

If the time frame is shortened to a five-year period (thereby measuring the pitchers at their absolute peak), Koufax usually gets the nod, although Appendix F shows that Grove won more games and had a higher winning percentage, a higher ERA differential and more pitching runs during his best five consecutive years than did Koufax. Randy Johnson had the third-best five-year period among left-handers, from 1998 through 2002 when he was 100–38 with a winning percentage differential of .190 and an ERA differential of 1.80.

If a time frame midway between five years and full career is used, Ford compares much better. Whitey did not have the longevity of Spahn or the peak brilliance of Koufax, but his best 10 consecutive years (1955–1964) have been bettered by only two left-handers in history: Lefty Grove (1928–1937) and Randy Johnson (1993–2002).

All things considered, Lefty Grove was probably the greatest southpaw ever, with Ford somewhere in the top five. However, there was one important difference between Ford and Grove: Whitey was one of the best-liked players of his era and a great teammate, while Grove had a reputation of being nasty when things didn't go his way. When he won 16 straight games in 1931 to tie the American League record shared by Walter Johnson and Smokey Joe Wood but then had the streak broken by a tainted run in a 1–0 loss to the lowly St. Louis Browns, Grove complained bitterly that teammate Al Simmons had cost him the record by sitting out the game with an injury. He never forgave Simmons for not playing that day, particularly since it was a misplay by Simmons' replacement that allowed the winning run to score.[8] Conversely, when Ford's 14-game winning streak in 1961 was snapped, Whitey made no excuses and took full responsibility for the loss. As Billy Martin said of Whitey in his 1987 autobiography *Billyball:* "If he messed up and lost a game, you'd never hear him complain, you'd never hear him alibi, you'd never hear him blame anybody else for losing. He'd just say, 'Hey, I screwed up. I'll get them next time.'"[9]

Ford's World Series record adds to his resume as one of the greatest pitchers of all time. He had a record of 10–8 with an ERA of 2.71 in 11 World Series, and with better support (runs, fielding and relief pitching), his record would have been much better. He retired with six World Series rings and his 10 wins are still a World Series record, as are his 33 consecutive scoreless innings.

One thing about which there is no doubt: Whitey Ford was the greatest Yankees pitcher in the long and storied history of the franchise. Several Yankees pitchers have had better individual seasons than Ford's best season, most notably Ron Guidry, whose 1978 season (25–3 with an ERA of 1.74 and nine shutouts) was one of the best individual seasons of all time. Lefty Gomez's 1934 season (26–5, 2.33 ERA) and Jack Chesbro's 1904 season (41–12, 1.82 ERA) also compare favorably with Ford's 1961 season (25–4, 3.21 ERA). However, no Yankees hurler comes close to Ford's career accomplishments. His club records of 236 wins, .690 winning percentage, 2.75 ERA and 45 shutouts haven't been approached in the 39 years since he retired and may never be broken.

Appendix A: Career Statistics

Year Team	W	L	Win %	G	GS	CG	SHO	SV	IP	Hits	Runs	ER	ERA	PR	BB	SO	HR	OAV	OOB
1950 New York (AL)	9	1	.900	20	12	7	2	1	112.0	87	39	35	2.81	22	52	59	7	.216	.309
1953 New York (AL)	18	6	.750	32	30	11	3	0	207.0	187	77	69	3.00	23	110	110	13	.245	.344
1954 New York (AL)	16	8	.667	34	28	11	3	1	210.7	170	72	66	2.82	21	101	125	10	.227	.319
1955 New York (AL)	*18**	7	.720	39	33	*18*	5	2	253.7	188	83	74	2.63	38	113	137	20	.208	.297
1956 New York (AL)	19	6	*.760*	31	30	18	2	1	225.7	187	70	62	*2.47*	42	84	141	13	.228	.303
1957 New York (AL)	11	5	.688	24	17	5	0	0	129.3	114	46	37	2.57	17	53	84	10	.237	.313
1958 New York (AL)	14	7	.667	30	29	15	*7*	1	219.3	174	62	49	*2.01*	*43*	62	145	14	.217	*.276*
1959 New York (AL)	16	10	.615	35	29	9	2	1	204.0	194	82	69	3.04	18	89	114	13	.250	.328
1960 New York (AL)	12	9	.571	33	29	8	*4*	0	192.7	168	76	66	3.08	17	65	85	15	.235	.299
1961 New York (AL)	*25*	4	*.862*	39	39	11	3	0	*283.0*	242	108	101	3.21	25	92	209	23	.229	.292
1962 New York (AL)	17	8	.680	38	37	7	0	0	257.7	243	90	83	2.90	31	69	160	22	.246	.298
1963 New York (AL)	*24*	7	*.774*	38	37	13	3	1	*269.3*	240	94	82	2.74	27	56	189	26	.241	.283
1964 New York (AL)	17	6	.739	39	36	12	8	1	244.7	212	67	58	2.13	41	57	172	10	.230	.276
1965 New York (AL)	16	13	.552	37	36	9	2	1	244.3	241	97	88	3.24	6	50	162	22	.258	.297
1966 New York (AL)	2	5	.286	22	9	0	0	0	73.0	79	33	20	2.47	8	24	43	8	.277	.333
1967 New York (AL)	2	4	.333	7	7	2	1	0	44.0	40	11	8	1.64	8	9	21	2	.247	.287
Totals	236	106	.690	498	438	156	45	10	3170.3	2766	1107	967	2.75	387	1086	1956	228	.235	.301

***Bold italic** print indicates led league

Appendix B: Ford's Yankees Record 236 Career Wins

Win #	Date	Opponent	Score	Win #	Date	Opponent	Score
1	07/17/50	Chicago	4–3	32	06/16/54	Baltimore (A)	2–0
2	07/26/50	St. Louis (A)	6–3	33	06/23/54	Detroit (A)	9–4
3	08/15/50	Washington (A)	9–0	34	07/06/54	Boston	4–1
4	08/20/50	Philadelphia (A)	5–2	35	07/16/54	Baltimore	3–2
5	08/25/50	St. Louis	10–0	36	07/20/54	Chicago	4–1
6	09/11/50	Washington (A)	5–1	37	07/29/54	Chicago (A)	10–0
7	09/16/50	Detroit (A)	8–1	38	08/03/54	Cleveland (A)	2–1
8	09/20/50	Chicago (A)	8–1	39	08/13/54	Boston	8–2
9	09/25/50	Washington	7–4	40	08/18/54	Philadelphia (A)	6–1
10	04/30/53	Chicago (A)	6–1	41	08/24/54	Baltimore	9–2
11	05/05/53	Cleveland (A)	11–1	42	08/29/54	Chicago	4–1
12	05/12/53	Cleveland	7–0	43	09/02/54	Cleveland	3–2
13	05/28/53	Washington	7–2	44	04/13/55	Washington	19–1
14	06/03/53	Chicago (A)	18–2	45	04/18/55	Baltimore (A)	6–0
15	06/07/53	St. Louis (A)	7–2	46	04/22/55	Boston	3–0
16	06/12/53	Cleveland (A)	4–2	47	05/13/55	Detroit	5–2
17	06/21/53	Detroit	6–3	48	05/17/55	Chicago	1–0
18	07/03/53	Philadelphia	4–0	49	05/27/55	Baltimore (A)	6–2
19	07/16/53	St. Louis (A)	7–3	50	06/01/55	Kansas City (A)	6–1
20	07/28/53	Cleveland	4–2	51	06/22/55	Kansas City	6–1
21	08/03/53	St. Louis	11–3	52	06/26/55	Cleveland	2–0
22	08/08/53	Chicago	1–0	53	07/01/55	Washington	7–2
23	08/12/53	Washington (A)	22–1	54	07/24/55	Kansas City (A)	7–3
24	08/17/53	Philadelphia (A)	10–3	55	07/29/55	Kansas City	3–2
25	09/01/53	Chicago (A)	3–2	56	08/14/55	Baltimore (A)	7–2
26	09/09/53	Chicago	9–3	57	08/19/55	Baltimore	8–0
27	09/20/53	Boston (A)	10–8	58	08/28/55	Chicago (A)	6–1
28	05/15/54	Detroit (A)	7–5	59	09/02/55	Washington	4–2
29	05/25/54	Washington (A)	9–3	60	09/07/55	Kansas City	2–1
30	06/04/54	Cleveland	8–3	61	09/20/55	Washington (A)	9–7
31	06/12/54	Chicago	2–0	62	04/20/56	Boston	7–1

Win #	Date	Opponent	Score	Win #	Date	Opponent	Score
63	04/25/56	Baltimore (A)	4–2	110	05/29/59	Baltimore	5–2
64	05/01/56	Detroit	9–2	111	06/04/59	Detroit (A)	14–3
65	05/06/56	Chicago	4–0	112	06/23/59	Kansas City (A)	10–2
66	05/11/56	Baltimore	3–2	113	07/03/59	Washington	4–3
67	05/17/56	Chicago (A)	10–3	114	07/14/59	Cleveland	1–0
68	05/28/56	Boston	2–0	115	07/19/59	Chicago	6–2
69	06/12/56	Chicago	4–2	116	08/07/59	Kansas City	3–0
70	06/26/56	Kansas City (A)	8–4	117	08/10/59	Boston (A)	7–4
71	07/05/56	Boston (A)	6–1	118	08/19/59	Detroit (A)	10–5
72	07/15/56	Chicago	2–1	119	09/01/59	Baltimore (A)	5–0
73	07/20/56	Kansas City	6–2	120	09/19/59	Boston	3–1
74	07/25/56	Chicago (A)	10–1	121	09/25/59	Baltimore	5–2
75	07/30/56	Cleveland (A)	13–6	122	04/22/60	Baltimore	5–0
76	08/31/56	Washington (A)	6–4	123	05/26/60	Baltimore	2–0
77	09/05/56	Boston (A)	5–3	124	06/21/60	Detroit (A)	6–0
78	09/09/56	Washington	2–1	125	06/26/60	Cleveland (A)	6–2
79	09/13/56	Kansas City (A)	3–2	126	07/06/60	Baltimore (A)	5–2
80	09/18/56	Chicago (A)	3–2	127	07/18/60	Cleveland (A)	9–2
81	04/16/57	Washington	2–1	128	07/28/60	Cleveland	4–0
82	04/22/57	Washington (A)	15–6	129	08/13/60	Washington	1–0
83	07/01/57	Baltimore (A)	3–2	130	08/16/60	Baltimore	1–0
84	07/02/57	Baltimore (A)	6–4	131	09/16/60	Baltimore	4–2
85	07/19/57	Cleveland (A)	9–1	132	09/21/60	Washington	10–3
86	07/30/57	Kansas City	10–4	133	09/28/60	Washington (A)	6–3
87	08/04/57	Cleveland	5–2	134	04/17/61	Kansas City	3–0
88	08/29/57	Chicago (A)	2–1	135	04/21/61	Baltimore (A)	4–2
89	09/07/57	Washington (A)	4–1	136	04/30/61	Washington (A)	4–3
90	09/13/57	Chicago	7–1	137	05/04/61	Minnesota (A)	5–2
91	09/20/57	Boston	7–4	138	05/21/61	Baltimore	4–2
92	04/18/58	Baltimore	3–1	139	05/25/61	Boston	6–4
93	05/10/58	Washington	8–0	140	06/02/61	Chicago (A)	6–2
94	05/16/58	Washington (A)	7–2	141	06/06/61	Minnesota	7–2
95	05/21/58	Chicago (A)	5–2	142	06/10/61	Kansas City	5–3
96	05/25/58	Cleveland (A)	6–1	143	06/14/61	Cleveland (A)	11–5
97	06/02/58	Chicago	3–0	144	06/18/61	Detroit (A)	9–0
98	06/07/58	Cleveland	6–3	145	06/22/61	Kansas City (A)	8–3
99	06/17/58	Cleveland (A)	4–0	146	06/26/61	Los Angeles (A)	8–6
100	06/28/58	Kansas City (A)	8–0	147	06/30/61	Washington	5–1
101	07/03/58	Washington (A)	11–3	148	07/04/61	Detroit	6–2
102	07/14/58	Chicago	5–0	149	07/08/61	Boston	8–5
103	07/20/58	Kansas City	8–0	150	07/17/61	Baltimore (A)	5–0
104	07/25/58	Cleveland (A)	6–0	151	07/25/61	Chicago	5–1
105	08/08/58	Boston	2–0	152	07/29/61	Baltimore	5–4
106	04/15/59	Baltimore (A)	3–1	153	08/10/61	Los Angeles	3–1
107	04/22/59	Washington (A)	1–0	154	08/19/61	Cleveland (A)	3–2
108	05/10/59	Washington	6–3	155	08/27/61	Kansas City (A)	8–7
109	05/24/59	Baltimore (A)	9–0	156	09/06/61	Washington	8–0

Win #	Date	Opponent	Score	Win #	Date	Opponent	Score
157	09/15/61	Detroit (A)	11–1	204	05/30/64	Kansas City (A)	9–1
158	09/23/61	Boston (A)	8–3	205	06/03/64	Minnesota (A)	3–0
159	04/21/62	Cleveland	3–1	206	06/07/64	Los Angeles (A)	9–3
160	04/29/62	Washington (A)	3–2	207	06/12/64	Chicago	3–0
161	05/09/62	Boston	4–1	208	06/16/64	Boston	7–5
162	06/21/62	Baltimore (A)	3–0	209	06/20/64	Chicago (A)	1–0
163	06/25/62	Detroit (A)	2–0	210	07/10/64	Washington (A)	4–1
164	06/29/62	Los Angeles	6–3	211	07/15/64	Baltimore	2–0
165	07/08/62	Minnesota (A)	9–8	212	08/25/64	Washington	4–1
166	07/16/62	Kansas City (A)	3–1	213	08/29/64	Boston	6–1
167	07/20/62	Washington	3–2	214	09/18/64	Kansas City	6–0
168	07/24/62	Boston	5–3	215	09/22/64	Cleveland (A)	8–1
169	08/01/62	Washington (A)	5–2	216	10/02/64	Cleveland	5–2
170	08/10/62	Detroit	8–0	217	04/25/65	California	3–2
171	08/14/62	Minnesota (A)	5–2	218	05/01/65	Baltimore	9–4
172	08/31/62	Kansas City	5–1	219	05/22/65	Washington	6–0
173	09/08/62	Boston	6–1	220	05/31/65	Detroit	3–1
174	09/12/62	Cleveland (A)	5–2	221	06/06/65	Chicago	6–1
175	09/25/62	Washington	8–3	222	06/13/65	California (A)	3–0
176	04/28/63	Cleveland	5–0	223	06/19/65	Minnesota	5–3
177	05/02/63	Los Angeles (A)	7–0	224	06/23/65	Kansas City	8–3
178	05/06/63	Detroit (A)	10–3	225	06/27/65	California	7–2
179	05/14/63	Minnesota	2–1	226	07/05/65	Detroit (A)	7–2
180	05/24/63	Washington	5–3	227	07/22/65	Chicago	3–1
181	05/31/63	Cleveland (A)	4–0	228	07/27/65	Detroit	4–3
182	06/05/63	Baltimore (A)	4–3	229	08/05/65	Chicago (A)	3–0
183	06/09/63	Detroit (A)	6–2	230	09/02/65	California (A)	8–1
184	06/18/63	Washington	10–5	231	09/11/65	Chicago (A)	3–1
185	06/22/63	Boston (A)	6–5	232	10/03/65	Boston (A)	11–5
186	06/26/63	Chicago (A)	3–2	233	07/16/66	Kansas City (A)	9–5
187	06/30/63	Boston	4–2	234	08/06/66	Cleveland (A)	5–4
188	07/04/63	Chicago	9–1	235	04/19/67	Chicago (A)	3–0
189	07/11/63	Los Angeles (A)	3–2	236	04/25/67	Chicago	11–2
190	07/20/63	Cleveland	5–4				
191	07/24/63	Los Angeles	8–4				
192	08/10/63	Los Angeles (A)	2–1				
193	08/24/63	Chicago	3–0				

World Series

Win #	Date	Opponent	Score
194	08/28/63	Boston	4–1
195	09/02/63	Detroit (A)	5–4
196	09/06/63	Detroit	2–1
197	09/11/63	Kansas City (A)	8–2
198	09/15/63	Minnesota (A)	2–1
199	09/24/63	Los Angeles	8–1
200	04/22/64	Chicago (A)	3–0
201	05/01/64	Washington	1–0
202	05/09/64	Cleveland (A)	6–2
203	05/17/64	Kansas City	8–0

#	Date	Opponent	Score
1	10/07/50	Philadelphia	5–2
2	09/28/55	Brooklyn	6–5
3	10/03/55	Brooklyn	5–1
4	10/06/56	Brooklyn	5–3
5	10/02/57	Milwaukee	3–1
6	10/08/60	Pittsburgh	10–0
7	10/12/60	Pittsburgh (A)	12–0
8	10/04/61	Cincinnati	2–0
9	10/08/61	Cincinnati (A)	7–0
10	10/04/62	San Francisco (A)	6–2

(A) Away game

Appendix C: Career Winning Percentage Leaders

1901–2005, minimum 200 decisions

Rank	Pitcher	Win %	Record
1	Pedro Martinez*	.701	197–84
2	Whitey Ford	.690	236–106
3	Lefty Grove	.680	300–141
4	Christy Mathewson	.665	373–188
5	Roger Clemens*	.665	341–172
6	Sam Leever	.660	194–100
7	Randy Johnson*	.659	263–136
8	Sandy Koufax	.655	165–87
9	Johnny Allen	.654	142–75
10	Andy Pettitte*	.654	172–91
11	Ron Guidry	.651	170–91
12	Lefty Gomez	.649	189–102
13	Mordecai Brown	.648	239–130
14	Dizzy Dean	.644	150–83
15	Grover C. Alexander	.642	373–208
16	Mike Mussina*	.638	224–127
17	Jim Palmer	.638	268–152
18	Deacon Phillippe	.634	189–109
19	Dwight Gooden	.634	194–112
20	Joe McGinnity	.634	246–142
21	Ed Reulbach	.632	182–106
22	Juan Marichal	.631	243–142
23	Mort Cooper	.631	128–75
24	Allie Reynolds	.630	182–107
25	Bartolo Colon*	.629	139–82

Still active as of 2006 season. (Statistics are as of end of 2005 season.)

Appendix D:
Career ERA Leaders

Post–1930, minimum 200 decisions

Rank	Pitcher	ERA
1	Hoyt Wilhelm	2.52
2	Pedro Martinez*	2.72
3	Whitey Ford	2.75
4	Sandy Koufax	2.76
5	Jim Palmer	2.86
6	Andy Messersmith	2.86
7	Tom Seaver	2.86
8	Juan Marichal	2.89
9	Rollie Fingers	2.90
10	Bob Gibson	2.91
11	Harry Brecheen	2.92
12	Dean Chance	2.92
13	Don Drysdale	2.95
14	Mort Cooper	2.97
15	Mel Stottlemyre	2.97
16	Carl Hubbell	2.98
17	Rich Gossage	3.01
18	Greg Maddux*	3.01
19	Dizzy Dean	3.02
20	Hal Newhouser	3.06
21	Lefty Grove	3.06
22	Bob Veale	3.07
23	Warren Spahn	3.09
24	Gaylord Perry	3.11
25	Joel Horlen	3.11

*Still active as of 2006 season. (Statistics are as of end of 2005 season.)

Appendix E: ERA Differential Versus League

Major League Baseball All-Century Team Nominees[†]

Rank	Pitcher	ERA	League ERA[‡]	ERA Differential	ERA %
1	Pedro Martinez*	2.72	4.45	1.73	61.1%
2	Ed Walsh	1.82	2.76	0.94	65.9%
3	Walter Johnson	2.17	3.24	1.07	67.0%
4	Lefty Grove	3.06	4.42	1.36	69.2%
5	Roger Clemens*	3.12	4.37	1.25	71.4%
6	Whitey Ford	2.75	3.84	1.09	71.6%
7	Randy Johnson*	3.11	4.34	1.23	71.7%
8	Mordecai Brown	2.06	2.85	0.79	72.3%
9	Christy Mathewson	2.13	2.92	0.79	72.9%
10	Greg Maddux*	3.01	4.07	1.06	74.0%
11	Cy Young	2.63	3.55	0.92	74.1%
12	Sandy Koufax	2.76	3.70	0.94	74.6%
13	Carl Hubbell	2.98	3.96	0.98	75.3%
14	Grover C. Alexander	2.56	3.40	0.84	75.3%
15	Jim Palmer	2.86	3.71	0.85	77.1%
16	Dizzy Dean	3.02	3.88	0.86	77.8%
17	Bob Feller	3.25	4.16	0.91	78.1%
18	Tom Seaver	2.86	3.65	0.79	78.4%
19	Warren Spahn	3.09	3.89	0.80	79.4%
20	Juan Marichal	2.89	3.56	0.67	81.2%
21	Bob Gibson	2.91	3.58	0.67	81.3%
22	Eddie Plank	2.35	2.88	0.53	81.6%
23	Nolan Ryan	3.19	3.71	0.52	86.0%
24	Robin Roberts	3.41	3.91	0.50	87.2%
25	Steve Carlton	3.22	3.62	0.40	89.0%

*Still active as of 2006 season (statistics are as of end of 2005 season).
[†]Plus Pedro Martinez and Randy Johnson (who clearly would have been in that group had it been selected several years later) and minus Dennis Eckersley and Rollie Fingers (relievers) and Satchel Paige (too little data).
[‡]Weighted based on innings pitched in each season.

Appendix F: Comparison of Best Left-Handers in Modern Baseball History

Category	Ford	Spahn	Koufax	Grove	Johnson	Carlton	Plank	Hubbell
Seasons	16	21	12	17	18	24	17	16
Wins	236	363	165	300	263	329	326	253
Loses	106	245	87	141	136	244	194	154
Winning %	.690	.597	.655	.680	.659	.574	.627	.622
Net Team Winning %	.587	.526	.544	.561	.481	.513	.567	.544
Winning % Differential	.103	.071	.111	.119	.178	.061	.060	.078
Pitcher Wins	35.1	43.3	27.8	52.6	71.2	35.3	31.4	31.8
20-win seasons	2	13	3	8	3	6	8	5
Games Started	438	665	314	457	513	709	529	431
Complete Games	156	382	137	298	96	254	410	260
Shutouts	45	63	40	35	37	55	69	36
Innings Pitched	3,170.3	5,243.7	2,324.3	3,940.7	3,593.7	5,217.3	4,495.7	3,590.3
ERA	2.75	3.09	2.76	3.06	3.11	3.22	2.35	2.98
League ERA	3.84	3.89	3.70	4.42	4.34	3.62	2.88	3.96
ERA Differential	1.09	0.80	0.94	1.36	1.23	0.40	0.53	0.98
Pitching Runs	387	470	244	595	490	236	265	393
Walks	1,086	1,434	817	1,187	1,349	1,833	1,072	725
Walks per 9 innings	3.1	2.5	3.2	2.7	3.4	3.2	2.1	1.8
Strikeouts	1,956	2,583	2,396	2,266	4,372	4,136	2,246	1,677
Strikeouts per 9 innings	5.6	4.4	9.3	5.2	10.9	7.1	4.5	4.2
Strikeout/ Walk Ratio	1.80	1.80	2.93	1.91	3.24	2.26	2.10	2.31
Hits/walks per 9 innings	11.0	10.8	10.0	11.6	10.4	11.3	10.5	10.6

Category	Ford	Spahn	Koufax	Grove	Johnson	Carlton	Plank	Hubbell
Opponents' Batting Ave.	.235	.244	.205	.255	.212	.240	.239	.251
Opponents' On Base %	.301	.297	.276	.311	.293	.308	.293	.291

Best 10 consecutive seasons

Years	'55–'64	'49–'58	'57–'66	'28–'37	'93–'02	'72–'81	'03–'12	'28–'37
Record	173–69	202–130	161–81	214–82	175–58	185–111	214–117	192–102
Winning %	.715	.608	.665	.723	.751	.625	.647	.653
Winning % Differential	.119	.080	.124	.166	.244	.129	.080	.093
ERA	2.69	2.93	2.70	2.88	2.73	2.94	2.16	2.79
ERA Differential	1.18	1.05	1.00	1.58	1.77	0.68	0.58	1.27
Pitching Runs	299	332	246	453	432	202	186	375

Best five consecutive seasons

Years	'60–'64	'53–'57	'62–'66	'29–'33	'98–'02	'77–'81	'11–'15	'32–'36
Record	95–34	102–55	111–34	128–33	100–38	94–47	103–42	111–53
Winning %	.736	.650	.766	.795	.725	.667	.710	.677
Winning % Differential	.125	.077	.224	.201	.190	.126	.115	.127
ERA	2.81	2.79	1.95	2.68	2.63	2.77	2.34	2.40
ERA Differential	1.02	1.22	1.60	1.73	1.80	0.90	0.76	1.46
Pitching Runs	140	182	246	273	254	128	102	245

Appendix G:
Yankees Career Wins List

Rank	Pitcher	Wins
1	Whitey Ford (L)	236
2	Red Ruffing (R)	231
3	Lefty Gomez (L)	189
4	Ron Guidry (L)	170
5	Bob Shawkey (R)	168
6	Mel Stottlemyre (R)	164
7	Herb Pennock (L)	162
8	Waite Hoyt (R)	157
9	Andy Pettitte (L)	149
10	Allie Reynolds (R)	131

Chapter Notes

One

1. Ford and Pepe, *Slick*, 78.

Two

1. Ford and Pepe, *Slick*, 42.
2. *New York Times*, October 13, 1960, 44.
3. Ford and Pepe, *Slick*, 21.
4. *New York Times*, October 13, 1960, 44.
5. John Drebinger, *New York Times*, September 17, 1950, 155.
6. Ford, Mantle and Durso, *Whitey and Mickey*, Appendix.
7. Arthur Daley, "Four Straight," *New York Times*, October 8, 1950, S2.

Three

1. Gallagher, *Explosion!* 29; also Louis Effrat, *New York Times*, April 18, 1953, 12.
2. Leonard Koppett, *New York Times*, March 15, 1966, 45.
3. Gallagher, p. 43.
4. John Drebinger, *New York Times*, February 24, 1954, 30.
5. *Ibid.*, February 28, 1954, S1.
6. Greg Maddux won three Cy Young Awards with the Braves and four overall (1992–1995), while Tom Glavine won the award in 1991 and 1998 and John Smoltz won it in 1996.
7. The 1971 Baltimore Orioles rotation consisted of Jim Palmer (20–9), Mike Cuellar (20–9), Dave McNally (21–5) and Pat Dobson (20–8).
8. Harry Agganis was one of the most storied high school and college athletes in Massachusetts history. After starring in football, basketball and baseball for Lynn Classical High School, Agganis went on to star in football and baseball at Boston University, where he was an All-American quarterback and set school records for passing yardage, touchdown passes, punting average, and interceptions while also starring for the baseball team. Following his graduation in 1953, Agganis opted for baseball and within one year was playing first base for the Red Sox. After a decent 1954 rookie season in which he hit .251 with 57 RBIs, "The Golden Greek" (as he was affectionately known) came into his own in 1955 and was batting .313 in mid-May when he began experiencing chest pain and was hospitalized. Six weeks later, he died of a massive pulmonary embolism at the age of 25.
9. Effrat, *New York Times*, September 13, 1954, 27.
10. The previous American League record was held by the Detroit Tigers, who won 100 games in 1915, one less than Boston. The major league record of 104 was shared by Brooklyn (second to St. Louis by two games in 1942) and Chicago (second behind Pittsburgh's 110 wins in 1909).

Four

1. Joseph M. Sheehan, *New York Times*, May 14, 1955, 14.
2. Mantle and Gluck, *The Mick*, 136.
3. Gallagher, *Explosion!*, 56–57.
4. Louis Effrat, *New York Times*, June 18, 1955, 11.
5. Gallagher, 58–59. Also Effrat, *New York Times*, June 22, 1955, 34.
6. Sheehan, *New York Times*, September 3, 1955, 10.
7. http://www.BaseballLibrary.com/baseballlibrary/ballplayers/F/Ford_Whitey.stm.
8. Ford and Pepe, *Slick*, 109.
9. Mantle and Herskowitz, *All My Octobers*, 52.
10. Ford, *Slick*, 110. Also Sheehan, *New York Times*, October 4, 1955, 42.
11. Effrat, *New York Times*, October 4, 1955, 41.
12. *Ibid.*

13. *Ibid.*
14. *Ibid.*

Five

1. Baseball Legend Video Ltd., "Mickey Mantle—The American Dream Comes To Life," 1988.
2. John Drebinger, *New York Times,* April 18, 1956, 36; Gallagher, *Explosion!* 72–73.
3. Arthur Daley, "A Reformed Man," *New York Times,* April 22, 1956, 202.
4. Joseph M. Sheehan, *New York Times,* April 22, 1956, 201.
5. Gallagher, 73–75.
6. Gallagher, 78–79; Mantle and Pepe, *My Favorite Summer, 1956,* 90–92.
7. Thorn, Palmer, Gershman, and Pietrusza, *Total Baseball,* 2104; Sheehan, *New York Times,* May 31, 1956, 30.
8. Gallagher, 80–81.
9. Drebinger, *New York Times,* July 21, 1956, 10.
10. Gallagher, 398. Mantle hit 13 homers off Early Wynn and 12 off Pedro Ramos.
11. Drebinger, *New York Times,* September 1, 1956, S10.
12. Ford and Pepe, *Slick,* 96.
13. Mantle and Pepe, *My Favorite Summer, 1956,* 184.
14. Kahn, *The Era,* 330.
15. Mantle, *My Favorite Summer, 1956,* 219.
16. Louis Effrat, *New York Times,* October 7, 1956, 202.
17. Mantle, *My Favorite Summer, 1956,* 239.
18. *Ibid.,* 269.
19. *Ibid.,* 271.

Six

1. Thorn, Palmer, Gershman, and Pietrusza, *Total Baseball,* 142.
2. *Ibid.*
3. For the purposes of this book, "pitcher wins" is defined as the difference between a pitcher's winning percentage and the winning percentage of his team in games in which he is not involved in the decision, multiplied by the pitcher's total number of decisions. For example, in 1961 Ford was 25–4 for a winning percentage of .862. The team's record was 109–53, meaning that it was 84–49 when Ford was not involved in the decision, for a winning percentage of .632. Ford's differential was therefore .230; when multiplied by his 29 decisions, the result is 6.7 pitcher wins, meaning that he was worth an extra 6.7 wins to the Yankees that year compared to the rest of the Yankees pitching staff. This measure is meant to level the sta-

tistical playing field for all pitchers, regardless of how good their teams are. "Pitching runs" (as used in *Total Baseball*) is defined as the total number of runs that a pitcher saves his team over the course of a season if his ERA is below the league average. (Pitching runs can be negative if the pitcher's ERA is worse than the league average.) An explanation of the calculation of Spahn's 1957 pitching runs is included in footnote 6 below.
4. Jim Murray, "A Joker Not Wild," *Los Angeles Times,* July 3, 1963, C1.
5. *Ibid.*
6. Spahn's 1957 ERA of 2.69 was 1.19 runs better than the National League average ERA of 3.88. He pitched 271 innings, the equivalent of 30.1 nine-inning games. The product of the two numbers is 35.8 pitching runs, representing the advantage that he gave the Braves over the average NL pitcher over the course of the season.
7. Mantle and Pepe, *My Favorite Summer, 1956,* 78–80; *New York Times,* June 4, 1957, 1 and 41.
8. *The New York Times,* June 4, 1957, 1 and 41.
9. Arthur Daley, "A Fine State of Affairs," *New York Times,* June 5, 1957, 42.
10. Ford and Pepe, *Slick,* 145.
11. Ford, Mantle, and Durso, *Whitey and Mickey,* 68.
12. Martin and Pepe, *Billyball,* 92.
13. Gallagher, *Explosion!* 95–97.
14. Ford and Pepe, *Slick,* 139.
15. Louis Effrat, *New York Times,* October 3, 1957, 35.
16. Effrat, *New York Times,* October 8, 1957, 57.
17. Ford, Mantle, and Durso, *Whitey and Mickey,* 63.

Seven

1. Louis Effrat, *New York Times,* June 3, 1958, 39.
2. Gallagher, *Explosion!* 106.
3. John Drebinger, *New York Times,* June 13, 1958, 16; also Gallagher, 106.
4. Gallagher, 398.
5. Drebinger, *New York Times,* September 15, 1958, 25.
6. Ford yielded 49 earned runs in 219⅓ innings in 1958; in his three starts between August 13 and August 23 he allowed 13 earned runs in 16⅔ innings. Excluding those three starts, he yielded 36 earned runs in 202⅔ innings, an ERA of 1.60.
7. Gallagher, 114.
8. Mantle and Herskowitz, *All My Octobers,* 99.
9. Effrat, *New York Times,* October 6, 1958, 43.

10. *Ibid.*
11. Effrat, *New York Times,* October 9, 1958, 50.
12. Mantle and Herskowitz, *All My Octobers,* 102.

Eight

1. John Drebinger, *New York Times,* April 24, 1959, 30.
2. Louis Effrat, *New York Times,* May 11, 1959, 34.
3. Gallagher, *Explosion!* 126.

Nine

1. Gallagher, *Explosion!* 144–145.
2. *Ibid.,* 150.
3. Mantle and Herskowitz, *All My Octobers,* 105, 125.
4. Ford and Pepe, *Slick,* 149–150.
5. Mantle and Herskowitz, *All My Octobers,* 126.

Ten

1. John Drebinger, *New York Times,* April 22, 1961, 20.
2. Mark Gallagher, *Explosion!* 160.
3. Joseph M. Sheehan, *New York Times,* July 1, 1961, 10.
4. Ford, Mantle, and Durso, *Whitey and Mickey,* 124–126. Also Ford and Pepe, *Slick,* 185–187.
5. Rick Telander, "The Record Almost Broke Him," *Sports Illustrated,* June 20, 1977, 69.
6. Mantle and Herskowitz, *All My Octobers,* 145.
7. Houk and Creamer, *Season of Glory,* 210.
8. *Ibid.,* 221.
9. Ford and Pepe, *Slick,* 162–163.
10. Houk and Creamer, 251–252.
11. Smith, *61*,* 135.
12. http://www.BaseballLibrary.com/baseballlibrary/ballplayers/F/Ford_Whitey.stm.
13. Gallagher, 176–177.
14. Sheehan, *New York Times,* October 9, 1961, 45.
15. Houk and Creamer, 272.

Eleven

1. Louis Effrat, *New York Times,* May 4, 1962, 36.
2. *Ibid.,* August 3, 1962, 16.
3. Ford, Mantle, and Durso, *Whitey and Mickey,* 138.

4. John Drebinger, *New York Times,* August 27, 1962, 38.
5. Foxx was 30 years and 248 days old; Mantle was 30 years and 325 days old. Ken Griffey Jr. (30 years, 141 days) and Alex Rodriguez (29 years, 316 days) have subsequently reached the 400-homer mark faster than Foxx. Tom Verducci, "New York State of Mind," *Sports Illustrated,* June 6, 2005, 41.
6. Ford's 257.7 innings equated to 28.63 nine-inning games, with an ERA differential of 1.07 per nine innings.
7. Drebinger, *New York Times,* October 5, 1962, 54.
8. Joseph M. Sheehan, *ibid.,* 53.
9. *Ibid.*
10. Effrat, *ibid.,* October 9, 1962, 49.
11. *Ibid.*
12. Sheehan, *ibid,* October 16, 1962, 68.
13. *Ibid.*

Twelve

1. Gallagher, *Explosion!* 188–190.
2. *Los Angeles Times,* May 3, 1963, B4.
3. Mantle and Herskowitz, *All My Octobers,* 167. Also Gallagher, 193.
4. Leavy, *Sandy Koufax,* 103.
5. Ford and Pepe, *Slick,* 205.
6. Leavy, 136.
7. Mantle and Herskowitz, 169.
8. Halberstam, *October 1964,* 326.
9. UPI, *New York Times,* October 7, 1963, 39.
10. Leavy, 143.
11. *Ibid.,* 209.
12. Tom Verducci, "The Left Arm of God," *Sports Illustrated,* July 12, 1999, 96.
13. Leavy, 212.
14. *Ibid.,* 240.
15. As of the end of the 2005 season, the career record for strikeouts per nine innings was held by Randy Johnson (10.95).

Thirteen

1. Joseph M. Sheehan, *New York Times,* October 9, 1961, 45.
2. Leonard Koppett, *New York Times,* April 23, 1964, 46.
3. Ford and Pepe, *Slick,* 195–196.
4. Gordon S. White Jr., *New York Times,* May 27, 1964, 27.
5. Ford, Mantle, and Durso, *Whitey and Mickey,* 142–144.
6. Koppett, *New York Times,* June 4, 1964, 45.
7. Joseph Durso, *New York Times,* August 5, 1964, 25.
8. *Ibid.,* August 9, 1964, S1.

9. *Ibid.*, August 13, 1964, 33. Also Gallagher, *Explosion!* 199–200.

10. Koppett, *New York Times*, September 14, 1964, 46.

11. *Ibid.*, August 26, 1966, 23.

12. Ford, Mantle, and Durso, *Whitey and Mickey*, 183.

13. Mantle and Herskowitz, *All My Octobers*, 188.

14. Ford and Pepe, *Slick*, 218. Also Koppett, *New York Times*, August 26, 1966, 23.

Fourteen

1. William N. Wallace, *New York Times*, April 26, 1965, 41.

2. Ford, Mantle, and Durso, *Whitey and Mickey*, 138. Also Ford and Pepe, *Slick*, 192–194.

3. Arthur Daley, "A Lucky Wild Pitch," *The New York Times*, September 6, 1953, S2.

4. Ford, Mantle, and Durso, *Whitey and Mickey*, 142.

5. Ford and Pepe, *Slick*, 192.

6. Joseph Durso, *New York Times*, January 9, 1966, 154.

7. *Ibid.*

8. Durso, *New York Times*, January 14, 1966, 49.

9. Ford and Pepe, *Slick*, 200–202. Also Ford, Mantle, and Durso, *Whitey and Mickey*, 136–137.

10. Durso, *New York Times*, July 8, 1966, 53.

11. Daley, "Chairman of the Board," *New York Times*, June 12, 1966, 222.

12. "Baseball is a Fun Game to Ford," *New York Times*, May 28, 1967, S2.

13. Leonard Koppett, *New York Times*, May 31, 1967, 31.

14. *Ibid.*

15. Daley, "The Chairman Retires," *New York Times*, May 31, 1967, 31.

16. Ford and Pepe, *Slick*, 249.

Fifteen

1. Ford was 228–100 with 110 no-decisions in 438 career starts, and 8–6 with 10 saves in 60 relief appearances.

2. Ford was 133–59 during his first eight and a half seasons in the majors (1950–1960), a winning percentage of .693. During the five seasons 1961–1965 when he averaged 37 starts, his record was 99–38, a winning percentage of .723.

3. Leavy, *Sandy Koufax*, 121.

4. Net team winning percentage is the team's winning percentage in games in which the pitcher in question was not involved in the decision. For example, in 1963 Ford was 24–7 and the Yankees' record was 104–57, meaning that they were 80–50 in games in which Ford was not involved in the decision. New York's net team winning percentage was thus .615. Since Whitey's winning percentage was .774, he had a differential that season of .159.

5. Clemens's statistics are as of the end of the 2005 season.

6. Ford was 207–83 (.714) with an ERA of 2.72 during this period (1953–1964), while Warren Spahn was 234–138 (.629) with an ERA of 3.05. No one else would merit serious consideration.

7. Pitching Runs: unless ERA differential is weighted by innings pitched, it doesn't measure the full value of a pitcher's favorable variance versus his league's average ERA. Pedro Martinez's ERA of 2.07 in 1999 was only 42.6 percent of the league's ERA of 4.86, but he pitched only 213 innings. Any manager would rather have the 1966 season of Sandy Koufax (whose 1.73 ERA was a slightly higher percentage of the league's ERA of 3.61) because Koufax provided his team with that advantage for 323 innings, 110 more than Martinez.

8. Thorn, Palmer, Gershman, and Pietrusza, *Total Baseball*, 191–192.

9. Martin and Pepe, *Billyball*, 91.

Bibliography

Newspapers

The New York Times, 1950–1967.
Los Angeles Times, 1962–1964.

Books

Ford, Whitey, and Phil Pepe. *Slick: My Life in and Around Baseball*. New York: William Morrow, 1987.

Ford, Whitey, Mickey Mantle and Joseph Durso. *Whitey and Mickey: A Joint Autobiography of the Yankee Years*. New York: Viking, 1977.

Frommer, Harvey. *The New York Yankee Encyclopedia*. New York: Macmillan, 1997.

Gallagher, Mark. *Explosion! Mickey Mantle's Legendary Home Runs*. New York: Arbor House, 1987.

Halberstam, David. *October 1964*. New York: Fawcett Columbine, 1994.

Houk, Ralph, and Robert W. Creamer. *Season of Glory*. New York: G. P. Putnam's Sons, 1988.

Kahn, Roger. *The Era*. New York: Houghton Mifflin, 1993.

_____. "Pursuit of No. 60: The Ordeal of Roger Maris." *Sports Illustrated,* September 26, 1994.

Leavy, Jane. *Sandy Koufax: A Lefty's Legacy*. New York: HarperCollins, 2002.

Mantle, Mickey, and Herb Gluck. *The Mick*. New York: Jove, 1986.

Mantle, Mickey, and Phil Pepe. *My Favorite Summer, 1956*. New York: Dell, 1991.

Mantle, Mickey, and Mickey Herskowitz. *All My Octobers*. New York: HarperCollins, 1994.

Martin, Billy, and Phil Pepe. *Billyball*. Garden City: Doubleday, 1987.

Shapiro, Milton J. *The Whitey Ford Story*. New York: Julian Messner, 1962.

Smith, Ron. *61**. St. Louis: The Sporting News, 2001.

Telander, Rick. "The Record Almost Broke Him." *Sports Illustrated,* June 20, 1977.

Thorn, John, Pete Palmer, Michael Gershman and David Pietrusza. *Total Baseball*. New York: Viking, 1997.

Verducci, Tom. "The Left Arm of God." *Sports Illustrated,* July 12, 1999.

Index

Aaron, Hank 75–76, 81–86, 96–97, 99–100, 118, 196, 215
Adams, Bobby 54
Adcock, Joe 76, 82–85, 96–97, 100, 118
Agganis, Harry 33–34
Aguirre, Hank 152–153, 165, 206
Alexander, Grover Cleveland 172, 174, 223, 225
Allen, Johnny 223
Allen, Richie 170, 186, 196
Allison, Bob 110, 129
Alou, Felipe 154–158
Alou, Matty 157, 159
Alston, Walter 50–51, 65–66, 69–70
Amoros, Sandy 50–52, 64–65, 68–69
Antonelli, Johnny 75, 166
Aparicio, Luis 57, 59, 89, 102
Arroyo, Luis 118, 125–129, 131–135, 137–140, 143–147, 153
Ashburn, Richie 15–16
Aspromonte, Ken 132
Avila, Bobby 32–33, 43

Bailey, Ed 156–157
Banks, Ernie 81, 196, 215
Barber, Steve 135–136
Bauer, Hank 1, 12, 14, 18, 26–30, 34, 37, 40–41, 43–44, 47, 49, 52, 54, 64, 67–70, 77–78, 82–83, 85, 89, 96–99, 101, 107, 125, 164
Beamon, Charlie 62
Belinsky, Bo 146, 150
Bell, Gary 147
Bennett, Dennis 186
Berra, Yogi 1, 11–15, 17–18, 23–26, 28–30, 31, 33, 36–37, 39–41, 43–44, 46, 49–52, 53–55, 59, 61, 64, 66–67, 77–78, 82–85, 90, 95, 97–101, 103–104, 107, 109, 114–116, 118–121, 125–126, 129, 131–132, 135, 140, 145, 148, 150–151, 153, 156, 161, 168, 175, 182–184, 188–189, 191, 193, 203, 209–210

Bertoia, Reno 110
Bessent, Don 48
Bevens, Bill 46
Bilko, Steve 146
Blanchard, Johnny 111, 117, 120, 126, 129, 134, 138, 140–142, 145, 150, 161, 188, 192
Bloodworth, Jimmy 17
Bolin, Bob 156
Bollweg, Don 27
Bonds, Barry 80, 149, 156
Boone, Ray 37, 58
Bouton, Jim 145, 148, 160–161, 168, 180, 184, 188, 191, 195
Boyd, Bob 24
Boyer, Clete 110, 120, 142, 145, 151, 153, 155–157, 160, 165, 169, 176, 179, 188–189, 192, 194
Boyer, Ken 187, 189, 191–192
Branca, Ralph 159
Brandt, Jackie 111, 147
Brecheen, Harry 224
Bridges, Marshall 147–153, 156–157
Briggs Stadium (Detroit) 13, 38, 56, 58, 95, 112
Bright, Harry 149, 168
Brock, Lou 186, 190, 192
Broglio, Ernie 186
Brown, Bobby 17–18
Brown, Hal 110
Brown, Mordecai 174, 223, 225
Bruton, Billy 76, 97–99
Buckner, Bill 159
Buhl, Bob 76, 83, 85
Bunning, Jim 58, 79, 90, 95, 110, 112, 133, 186
Burdette, Lew 10, 76, 82–83, 85–86, 95–100, 119, 197
Burgess, Smoky 116, 119–120
Busby, Jim 88, 112
Busch, Gussie 192
Busch Stadium (St. Louis) 187

235

Buzhardt, Johnny 145
Byrne, Tommy 10, 12–13, 15, 36, 43, 45, 47, 49–51, 64, 66, 84, 86

Callison, Johnny 186
Campanella, Roy 26–27, 29, 46–47, 49–51, 64–67, 69, 153, 215
Carey, Andy 33–34, 37–38, 49, 56–57, 59, 67–69, 76, 82, 89, 101
Carlton, Steve 213, 225–227
Casey, Hugh 46, 158
Cash, Norm 148, 201, 203
Castro, Fidel 99
Cepeda, Orlando 154, 156, 158–159, 165
Cerv, Bob 50, 52, 62, 95, 110, 116–117, 129
Chacon, Elio 141–142
Chance, Dean 146, 151, 162, 164, 184–185, 224
Chandler, Spud 177, 184
Chapman, Sam 15
Chavez Ravine (Los Angeles) 146–147
Chesbro, Jack 131, 163, 217
Cimoli, Gino 116–117, 120
Clarke, Horace 208
Clemens, Roger 72, 131, 211, 213–214, 216, 223, 225
Clemente, Roberto 113–114, 116, 118, 120, 172, 196, 215
Clevenger, Tex 125, 143
Coates, Jim 114, 120–121, 137, 142–143, 147–148, 152, 156–157
Cobb, Ty 51, 153
Colavito, Rocky 95
Coleman, Jerry 17–18, 30–31, 82, 84–86
Coleman, Rip 45
Collins, Joe 17, 26–29, 40, 48, 50–51, 54, 57, 62, 64, 66–67, 70
Colon, Bartolo 223
Combs, Earle 11, 30, 143
Comiskey Park (Chicago) 14, 38, 55, 109, 207
Conley, Gene 83
Consuegra, Sandy 24
Cooley, Dr. Denton 193, 196, 202, 205
Coombs, Jack 184
Cooper, Mort 223–224
Copacabana Incident 77–78
Cottier, Chuck 164
County Stadium (Milwaukee) 83–84, 96
Covington, Wes 76, 82–86, 97, 99
Cox, Billy 27, 29
Craig, Roger 50, 66, 70, 189
Crandall, Del 97, 100
Culp, Ray 186

Daley, Arthur 18, 205, 209

Daley, Bud 132, 147, 152
Dark, Alvin 157, 178–179
Davenport, Jim 155, 157–158
Davis, Sammy, Jr. 77
Davis, Tommy 154, 168
Davis, Willie 169
D.C. Stadium (Washington) 205
Dean, Dizzy 17, 166, 223–225
Delock, Ike 125
DeMaestri, Joe 120–121
Dente, Sam 34
Devine, Bing 186
Dickey, Bill 30–31, 37, 62
DiMaggio, Joe 3, 10, 12–13, 15, 17–18, 30–31, 37, 46, 58, 60, 62, 90, 95, 113, 129–130, 153, 184, 202, 208–210
Ditmar, Art 93, 99, 111, 114, 118, 126, 140
Doby, Larry 32–34, 56, 61
Dodger Stadium (Los Angeles) 146, 168
Donatelli, Augie 84
Donovan, Dick 38, 59, 78, 93
Donovan, Wild Bill 139
Downing, Al 138, 160–161, 168, 180, 187, 189, 192, 200, 207
Drebinger, John 14
Dressen, Charlie 26–28, 203
Dropo, Walt 15, 38, 41, 61, 89, 112
Drysdale, Don 68, 73, 153–154, 168, 171–172, 224
Durante, Sal 138
Duren, Ryne 78, 89–90, 93, 95–97, 99–100, 104, 106, 120
Durocher, Leo 2, 192
Durso, Joseph 202
Dykes, Jimmy 66, 110

Easter, Luke 13
Ebbets Field (Brooklyn) 15, 26–28, 47, 49, 50, 65–68, 70, 82, 87
Eisenhower, Dwight 53, 59, 65
Ennis, Del 16, 18
Erskine, Carl 26–29, 50, 65, 67–68, 168
Evers, Hoot 43
Evers, Johnny 158

Face, Elroy 113–114, 117–118, 120–121
Feller, Bob 13, 32, 58, 89, 103, 138, 166, 171, 225
Fenway Park (Boston) 25, 34, 57, 61–62, 75, 87, 107, 129, 137, 183, 199, 202, 205
Ferrick, Tom 11, 13
Fingers, Rollie 224
Finigan, Jim 43
Fischer, Bill 102, 110, 162
Fisher, Eddie 199

Fisher, Jack 137
Flood, Curt 172, 187, 189–190
Foran, Joan 5, 19
Foran, Joe 5
Forbes Field (Pittsburgh) 118–119
Ford, Eddie, Jr. 6, 92
Ford, Russ 93, 184, 198
Ford, Tommy 92
Ford, Whitey: all-star games 32, 39–40, 57, 101, 106, 128; arm operations 193, 196–197, 205; Babe Ruth Award 142; career statistics 219, 220–222; Cy Young Award 139; Hall of Fame election 210; high school years 5–6; home runs (as batter) 40, 103, 162; illegal pitches (mud ball, cut ball, spitter) 128, 149–150, 178–179, 197–198; major league debut 10–11; Mexico (winter ball) 8–9; milestone wins (1st) 11; (100th) 91; (200th) 176; (232nd) 201–202; minor league years 8–10; no-hit bids 22, 41–43, 56, 110, 146–147; retirement 208–209; salary 19–20, 31, 77, 139, 202, 206; sandlot ball 3–6; signed by Yankees 6–7; strikeout records 58, 89, 102–103, 139, 165, 187; wedding 19; Whitey Ford Day 134; winning percentage records 2, 91, 176–177, 215; winning streaks 131, 163; World Series records 141, 155, 187; World Series wins 18, 47–49, 50–51, 66–67, 82, 116, 118, 141–142, 154–155; Yankee records 102–103, 131, 139, 165, 179, 181, 184, 201–202
Fox, Nellie 38, 56, 59, 61, 102
Fox, Terry 135
Foxx, Jimmie 38, 46, 61, 90, 132, 134–135, 137, 152–153
Foy, Joe 207
Foytack, Paul 93, 112
Francona, Tito 62, 89
Frick, Ford 128, 135, 137
Friend, Bob 114, 121
Frisch, Frankie 100
Furillo, Carl 26, 29, 47, 49–51, 64–67, 69

Garcia, Mike 32–35
Gardner, Billy 54, 111
Gastall, Tom 54
Gaynor, Dr. Sidney 204, 208
Gehrig, Lou 30, 37, 62–63, 66, 70, 82, 97, 99, 132, 143, 184, 206, 208
Geiger, Gary 145
Gentile, Jim 147, 151
Gernert, Dick 142
Gibbon, Joe 115
Gibson, Bob 1–2, 173, 186–188, 190–192, 196, 211–214, 224–225

Gilliam, Jim 26, 28–29, 49, 51–52, 65–66, 69–70, 169
Gionfriddo, Al 46
Goliat, Mike 17–18
Gomez, Lefty 6, 8, 30, 217, 223, 228
Gooden, Dwight 91, 223
Goodman, Billy 34
Gorman, Tom 28, 61
Gossage, Rich 224
Grant, Mudcat 162, 178–179, 200
Green, Fred 114–116
Greenberg, Hank 61, 90, 135, 137
Griffey, Ken, Jr. 134
Griffith Stadium (Washington) 21, 53, 60
Grim, Bob 31, 33–34, 36, 49–50, 62, 64, 77, 84
Grimm, Charlie 76
Groat, Dick 113–114, 116, 120, 189–191
Grove, Lefty 63, 91, 136, 139, 173–174, 177, 211, 213, 216–217, 223–227
Guidry, Ron 6, 74, 131, 217, 223, 228

Haddix, Harvey 118, 121
Hall, Dick 136
Haller, Tom 156
Hamilton, Steve 191–193, 200–201
Hamner, Granny 17–18
Haney, Fred 76, 82, 85, 99–100
Hannan, Jim 205–206
Hansen, Ron 112
Harrelson, Ken 183
Hartnett, Gabby 64
Hatfield, Fred 59
Hatton, Grady 44
Hazle, Bob "Hurricane" 76, 85
Hegan, Jim 33
Heintzelman, Ken 17
Henrich, Tommy 13, 15, 31, 46, 158
Herbert, Ray 152, 182
Hiller, Chuck 155–157
Hoak, Don 113–114, 116–117, 119
Hodges, Gil 26, 28, 47, 50–51, 64–66, 68–69
Hoeft, Billy 40, 56
Honochick, Jim 203
Horlen, Joel 185, 224
Hornsby, Rogers 63
Houk, Ralph 96, 122–126, 129, 133, 135, 138, 145, 147, 150, 155–159, 161–162, 164–165, 175, 193, 202, 204, 207, 210
Houtteman, Art 32
Howard, Elston 1, 31, 42, 47, 52, 54, 70, 84, 92, 96, 98–101, 107, 114–116, 124, 132, 134, 140–141, 145–147, 149–151, 153, 160, 161, 163, 165, 168, 175, 181, 185, 187–191, 194, 196, 198, 200, 207

Howard, Frank 167, 169
Hoyt, Waite 228
Hubbell, Carl 114, 165, 224–227
Hunt, Ken 178
Hunter, Billy 38, 61

Jay, Joey 141
Jensen, Jackie 10, 13, 33, 45, 80, 91–92, 95, 125–126
John, Tommy 170, 199
Johnson, Connie 88
Johnson, Darrell 141–142
Johnson, Randy 174, 216–217, 223, 225–227
Johnson, Walter 89, 94, 99, 101, 166, 172–174, 184, 211, 213, 216–217, 225
Jones, Sam 103
Jones, Vernal "Nippy" 84
Jones, Willie 16, 18
Jucker, Ed 166

Kahn, Roger 47
Kaline, Al 40, 55, 58, 61–63, 135, 152, 165, 205
Keane, Johnny 186, 190, 192–193, 199–200, 204
Kell, George 38–39
Keller, Charlie 37
Kellner, Alex 39
Killebrew, Harmon 110, 146, 185
Kinder, Ellis 44
Kiner, Ralph 43, 61, 134
Klaus, Billy 44–45
Kluszewski, Ted 118
Konstanty, Jim 15, 17–18, 40, 44
Koufax, Sandy 1–2, 72, 153–154, 165–174, 180, 184, 189, 211–214, 216–217, 223–227
Kraly, Steve 24
Krichell, Paul 5, 7, 10
Kubek, Tony 1, 83–85, 90, 98, 106, 109–110, 114, 116–117, 120, 142, 145, 150–151, 156, 158–160, 167, 185, 194
Kucks, Johnny 36, 38, 40, 50, 64, 66, 68, 70, 77, 79
Kuenn, Harvey 40, 55, 157
Kuzava, Bob 24, 29

Labine, Clem 26, 28, 47, 50, 70, 115–116
Landis, Jim 79, 89
Larsen, Don 22, 36, 43, 45, 47, 50, 64, 66, 68–70, 83, 85, 89, 97, 100, 118, 155, 157
Lary, Frank 55, 63, 88, 90, 106, 109, 126, 132, 135, 139, 148, 165
Lavagetto, Cookie 102
Law, Vernon 113–114, 116–117, 119–120
Lazzeri, Tony 30, 37, 143

Lee, Don 110
Leever, Sam 223
Lemon, Bob 31–35, 38–39, 45, 58
Lemon, Jim 45, 60–61, 91, 111, 126
Lenhardt, Don 34
Lepcio, Ted 34
Linz, Phil 147, 182, 188–192, 197
Loes, Billy 4, 26, 28, 49, 58, 87
Logan, Johnny 82–85, 97–100
Lolich, Mickey 183, 201, 203
Lollar, Sherman 62, 89–90
Long, Dale 118, 121, 151
Lopat, Ed 1, 10–13, 15, 17, 20–22, 24–27, 30–31, 33–34, 36, 40, 180
Lopata, Stan 18
Lopez, Hector 43, 112, 114, 142, 147, 150, 152, 161, 163, 168, 170, 200
Lumpe, Jerry 103, 200

Maas, Duke 97, 110
Maddux, Greg 174, 216, 224–225
Maglie, Sal 64–66, 68–69
Mahaffey, Art 186
Malzone, Frank 145
Mantle, Mickey 1–2, 14, 19–30, 31–34, 36–44, 46–50, 52, 53–70, 77–79, 82–83, 86, 87–93, 95, 97–101, 102–105, 107, 108–118, 120–121, 123–135, 137–138, 140–142, 144–153, 155–156, 160, 161–162, 164, 167, 169–171, 175, 180–185, 187–192, 194, 200–202, 203–206, 207–210; Hall of Fame election 210; memorable home runs 20–21, 28–29, 37–39, 53–56, 78–79, 90, 95, 104, 112, 115, 126–127, 148–149, 161–162, 169, 182, 189, 205–206, 208; milestone home runs, (No. 100) 39; (No. 200) 79; (No. 300) 109; (No. 400) 152; (No. 500) 208; Most Valuable Player Awards 64, 81, 153; relationship with fans 104–106, 130; runner-up 113, 138–139, 185; switch-hit home runs in same game 37, 41, 54–55, 57, 92, 107, 124, 145, 182; Triple Crown 61–63; World Series home run record 189
Marichal, Juan 1–2, 73, 154, 156, 173, 196, 223–225
Maris, Roger 1, 30, 90, 109–116, 118, 120–121, 123–138, 140–142, 144–145, 147–151, 153–156, 158–160, 161, 167, 182–185, 188–189, 191–192, 194
Marquard, Rube 127, 131, 158
Martin, Billy 1, 6–7, 10, 21, 23–31, 41–45, 47–48, 52, 61–62, 66–70, 77–79, 217
Martin, Johnny 4–5, 7
Martin, Pepper 30

Martinez, Pedro 139–140, 172, 174, 215–216, 223–225
Mathews, Eddie 75–76, 81–82, 84–86, 96, 98
Mathewson, Christy 70, 72, 86, 119, 141, 158, 167, 174, 211, 213, 223, 225
Mauch, Gene 186
Mauch, Gus 14
Maxvill, Dal 192
Maxwell, Charlie 55
Mays, Willie 35, 40, 57, 61, 73, 82, 106–107, 128, 134, 154–159, 165, 171, 196, 215
Mazeroski, Bill 113–114, 116–117, 119, 121, 158–159
McCarthy, Joe 30, 193
McCarver, Tim 187–188, 191, 193
McCormick, Mike 164, 205
McCovey, Willie 82, 154–157, 159, 165, 196
McDonald, Jim 28–29
McDougald, Gil 22, 27–29, 31, 41, 45, 51–52, 57, 64, 68–69, 83–84, 86, 88, 98–100, 106, 109, 116–118, 121
McDowell, Sam 181
McGinnity, Joe 223
McGraw, John 75
McGwire, Mark 134
McKinley, Bill 188
McLain, Denny 199
McMahon, Don 100, 205
McNally, Dave 172, 181
Memorial Stadium (Baltimore) 94, 112, 135, 164
Merkle, Fred 158
Messersmith, Andy 172, 224
Meusel, Bob 143
Meyer, Russ 17, 26, 28–29
Mikkelsen, Pete 179, 183, 190–191, 199
Miller, Bob 18, 37
Miller, Marvin 171–172
Miller, Stu 155
Minoso, Minnie 57
Mitchell, Dale 22, 69
Mize, Johnny 15, 17, 23–24, 27–28, 30, 37, 47, 61
Mizell, Vinegar Bend 116
Monbouquette, Bill 137–138, 145
Moore, Ray 90
Morgan, Tom 39, 45, 57, 61, 147
Moses, Wally 175
Mossi, Don 43, 132
Municipal Stadium (Cleveland) 33, 35, 38, 91
Municipal Stadium (Kansas City) 126
Murray, Eddie 182
Murray, Jim 73
Murray, Spud 115

Murtaugh, Danny 114, 116, 119, 121
Musial, Stan 32, 40, 46, 57, 73, 152–153, 202
Mussina, Mike 223

Narleski, Ray 89
Neal, Charlie 67
Nelson, Rocky 119, 121
Newcombe, Don 15, 26, 47–48, 50, 64–66, 70, 214
Newhouser, Hal 13, 23, 32, 138, 174, 224
Nieman, Bob 62, 103, 157
Nixon, Willard 33
Noren, Irv 32–33, 36, 42–43

O'Dell, Billy 154–155
Oliva, Tony 185
Olson, Karl 44
O'Malley, Walter 171
Osteen, Claude 171
O'Toole, Jim 141–142
Owen, Mickey 46, 158

Pafko, Andy 82–83, 99–100
Pagan, Jose 155
Page, Joe 10, 46, 128, 137
Pagliaroni, Jim 145
Paige, Satchel 23–24
Palmer, Jim 172, 208, 223–225
Pappas, Milt 112, 136
Pascual, Camilo 53, 55–56, 59–60, 89, 111, 153
Patterson, Arthur "Red" 21
Paul, Gabe 6
Paula, Carlos 41–42
Pearson, Albie 146
Peckinpaugh, Roger 198
Pennock, Herb 228
Pepitone, Joe 146–147, 150, 161, 168–169, 178, 183, 188, 190–191, 194, 203, 206
Perry, Gaylord 224
Pesky, Johnny 158–159
Peters, Gary 176, 179
Peterson, Fritz 206
Pettitte, Andy 223, 228
Phillippe, Deacon 223
Phillips, Bubba 89
Pierce, Billy 37–38, 40–41, 45, 57, 61, 80, 89–90, 131, 154, 156–158
Piersall, Jimmy 44, 59, 132
Pillette, Duane 23, 32
Pinelli, Babe 69
Pinson, Vada 141
Pizarro, Juan 99, 131
Plank, Eddie 70, 158, 225–227
Podres, Johnny 26, 28, 49, 51–52, 65, 168

Polo Grounds (New York) 4, 6–7, 35, 87, 146
Porterfield, Bob 41, 63
Portocarrero, Arnie 42–43
Powell, Boog 185
Power, Vic 200
Priddy, Gerry 13
Purkey, Bob 141

Ramos, Pedro 55, 124, 129, 183–185, 188, 199–200, 203
Raschi, Vic 1, 10, 15, 17, 20, 23, 25, 27, 30–31, 36, 40
Reed, Jack 148
Reese, Pee Wee 26, 47, 50–52, 64–67, 69–70, 72
Reniff, Hal 143, 162
Reulbach, Ed 223
Reynolds, Allie 1, 10, 13–15, 17–18, 20, 22, 25–27, 29–31, 33–36, 140–141, 223, 228
Rhodes, Dusty 35
Rice, John 179
Rice, Sam 30
Richardson, Bobby 1, 6, 77–78, 110, 113–118, 120–121, 131, 142, 150–151, 153–154, 156, 159–160, 167–168, 181, 188–190, 192, 200
Richardson, Gordon 191
Rigney, Bill 147
Rivera, Jim 62
Rivera, Mariano 155
Rizzuto, Phil 1, 13, 15, 17–18, 24, 28–31, 41, 43–44, 51–52, 54, 59
Roberts, Robin 15, 17, 40, 151–152, 225
Robinson, Brooks 147, 162, 185
Robinson, Eddie 33, 38
Robinson, Frank 140–141, 196, 206, 208, 215
Robinson, Jackie 26–29, 46–51, 64–65, 67–71, 196, 214–215
Rodgers, Bob 147
Rodriguez, Alex 63, 134
Roe, Preacher 26–27, 139
Roebuck, Ed 68, 154
Rohr, Billy 207
Rolfe, Red 13
Rosar, Buddy 103
Roseboro, Johnny 168
Rosen, Al 25, 32–33, 35
Rowe, Schoolboy 127
Ruffing, Red 30, 67, 140–141, 165, 179, 181, 201–202, 228
Runnels, Pete 153
Rush, Bob 97, 99
Russell, Jim 37

Ruth, Babe 9, 30, 37, 53, 56–57, 61, 66, 77, 80, 82, 93, 99, 110–111, 115–116, 123–124, 127–128, 130, 132, 134–138, 141–143, 149, 169, 175, 183–184, 189, 208
Ryan, Nolan 171, 173, 211–213, 225

Sadecki, Ray 187, 189
Sain, Johnny 20, 25–26, 28, 34, 36, 82, 96, 123
Sanford, Jack 154–159
Sawyer, Eddie 17
Scheffing, Bob 152
Schoendienst, Red 37, 76, 82–84, 86, 95, 97–99, 101
Schultz, Barney 188–189, 191
Schwall, Don 138, 152
Score, Herb 39, 43, 45, 58, 64
Seaver, Tom 224–225
Selkirk, George 9
Seminick, Andy 18
Shannon, Mike 187, 189, 191–192
Shantz, Bobby 80, 82–83, 85–86, 89, 110, 112, 115, 120, 213
Shawkey, Bob 103, 228
Shea Stadium (New York) 146, 181, 210
Sheldon, Rollie 126, 132, 138, 140, 151, 181, 192, 204
Sherry, Norm 166–167
Shibe Park (Philadelphia) 17
Short, Chris 186
Shuba, George 26
Siebern, Norm 96, 98
Sievers, Roy 80–81, 95
Silvera, Charlie 30
Simmons, Al 217
Simmons, Curt 16–17, 188, 191
Simpson, Harry 43, 78, 84
Sisler, Dick 15–16
Sisler, George 16
Skinner, Bob 114, 119
Skowron, Bill 1, 14, 36, 40, 48–50, 52, 54, 64, 70, 84, 86, 88, 90, 96–101, 102, 104, 109, 114–118, 120, 126–127, 131–132, 135, 140–142, 144–145, 153, 156, 160, 161, 167–168, 200, 202
Slaughter, Enos 40, 43, 58–59, 62, 65, 67, 70, 80, 83, 90, 97, 159
Smith, Hal 93, 120
Snider, Duke 26, 28–29, 47, 49–50, 64–70, 97, 99, 115, 149
Soares, Joe 179
Sosa, Sammy 134
Spahn, Warren 1–2, 57, 72–77, 81–86, 95–101, 123, 139, 173, 179, 210–211, 213, 215–217, 224–227
Spooner, Karl 50

Stafford, Bill 119–120, 126, 133, 140, 148, 150, 153, 156, 180–182, 195
Staley, Gerry 134
Stallard, Tracy 138
Stange, Lee 165
Stanky, Eddie 207
Stargell, Willie 196
Steinbrenner, George 6
Stengel, Casey 10, 12–13, 15–16, 18, 20–21, 24–30, 31–32, 34–35, 37–39, 45, 49, 51, 53–54, 60–66, 68, 70, 72, 78, 80, 82–85, 87, 93, 97–100, 105–106, 108, 111–114, 118–122, 123, 209, 211–212
Stobbs, Chuck 21, 61, 102–103, 113
Stoneham, Horace 128
Stottlemyre, Mel 160, 182–185, 188, 190–192, 194, 196, 200, 206–207, 224, 228
Stuart, Dick 116, 121, 164
Sturdivant, Tom 64, 67–68, 80, 83, 85
Sullivan, Ed 50
Sullivan, Frank 40, 44–45
Sullivan, Haywood 129
Summers, Bill 49
Surkont, Max 58

Taylor, Joe 94
Taylor, Ron 190
Terry, Ralph 107–108, 111, 116–117, 121, 133, 140, 143–144, 149, 151–153, 155–161, 168, 180
Thomas, Frank 186
Thomson, Bobby 19, 75–76, 159
Throneberry, Marv 96
Tiant, Luis 181
Torre, Frank 83–86, 100
Tracewski, Dick 168
Tresh, Tom 145–146, 150–151, 153–154, 156–157, 159–161, 163–164, 167–168, 170, 187–188, 190, 192, 200, 206
Triandos, Gus 112
Trout, Dizzy 13
Turley, Bob 36, 43, 45, 47, 49, 64, 68, 70, 82–83, 85, 89, 93–103, 111, 115, 119, 126, 140, 147–148
Turner, Jim 10–11, 69
Tuttle, Bill 40, 55, 129

Valentinetti, Vito 6

Vander Meer, Johnny 103
Veale, Bob 224
Vernon, Mickey 41–42, 45
Versalles, Zoilo 129
Vincent, Fay 129
Virdon, Bill 114–117, 120, 210

Waddell, Rube 171
Wagner, Leon 150
Waitkus, Eddie 16
Walsh, Ed 184, 211, 215–216, 225
Ward, Pete 202
Warwick, Carl 187, 189
Weiss, George 9, 20–21, 31, 77–78, 108
Wertz, Vic 13, 23, 33–34, 126
White, Bill 187, 190–192
White, Sammy 34
Whitfield, Fred 201
Whitman, Dick 17, 175
Wiesler, Bob 89
Wilhelm, Hoyt 94, 103, 137, 215, 224
Williams, Billy 196
Williams, Stan 154, 161, 182
Williams, Ted 33–34, 45, 56–57, 61–63, 77, 79–81, 95, 112–113, 137, 202
Wills, Maury 74, 153–154, 196
Wilson, Hack 61, 137
Wilson, Jim 89
Wilson, Red 55
Wood, Jake 148
Wood, Smokey Joe 139, 217
Woodling, Gene 13, 17–18, 22, 24, 27–30, 88
Woods, Dr. Robert 162
World Series: (1941) 46; (1947) 46; (1949) 47; (1950) 15–18; (1952) 47; (1953) 25–30; (1954) 35; (1955) 46–52; (1956) 65–71; (1957) 82–86; (1958) 96–101; (1960) 113–122; (1961) 140–143; (1962) 154–159; (1963) 167–170; (1964) 187–192; (1965) 171; (1966) 172
Wynn, Early 15, 22, 31–35, 38–40, 56, 58, 90–91

Yastrzemski, Carl 145
Young, Cy 72, 211, 213–214, 216, 225

Zimmer, Don 47, 49, 51, 178